JOURNAL FOR THE STUDY OF THE OLD TESTAMENT
SUPPLEMENT SERIES

415

Antony F. Campbell, SJ

Seeing Signals, Reading Signs

The Art of Exegesis

Studies in Honour of Antony F. Campbell, SJ
for his Seventieth Birthday

edited by

Mark A. O'Brien and Howard N. Wallace

T & T CLARK INTERNATIONAL
A Continuum imprint
LONDON • NEW YORK

Copyright © 2004 T&T Clark International
A Continuum imprint

Published by T&T Clark International
The Tower Building, 11 York Road, London SE1 7NX
15 East 26th Street, Suite 1703, New York, NY 10010

www.tandtclark.com

British Library Cataloguing-in-Publication Data
A catalogue record for this book is available from the British Library

Typeset and edited for Continuum by Forthcoming Publications Ltd
www.forthcomingpublications.com

Printed on acid-free paper in Great Britain by Antony Rowe, Chippenham, Wilts.

ISBN 0-8264-7158-7

CONTENTS

LIST OF CONTRIBUTORS

Suzanne Boorer is Lecturer in Old Testament Studies at the Perth College of Divinity, Murdoch University, Australia

Mark G. Brett is Professor of Old Testament Studies at Whitley College, Evangelical Theological Association, Melbourne College of Divinity, Australia

Brendan J. Byrne is Professor of New Testament Studies at the United Faculty of Theology, Melbourne College of Divinity, Australia

John Hill is Lecturer in Old Testament Studies at the Yarra Theological Union, Melbourne College of Divinity, Australia

Wonil Kim is Associate Professor of Jewish Bible/Old Testament Studies at the School of Religion, La Sierra University, Riverside, California, USA

Rolf P. Knierim is Emeritus Professor of Religion (Hebrew Bible) at the School of Religion, Claremont Graduate University, California, USA

Norbert Lohfink is Professor of Old Testament Studies at the Hochschule Sankt Georgen, Frankfurt, Germany

Sean McEvenue is Emeritus Professor of Old Testament Theology at Concordia University, Montreal, Canada

Steven L. McKenzie is Professor of Religious Studies at Rhodes College, Memphis, Tennessee, USA

Mark A. O'Brien is Lecturer in Old Testament Studies at the Yarra Theological Union, Melbourne College of Divinity, Australia

Brian Peckham is Professor of Religion Studies, Department of Near and Middle Eastern Civilizations at the University of Toronto, Canada

Marvin A. Sweeney is Professor of Religion (Hebrew Bible) at the School of Religion, Claremont Graduate University, California, USA

Howard N. Wallace is Professor of Old Testament Studies at the United Faculty of Theology, Melbourne College of Divinity, Australia

T. John Wright is Professor of Biblical Studies at the School of Theology, University of Auckland, New Zealand

ABBREVIATIONS

AB	Anchor Bible
ABD	David Noel Freedman (ed.), *The Anchor Bible Dictionary* (New York: Doubleday, 1992)
ANET	James B. Pritchard (ed.), *Ancient Near Eastern Texts Relating to the Old Testament* (Princeton: Princeton University Press, 1950)
ATANT	Abhandlungen zur Theologie des Alten und Neuen Testaments
ATD	Das Alte Testament Deutsch
AusBR	*Australian Biblical Review*
AV	Authorized Version
BASOR	*Bulletin of the American Schools of Oriental Research*
BBB	Bonner biblische Beiträge
BETL	Bibliotheca ephemeridum theologicarum lovaniensium
BEvT	Beiträge zur evangelischen Theologie
BHQ	*Biblia Hebraica Quinta: Librum Ruth praeparavit Jan de Waard* (Stuttgart: Deutsche Bibelgesellschaft, 1998)
BHS	*Biblia hebraica stuttgartensia*
BJ	*La Bible de Jerusalem*
BJS	Brown Judaic Studies
BKAT	Biblischer Kommentar: Altes Testament
BTB	*Biblical Theology Bulletin*
BTS	Biblisch-theologische Studien
BWANT	Beiträge zur Wissenschaft vom Alten und Neuen Testament
BZ	*Biblische Zeitschrift*
BZAW	Beihefte zur *ZAW*
CBQ	*Catholic Biblical Quarterly*
ConBOT	Coniectanea biblica, Old Testament
DH	The Deuteronomistic History (Deuteronomy–2 Kings)
DJD	Discoveries in the Judaean Desert
Dtr	Deuteronomistic (in relation to the composition of the DH)
ETL	*Ephemerides theologicae lovanienses*
EvT	*Evangelische Theologie*
FAT	Forschungen zum Alten Testament
FOTL	The Forms of the Old Testament Literature
FRLANT	Forschungen zur Religion und Literatur des Alten und Neuen Testaments
GNB	*Good News Bible*
HAR	*Hebrew Annual Review*

HAT	Handbuch zum Alten Testament
HCOT	Historical commentary on the Old Testament
HALAT	Hebraisches und Aramaisches Lexikon zum Alten Testament
HS	*Hebrew Studies*
HSLuth	*Die Bibel oder die ganze heilige Schrift des Alten und Neuen Testaments, nach der deutschen Uebersetzung D. Martin Luthers* (Cologne, 1877)
HSLuthR	*Die Bibel oder die ganze heilige Schrift des Alten und Neuen Testaments, nach der deutschen Übersetzung Martin Luthers* (Revidierter Text. Deutsche Bibelstiftung Stuttgart, 1975)
HSS	Harvard Semitic Studies
HTR	*Harvard Theological Review*
HUCA	*Hebrew Union College Annual*
IBS	*Irish Biblical Studies*
ICC	International Critical Commentary
IDBSup	*IDB*, Supplementary Volume
Int	*Interpretation*
ITC	International Theological Commentary
JANESCU	*Journal of the Ancient Near Eastern Society of Columbia University*
JB	*Jerusalem Bible*
JBL	*Journal of Biblical Literature*
JETS	*Journal of the Evangelical Theological Society*
JNSL	*Journal of Northwest Semitic Languages*
JSOT	*Journal for the Study of the Old Testament*
JSOTSup	*Journal for the Study of the Old Testament*, Supplement Series
JSS	*Journal of Semitic Studies*
KAT	Kommentar zum Alten Testament
LB	Living Bible
LXX	Septuagint
MT	Masoretic Text
NAB	*New American Bible*
NASB	New American Standard Bible
NCB	New Century Bible Commentary
NEB	*New English Bible*
NEchtB	*Neue Echter Bibel*
NIB	*The New Interpreter's Bible*
NICOT	New International Commentary on the Old Testament
NIV	New International Version
NJB	*New Jerusalem Bible*
NJPS	*New Jerusalem Publication Society* (Tanakh: The Holy Scriptures: The New JPS Translation according to the Traditional Hebrew Text).
NJPSV	*New Jerusalem Publication Society Version*
NRSV	New Revised Standard Version

OBO	Orbis biblicus et orientalis
Or	*Orientalia*
OTL	Old Testament Library
QD	Quaestiones disputatae
RB	*Revue biblique*
REB	*Revised English Bible*
RSV	Revised Standard Version
RV	Revised Version
SBLDS	SBL Dissertation Series
SBLSCS	SBL Septuagint and Cognate Studies
SBT	Studies in Biblical Theology
SEÅ	*Svensk exegetisk årsbok*
SJOT	*Scandinavian Journal of the Old Testament*
SNTSMS	Society for New Testament Studies Monograph Series
Tanak	*Torah, Nebiim, Ketubim (The Hebrew Bible)*
ThWAT	G.J. Botterweck and H. Ringgren (eds.), *Theologisches Wörterbuch zum Alten Testament* (Stuttgart: W. Kohlhammer, 1970–)
TOB	*Traduction oecuménique de la Bible*
TM	Calwever theologische Monographien
TTod	*Theology Today*
UF	*Ugarit-Forschungen*
VT	*Vetus Testamentum*
VTSup	*Vetus Testamentum*, Supplements
WBC	Word Biblical Commentary
WMANT	Wissenschaftliche Monographien zum Alten und Neuen Testament
ZAH	*Zeitschrift für Althebraistik*
ZAW	*Zeitschrift für die alttestamentliche Wissenschaft*
ZB	*Zürcher Bibel*
ZBKAT	Zürcher Bibelkommentare Altes Testament
ZTK	*Zeitschrift für Theologie und Kirche*

Antony F. Campbell, SJ: A Tribute

Brendan Byrne, SJ

Tony Campbell, by birth a New Zealander of English, Scottish and Irish background, was educated by the Marist Fathers at Greenmeadows. In 1953 he crossed the Tasman Sea to enter the Society of Jesus (Jesuits) at Loyola College, Watsonia, Victoria. After studying philosophy, he began his path in biblical studies by taking a combined Greek and Hebrew major in his honours degree at the University of Melbourne. Tony's artistic appreciation and keen eye for detail attracted him also to archaeology. Under the inspiration of William Culican, biblical archaeology became for a time a major interest and potential area of specialization.

After a year's teaching at St Aloysius' (secondary) College, Milsons Point, Sydney, Tony left for Fourvière, near Lyon, France, to pursue the theological studies required for priesthood. The choice of this theological institute stemmed from the leading role played by French theologians in the rediscovery of the Bible in Catholic theology. Living and studying at Fourvière in the years immediately after the Second Vatican Council, when the shadows and memories of wartime occupation still lingered, Tony experienced the turmoil as well as the liberation that swept through such institutions at the time. The experience contributed to an abiding conviction that any theology claiming to be genuine must submit to a rigorous checking out against the human experience it purports to address.

Following ordination to the priesthood in July 1967, Tony moved to Rome to obtain the Licentiate in Sacred Scripture from the Pontifical Biblical Institute. The competence in biblical languages already gained in Melbourne enabled him to complete this degree in record time and then proceed to doctoral studies in Claremont, California, under the direction of Rolf Knierim. Here a fascination with biblical narrative—its genesis, its evolution, its ability to communicate meaning—was nurtured and honed into strict scholarly method, to become a life-long avocation.

One has only to meet Tony to grasp how significant a part those years in the California of the mid-1970s played in his personal, as well as his scholarly formation. Throughout that period, he lived in the university parish of St Mary of the Angels, Claremont, where Monsignor Bill Barry was pastor for many years. A richly cultivated man, of keen theological as well as pastoral gifts, Barry offered both academic and physical hospitality to a whole generation of priest graduate students at Claremont. Tony's debt to him and to the parish community is shown by his return, time and time again, when on study leave, to that same community, and to the friendship and companionship it offered.

His Claremont doctorate gained (and soon to be published in the SBL Monograph series as *The Ark Narrative* [SBLMS, 16; Missoula, MT: Scholars Press, 1975]), Tony returned to Australia in 1975 to take up the academic position in which he has remained ever since: teaching Older Testament at Jesuit Theological College (JTC), Parkville, within the United Faculty of Theology and the wider ambit of the Melbourne College of Divinity. Because of his theological studies in France, Tony had not been part of the foundation generation of students at JTC. He adapted, nonetheless, with alacrity to its distinctive style of living, finding that it offered an appropriate balance between community participation and the freedom required for continued scholarly work at the highest level.

Immediately on joining the faculty Tony became Dean of JTC, a position he held for many years. Here he made a truly lasting administrative contribution. Prior to his arrival the organization of studies reflected the upheaval in theology unleashed by Vatican II—rather much a time when 'each one did what was good in their own eyes'. JTC had also just become a full member of the United Faculty of Theology (UFT) and much work needed to be done to bring its course requirements into line with those of the other colleges and, in particular, the Bachelor of Theology degree of the Melbourne College of Divinity. With his clarity of vision, capacity for organization, and concern to see prescription include due allowance for individual need and exception, Tony devised a pattern of structures that have endured, with remarkably little revision, to this day. Successors in administration, over thirty years, have merely tinkered with the arrangements he set in place.

Besides administration, first as Dean and later as Principal of JTC (at times holding both offices simultaneously), Tony's main contribution has been as teacher of Older Testament. From the start, students in his classes, in both introductory courses and those of higher level, found themselves in the hands of a gifted and exciting teacher, effectively relating texts from a faraway past to universal human concerns and preoccupations. A scholar of international standing was mediating to them through his own formation under Knierim a tradition going back to the great German scholars of the nineteenth century. For many years, along with his former graduate student and now long-time associate, Mark O'Brien, OP, Tony ran a research seminar on biblical narrative. This seminar forged a whole generation of students, including some of no great achievement hitherto, into a collective research team. The results of this cooperation emerged in a series of scholarly publications, notably the monumental study of source criticism, *Sources of the Pentateuch* (Philadelphia: Fortress Press, 1993), and its later companion, *Unfolding the Deuteronomistic History* (Philadelphia: Fortress Press, 2000), both with Mark as co-author. Tony's research seminar has a lasting place in UFT history—and legend!

At a higher level still, Tony has had a steady stream of doctoral candidates enter into the scholarly guild under his direction. Attending an overseas conference some years back he was bemused and not entirely ungratified to hear talk of a 'Campbell-*Schule*'. His gifts for analysis and sense of process have guided many students through research thickets to academic pastures that truly matched their capacities. The same gifts, along with a high concern for fairness and due process, have made him a valued and challenging contributor on boards and in meetings associated with the Melbourne College of Divinity and other academic bodies. In recognition both of his scholarly attainment and the esteem in which he is held by his peers, the College in 1994 conferred upon him its highest award, the Doctorate of Divinity.

Tony has been most generous in placing his flair for organization and the preparation of material for publication at the disposal of various scholarly associations. He was for many years secretary of the Fellowship for Biblical Studies (Melbourne), whose academic journal the *Australian Biblical Review* he set up in print-ready copy for over two decades. He has also been an active member and office bearer in the Australian Catholic Biblical Association. Along with his publications, his participation in these and similar bodies has notably contributed to ensuring that Australian biblical scholarship operates at the highest international standards.

Tony has always sought, both in writing and in external lectures, workshops and the like, to make his scholarship available to a wider audience. An interest in psychology led him to work for many years on an inter-disciplinary basis with Professor Edmond Chiu of Melbourne University's Department of Psychiatry. More recently, he has brought biblical insights to the area of grief-counseling, particularly in association with Sr Nicole Rotaru, RSM. His recently published *God First Loved Us: The Challenge of Accepting Unconditional Love* (New York: Paulist Press, 2000) draws on a keen perception of human experience to communicate in engaging and accessible terms something in which he passionately believes: God's unconditional love. Many have found the book transforming.

Behind all this lies something that anyone who knows Tony well would readily concede. While he can at times present a formidable front—particularly if stirred early in the day—Tony is possessed of a deeply compassionate heart. Many are those who have approached him—often in the dead of night or wee hours of morning—with some deep burden and come away feeling welcomed, heard, understood, wisely counseled. Tony's capacity for process is never more effectively in play than in such situations. In a non-judgmental and non-directive way, he sits down and helps trapped and troubled people find possibilities, ways to go, and the appropriate order in which to take them. Women, particularly those bruised and hurt in the name of religion, have found in him not only great reserves of compassion but also high capacity for friendship and support. It is here that Tony's scholarship, priesthood and human qualities flow together in a rich unity.

Besides his work as scholar and teacher, Tony for some years had oversight over the financial affairs of the Australian Jesuit province, of which he has been for over fifty years a well-loved and respected member. His vigorous and colorful personality is widely held to belie the adage that all the 'characters' in the community have long since died out. While long committed to teaching and working on an ecumenical basis, his loyalty to the Catholic tradition and to the Society of Jesus within that tradition is patent. The remaining contributions in this volume will testify to the scholarly esteem in which he is held. It has been my privilege to complement that with this tribute to Tony as colleague, teacher and pastor—and altogether memorable human being.

Mark A. O'Brien and Howard N. Wallace

For Antony Campbell, exegesis is an artistic endeavour, requiring sensitivity to the literary signals in the text and an artist's eye for 'reading the signs'. Literary signals are like signposts. As he notes in his 2003 commentary on 1 Samuel, 'several signposts, pointing in different directions to the same destination, invite reflection... Several routes can lead to the same goal' (p. 12). His experience of the biblical text 'suggests that reflection is being invited constantly'. A biblical text can appear disarmingly simple or profoundly challenging. Overall, the books of the Old Testament form a rich and varied tapestry.

This volume of essays is a fitting testimony to Campbell's contribution to the challenge of biblical exegesis. A diverse group of international scholars takes up the challenge of applying their exegetical skills and sensitivity to seeing signals and reading signs in the text. The essays reflect first of all on aspects of the biblical/canonical text itself, then on specific areas of the Pentateuch, the Former Prophets, and the Latter Prophets. It concludes with two essays that focus more on Biblical Theology. A wide variety of perspectives on a wide variety of biblical texts.

1. *In Text and Canon*

Seeing signs and reading signals is not just a matter of detecting those things in a text that affect meaning on a grander scale. It also involves an awareness of how a text has been constructed, how it is to be translated, and even how it should be punctuated. Brian Peckham's essay, 'Punctuation is the Point', is concerned with the signs and signals associated with this last issue, punctuation. Clause sequencing is the key and translators/interpreters of the text need to use all their skills in observing word order, noting the cadences and rhythms of clause types and how they are used individually and in sequence, noting sameness and difference within sequences, and employ attentiveness to 'sight and sound and a sense of direction'. All this is necessary in the process of translation from Hebrew into 'the incompatible grammar, syntax and punctuation' of a modern language. Syntax was the guide to punctuation in ancient Hebrew, Peckham argues, because meaning was attached to word order, clause type and sequencing, and to the structure of texts. The essay helps plot some of these issues, and some of the complexities that can arise. Peckham spends most time dealing with sequences indicating 'stops', both of consecutive and non-consecutive types, but also looks at subordinate and mixed sequences. He gives special attention to punctuation in quotations, dialogue, discourse and soliloquy. Poetry and prose examples are examined. This is an important contribution to understanding the punctuation of a Hebrew text and ultimately to discerning meaning in a Hebrew text.

Norbert Lohfink's study of 'Canonical Signals in the Additions in Deuteronomy 1.39' also has important implications, in this case for our understanding of the growth of the biblical text and the factors affecting its growth. By a close analysis, in particular of the Masoretic text, the Septuagint and the Samaritan Pentateuch, Lohfink is able to plot the development of Deut. 1.39 in a much more satisfactory way than previously thought. As well, he is able to point to 'canonical signals' in the development of the present Masoretic text. Additions to earlier stages of the text are carefully embedded signals designed to allude to other, similar passages within the emerging Pentateuch. Thus, Deut. 1.39 has been delicately reworked to create a certain harmonization with Num. 14.31—two texts that deal with the fate of Israel's 'baggage-train' (Lohfink's translation; NRSV renders 'little ones'). As the Pentateuch moved towards its final stage, canonical signals were added to texts in order to point to their inter-relationship, particularly where such texts provided differing accounts of the same or similar issue. Lohfink argues that these 'canonical signals' served as guides to assist the reader in the task of understanding. They were not meant to impose: 'The outcome was the reader's business'. Lohfink's essay underlines the crucial role of text criticism in reconstructing the stages of a text's growth and the implications of this for a 'canonical exegesis' (focus on the present text).

2. *In the Pentateuch and Former Prophets*

In her wide ranging 'The 'Paradigmatic' and 'Historiographical' Nature of the Priestly Material as a Key to its Interpretation', Suzanne Boorer seeks to identify the signs and read the signals that contribute to an understanding of the nature/genre of the Priestly document as a whole. This is the necessary task before one can discuss the meaning of P, either as a document validating past traditions or setting a programme for the future restoration of the community. She notes linear sequencing and repeated patterns in the stories of P. There are parallels between the story of the cosmos and that of the nation with echoes of ancient myths. P moves by means of genealogies or by way of desert itineraries, incorporating traditions from the past, reflections on the present and visions for the future in a series of 'timeless realities'. But how can one interpret P as a whole while doing justice to the nature of the work? She highlights the debate over the designation of P as either 'paradigmatic' or 'historiographic', and Van Seters' discussion of the 'historicization of myth' and the 'mythologization of history'. Boorer applies these discussions to P, debating a number of scholars on the way. She argues that there is a reflection of all time (past/present/future) in P. In the context of the early post-exilic community, each section of P is seen to function paradigmatically and historically while inter-relating cosmic and national material. As the reader enters the world of the text and follows the rituals set out therein, they 'experience...glimpses of the known combined with visions of the future not yet experienced, both at each point... At the same time...the reader is provided with the means of entering into, and embodying, the world of the text, the fulfillment of this complex "eschatological" paradigm with its future...'

Mark O'Brien's 'At "Sixes and Sevens" in Exodus 6 and 7?' traces the complex of signals in the dialogues between Moses and God in Exod. 5.22–6.8; 6.10-12; 6.28–7.5. He identifies three key elements in 5.22-23: God's relationship to the people (your people), Moses' role, and the fate of Pharaoh (and the Egyptians). The signals associated with Moses' role are elusive, particularly when read in relation to different passages in the surrounding context. The following dialogue texts in 6.1, 2-8, 10-12, 6.28–7.5 are then examined to see whether and in what way they take up these elements. Exodus 6.1 highlights the overthrow of Pharaoh, with the other elements given only a subsidiary role. Even though it may be from another hand, God's speech in 6.2-8 is noteworthy for the way it highlights elements left 'undeveloped' in 6.1—the role of Moses and God's relationship to the people. Moses is elevated to the status of an ancestor like Abraham, ushering in a new epoch in God's relationship with the people. Israel is already God's people in 3.7; the new element in 6.2-8 is Israel's coming to *know* that *Yhwh* is their God and that they are *Yhwh*'s people. There is a dynamic quality to Israel's status as God's people which will be fully realized in the land. The short dialogue in 6.10-12 ends with issues unresolved. The fuller version in 6.28–7.5 focuses on the role of Moses (in relation to God and to Aaron) and the fate of Pharaoh and the Egyptians. It provides a fitting prelude to the story of the plagues. On this reading, the text looks to have direction and a dominant meaning. But, there are enough competing signals to caution the reader too eager to achieve closure. As well as resisting closure, these counter signals invite one to explore alternative pathways of meaning.

Mark Brett begins his 'Genocide in Deuteronomy: Post-Colonial Variations on Mimetic Desire' by asking what purposes the biblical discussion on the 'ban' on the prior inhabitants of Canaan served and how does the ancient concept of *herem* relate to modern cases of genocide? He admits that there is no easy neutral way to approach such questions in many contemporary situations, especially for those living in post-colonial contexts. To address this question and deal with contemporary issues of reconciliation with aboriginal peoples, Brett explores texts within Deuteronomy, specifically Deuteronomy 13 with its demand for loyalty to *Yhwh*, and Deuteronomy 20 with its laws on warfare. As no single literary category suits the mix of traditions in Deuteronomy, Brett employs an approach similar to the approaches to discourse in post-colonial studies which relate 'cultural hybridity' to particular socio-cultural struggles. He enters into dialogue with the studies of Lohfink and Matties on the concept of 'mimetic desire' and especially the fear of mimicry of Canaanites in Deuteronomy. Given recent arguments that Israel was in fact indigenous to the land of Canaan, Brett argues that the civil strifes behind the texts on the 'ban' in Deuteronomy involved 'not so much "indigenous" peoples but close kin who held different religious views and practices'. He concludes that 'What appears on the surface of

Deuteronomy 20 as a programme for genocide is actually part of an internal social and religious reform'. The essay finishes with a postscript on contemporary aspects of mimetic desire, especially in the context of 'globalized capital' in Western thought.

The essays on the Former Prophets begin with Wonil Kim's 'The Rhetoric of War and the *Book* of Joshua'. For many contemporary readers of the Bible, the war texts in the book of Joshua send disturbing signals. What relationship do these texts bear to Israel's history? Kim finds useful material on the function of texts from a debate between two schools of Marxist literary criticism. The Plekhanov school believes the literary artist passively 'intuits the world' in his/her work while the Bogdanov school believes the primary function of an artistic work is its impact on society. According to Kim, one can see the interplay of these two approaches in the work of Norman Gottwald, who employs aspects of Marxist theory in his analysis of biblical texts. Gottwald is alert to the rhetorical impact of the war texts on a reader but his primary interest is in what they reveal of the social reality of Israel. From quite another perspective, James Barr also favours extra-textual factors for the interpretation of biblical text. More recent exponents of the rhetorical impact of texts who employ Marxist theory are Terry Eagleton and Pierre Macherey. For Macherey in particular, every text is a rewriting, a reproduction (the image of a palimpsest). A reader must 'rewrite' the text from the internal relations perceptible in it. Kim finds that Rolf Knierim reads biblical texts in a 'Machereyian way', although he is neither Marxist nor influenced by Macherey. According to Knierim, the texts reporting the extermination of the Canaanites are part of the theology of 'the land of Israel'. As such, it is a reproduced literature with reproduced 'God effects' that bring it into conflict with the 'God effects' of, for example, Genesis 1. These textual conflicts have an impact on the task of biblical theology.

Marvin Sweeney's essay, 'On the Literary Function of the Notice Concerning Hiel's Re-establishment of Jericho in 1 Kings 16.34', amounts to a major reassessment of a text that interpreters tend to regard as an editorial aside of little significance. 1 Kings 16.34 does not 'fit' neatly into the typical statements that characterize the regnal formulas in the books of Kings. Nevertheless, as Sweeney points out, there is a definite link to the preceding text via the third masculine singular pronoun ('in *his* days'). The *waw*-consecutive verb which commences the next verse (1 Kgs 17.1) implies a syntactical relationship with the story of Elijah. Thus the verse looks both back and forward. Sweeney notes that 1 Kgs 16.34 and the story of Elijah 'share an interest in the fulfillment of *Yhwh*'s word'. As God's word to Joshua was fulfilled, so will God's word to Elijah concerning Ahab and his dynasty. Joshua's curse in 6.26 is made in the context of Jericho as the first Canaanite city given by God to Israel. Its rebuilding by Ahab represents a 're-Canaanization' of the land—exemplified in his worship of Baal—which evokes the curses in Deuteronomy. Elijah's task is to turn the people back to *Yhwh* and to eliminate the house of Omri/Ahab, the source of the apostasy. The Ahab factor, and its links to Joshua's curse, can be followed through to the end of 2 Kings. Because of the marriage of Jehoram of Judah to Athaliah, every subsequent Davidide is also a descendant of Ahab. Elijah's curse against the northern dynasty touches the Davidic dynasty as well, as can be seen in the texts on Manasseh (2 Kgs 21; 23.26-27; 24.3-4) and the fate of Judah's last king, Jehoiachin (2 Kgs 25.25-30). 1 Kings 16.34 may have been part of an editorial process, but a careful synchronic analysis reveals the strategic nature of its location and its far reaching function.

3. *In the Latter Prophets*

For his essay 'Harvesting the Vineyard: The Development of Vineyard Imagery in the Hebrew Bible', Howard Wallace examines a different set of signs and signals within the biblical text, namely those associated with the images of vineyards, grapevines and wine, to see how they are employed within biblical texts and in the development of the language of faith. He first looks at a series of brief texts employing aspects of this set of metaphors. These especially concern the relation of *Yhwh* to the people. Different aspects of the imagery are employed—the growth of the vine, its fruitfulness, and so on—to portray the history of the people and their faithfulness, or otherwise. The imagery is also used in brief references to speak of the kings of Israel and Judah. The bulk of the essay is, however, concerned with a number of longer texts that develop either a single aspect of the imagery at length, or play with the complexity and inter-relationships of the imagery. The 'song of the vineyard' in Isa. 5.1-7, or the tradition behind it, is the starting point and fundamental to the development of the imagery in the texts that follow. This passage is exegeted and developed in Isa. 27.2-6, and, arguably, 'completed' in Isa. 63.1-6. While the tradition associated with Isa. 5.1-7 is probably Judean in origin, it is combined with an Ephraimite tradition in Psalm 80. Specifically, traditions of the vineyard and the vine are brought together. Two passages in Ezekiel (15.2-8 and 19.10-14) are discussed briefly. Finally, the development of the imagery in the Gospel parable of the wicked tenants (Mt. 21.33-46//Mk 12.1-12//Lk. 20.9-19) and in Jn 15.1-11 is noted. In the former, the development of the imagery via the LXX and Isaiah Targum is explored. The complex, yet rich history of the growth of this set of signs stands alongside the individual contributions of particular writers and editors.

Jeremiah 40.1-6 is a complex text that has attracted much diachronic analysis but with little attention to its present shape and function within the book of Jeremiah. In order to redress this imbalance, John Hill, in his 'Jeremiah 40.1-6—An Appreciation', provides a detailed analysis of the constituent parts of the passage: the report of the word to Jeremiah in v. 1; Nebuzaradan's explanation of Jerusalem's destruction in vv. 2b-3; his offer to Jeremiah in vv. 4-5b; and Jeremiah's decision to join Gedaliah in Mizpah in vv. 5b-6. Hill argues that Nebuzaradan's speech reflects the Dtr question and answer pattern; it provides an answer to the implied question 'Why has this disaster come about?' Nebuzaradan is cast as a Dtr prophet. This portrait of the foreigner has troubled some scholars, leading to proposals that the introductory v. 1 has been tampered with and earlier material displaced. However, Hill is able to show that 'the privileging of non-

Jewish characters is an important literary device' in the book of Jeremiah. The portrait of the foreigner is integral, not foreign, to the book. Verses 4-5 allow the reader to see further evidence of this privileging of the foreigner. Nebuzaradan's statement in v. 4b that 'the land is before you' echoes Gen. 20.18, where the Philistine Abimelech offers land to Abraham, and Gen. 47.6, where Pharaoh makes the same offer to Joseph. Jeremiah 40.4b also suggests a link with Gen. 13.9 where Abraham offers land to Lot. The separation of Jeremiah from the exiles (40.1) and his decision to settle in Mizpah (vv. 5b-6) enhance the status of the community left in the land. According to Hill, 40.1-6 and 7-12 do not support Pohlmann's contention that they are among the pro-*Golah* passages in chs. 37–44.

In '*Ruach* in Ezekiel 37', John Wright examines the signs and signals that relate to the meaning of a lexeme in its context. The problems of communication and translation are all too evident, especially with an ancient language. Moreover, individual ancient authors brought their own interpretations to the words they used. Wright examines an evolutionary understanding of the development of a lexeme and traces how this has been applied to the Hebrew word *ruach*, with stages in meaning from a literal 'wind' through to understanding the term as designating the power of God at work. Building on the work of Barfield and Prickett and the notion of 'sentient meaning', Wright argues that the meaning of words like *ruach* does not begin with the literal and develop from there, but that 'inner' and 'outer' meanings are there from the start. The ancient world did not distinguish between 'wind', 'breath', 'spirit' and 'life' as we might want today. There is a latent meaning to a lexeme which cannot be understood fully without attention to contextual matters. Wright then explores how the author of Ezekiel 37 utilizes the latent meaning of *ruach* for their own purposes. He notes the ambiguity of *ruach* in the text, something which many modern translators have struggled with. For Wright it is not just a matter of coping with ambiguity, but recognizing that 'the word expresses a concept and reflects an "entity" that is almost impossible for us moderns to grasp without dividing that entity up into signifiers of the literal'. Nor is translation simply a matter of selecting an alternative. It is a question of whether there is something inherent in the lexeme which enables its use. 'What the author is doing in ch. 37 is rediscovering synonymy, and making the whole a riddle.' The signs and signals may well lead in more than one direction in the one text.

Steven McKenzie begins his study of 'The Genre of Jonah' by acknowledging the work of Campbell in the area of Form Criticism. In particular he wants to take up Campbell's call for a refocus on the method with a concern for both the shape or structure of a text and its genre. McKenzie analyses the book of Jonah as a way of demonstrating the value of heeding this call. He concludes that the form of Jonah is a well organized work of narrative literature, unique among the prophets. The character of Jonah is central, with the contents of the book revolving around the interaction between Jonah and the other characters. But, as Campbell emphasizes, form is not determinative of genre. In Jonah, McKenzie argues that there are good indications that we are dealing with the genre of story, and in particular with short story or novella. Moreover, the final scene in the book suggests that this short story is intended to be didactic. A close study of the characters in the book clarifies its purpose or intent. All characters are really caricatures and the purpose of the book is 'to satirize Jonah or the people or attitude he represents'. The real object of the ridicule in the book is, however, not just Jonah but 'the book's intended readership'. 'The humour and hyperbole', McKenzie concludes, 'help the book's audience to perceive in Jonah the silliness of their own attitudes and the ridiculous lengths to which arrogance and prejudice can lead them. Jonah's character is thus something of a mirror for the book's audience.' He locates the *Sitz im Leben* of the book in the post-exilic period, seeing it as intended to contribute to the theological debate of the time, possibly even 'as a response to the narrow perspective of Ezra–Nehemiah'. The essay ends helpfully with a further reflection on Form Criticism and the significance of Jonah for modern faith.

4. *In Biblical Theology*

In 'The Truth Trap in Interpretation', Sean McEvenue begins by saluting the contribution to Bible study made by historical-critical analysis over the past few hundred years. But, a price has been paid: biblical scholars were pressured by the objective, scientific aims of the Enlightenment to establish the objective, histori-cal 'truth' of the Bible. Academic history writing added to this pressure. Accord-ing to McEvenue, not only did this put unreal demands on the Bible, it also, and more fundamentally, misread the signals in the biblical text. The Bible is primarily a work of literature: 'it may not refer to facts at all, or when it does use facts, or hard data, its primary focus is to evoke a personal (subjective) experi-ence of them'. McEvenue suggests that 'good or bad' may be a better term to measure literature like the Bible than 'true or false'. As a work of (religious) lit-erature, the Bible is primarily about God, or what one may call the literary articu-lation or evocation of a believer's experience of God. 'The Bible cannot be read as history, in our sense of that word, but rather as inspiration or revelation.' McEvenue fleshes this statement out with definitions of experience, revelation and inspiration. He then tests his understanding of biblical literature in a narrative text (1 Sam. 9–31) and two prophetic passages (Zeph. 3.14-18a and Hos. 1–3). Each text is seen as an evocation of a particular faith experience. But what an author has learned about God is always true about God. Historical and philologi-cal questions asked of the biblical text must not interfere with the central task of interpretation which is to fully understand 'by experiencing what the writer evokes through the text'.

   It is fitting that this volume concludes with an essay by Rolf Knierim, 'Antony Campbell's *God First Loved Us* and the Task of Biblical Theology', under whose supervision Campbell wrote his doctoral dissertation (later published as *The Ark Narrative*) and with whom he has collaborated in the Forms of Old Testament Literature project (FOTL). It is also fitting that Knierim, who is well known for his reflections on the task of Old Testament theology, should write a lengthy appreciation and critique of Campbell's *God First Loved Us: The Challenge of*

Accepting Unconditional Love, a book that questions much traditional thinking about God. Knierim provides a brisk summary of each part of Campbell's book, along with pertinent comments on areas that he considers particularly important. He draws attention to two features of Campbell's presentation. The first is that accepting God's unconditional love for us challenges 'the ethical, or moral, foundation of our existence'. In relation to this, he notes that Campbell's focus on our being loved by God differs from a focus on our being justified by God. The second is that Campbell's discussion of God's unconditional love 'takes place on the fields of biblical theology as well as of systematic theology or theological doctrine'. This points to 'the difference between the tasks of the exegesis of the theologies of the biblical texts and of biblical theology built from the exegeted texts and their theologies'. In a more critical vein, Knierim questions whether the theology of unconditional love and redemption theology are at odds, as Campbell argues. Knierim believes that the fundamental New Testament texts 'consider God's reconciliation of the world to God as the fulfillment of God's love for the world in its redemption through the sacrificial death of Jesus Christ'. Appropriately, the collection of essays ends with questions and an opportunity for further reflection.

Part I

IN TEXT AND CANON

PUNCTUATION IS THE POINT

Brian Peckham

Everybody knows about Hebrew punctuation. The best known, and the common-est, is the period, the full stop disjunctive clause, at the end of a sequence of consecutive clauses: 'And the girl [was] exceedingly pretty, *and* she became the king's bed mate, *and* she took care of him: the king did not know her' (1 Kgs 1.4). The sequence sometimes is very long, sometimes no more than the two clauses of this Abishag interlude, and often is introduced by one or more clauses that are not consecutive. The syntax is marked and perfectly clear in Hebrew: pretty Abishag is described in a paratactic ('and') nominal clause, her sorry tale is told in two consecutive ('*and*') verbal clauses, and the king's dotage is disjunc-tive. The syntax is not too obvious in translation, but punctuation does the trick.

The syntax is a matter of word order and clause type. A consecutive clause is verbal, and its verb is bound with *waw* in initial position—*wattiqtol* in Abishag's instance—and the remaining word order does not matter to the syntax. A disjunc-tive clause is also verbal, but its initial *waw* is bound to the subject—והמלך לא ידעה in poor Abishag's case—or to the object or to an adverbial modifier, but not to the verb, and syntactically, again, it is only this opening word order that counts. The syntax is formal, functional and clearly marked: clause types are distinguished as verbal or not and by how they begin. A consecutive clause is narrative—sweet Abishag's story is that she kept the king warm and took care of him—and a disjunctive clause is explanatory—even though she shared his bed he did not take advantage of her—but while this is all very charming, and certainly misled Adonijah, the syntax does not depend on it.

This syntax is the gist of the sequence of clauses. A sequence, as in the Abishag interlude, is a series of clauses of the same type, introduced or not by unlike clauses, stopping with a clause of another type. Each type has a predict-able value, as consecutive suggests 'story' and disjunctive forebodes an explana-tion, but syntax just tracks the meaning and is not confused with it. Clause type and word order, consequently, can be distinguished apart from their meaning by the features that make them syntactically significant.

Clause types are verbal or nominal and each is distinguished by how it begins. In both, there are two choices—each can start with or without *waw*—and the first choice after that limits the possibilities. In nominal clauses, the choice could be a preposition or a conjunction or neither, depending on whether subordination or coordination is going to be expressed, followed or not by an explicit subject (noun or pronoun), object (marked by את) or predicate (either an infinitive or a participle). In verbal clauses, what immediately follows *waw* can be a verb, in either tense (*qatal* or *yiqtol*) or mood (indicative or modal), or it can be the subject, the object or the modifier of the verb—but which of these and their order makes no difference, and what follows the verb also does not count in the definition of clause type. The only significant element of word order in clauses beginning without *waw* is an initial conjunction. Word order has many other uses, prosodic, temporal and aspectual among them, but the sequence of clauses relies on a small sampling of orders, marked at the start, and easily distinguishable:

1.　　nominals begin with *waw* (and are called <u>paratactic</u> or, if they have an explicit subject, object or predicate, <u>disjunctive</u>), and without *waw* (called <u>asyndetic</u>), or with a preposition or a conjunction (called <u>prepositive</u>, <u>conjunctive</u>);

2.　　verbal clauses are <u>asyndetic</u> (*qatal*, or *yiqtol* or modal in any position), <u>consecutive</u> (positive $w^e qatal$ or *wayyiqtol*, negative $w^e lo'$ *qatal* or $w^e lo'$ *yiqtol*), <u>disjunctive</u> (*waw* + X + *qatal*, or + X + *yiqtol*), <u>paratactic</u> (w^e + *qatal*, w^e + *yiqtol*, or modal), or <u>conjunctive</u> (with a conjunction).

All in all there are limited choices, but each type of clause is identified from the beginning, and its place in the sequence—as sequential, coordinate or subordinate—is marked by its kind and its cadence and is easily learned.

Sequences are like sentences and paragraphs. They can be, but rarely are, simple, with all their clauses of the same type, except the last of which functions as their period. A sequence is often complicated or elaborated by subordinate and coordinate clauses of any type, or it has embedded dialogue or speeches or snippets of verse. Sometimes the clause that punctuates is not last in the sequence, but is continued by one or more coordinate or subordinate clauses. Sometimes it is not the end of the sequence that is marked, but the beginning of the next sequence that punctuates the text. Texts are organized according to their sequences, as by sentences and paragraphs, and might be composed of the same kind of sequence, or of different kinds in particular patterns, or of any kind that suits the form, or style or mood of the piece. Sequences create expectations, their aural and visual alignments produce familiar resonances, and variations on them are notable surprises, not just in poetry, but in any text that was meant to be studied, murmured, or read aloud.

1. *Sequences with Simple Stops*

Since sequence is a series of clauses of the same type, a consecutive sequence is punctuated by a non-consecutive clause: by a clause without *waw* (asyndetic, and either nominal or verbal), or by a clause with a different kind of *waw* (disjunctive or paratactic, and either nominal or verbal), or by a clause with a different tense (*qatal* or *yiqtol*) or mood (indicative or modal). There are also other kinds of sequences that are not consecutive—nominal or verbal, and in each instance either asyndetic, disjunctive or paratactic—and so there are other stops which are not disjunctive. The principle is sequence—a series of the same type of clause—and punctuation, that is, the change to something different, always makes the point. Following are some examples.

a. *Consecutive Sequences*

Consecutive sequences are narrative or discursive, following a logical, chronological or topical order. The Deuteronomistic explanation of the fall of Samaria
(2 Kgs 17.6-18) is that Israel had sinned. This idea is developed in four consecutive clauses (17.6, 18a)—this main clause sequence is modified by a subordinate
sequence (17.7-17) also composed entirely of consecutive clauses—and the
sequence ends abruptly in an *asyndetic* clause: 'In the ninth year of Hoshea, the
king of Assyria captured Samaria, *and* he exiled Israel to Assyria, *and* he settled
them..., *and Yhwh* was very angry at Israel, *and* he removed them from his
sight—*none was left except the tribe of Judah'*. The ritual encirclement of
Jericho (Josh. 6.15) takes three consecutive clauses and it also stops in an
asyndetic verbal clause: '*And* it was on the seventh day, *and* they got up at
sunrise, *and* they circled the city in this way seven times—only on this day did
they circle the city seven times'. The choice of Othniel (Judg. 3.7-9) occurs in an
asyndetic nominal clause at the end of the usual cycle of crime and punishment
that takes up nine consecutive clauses: '*And* Israel did evil..., *and* they forgot...,
and they served..., *and Yhwh* became angry at Israel, *and* he sold them..., *and*
they served..., *and* they cried out..., *and Yhwh* raised up a saviour..., *and* he
saved them—that is, Othniel, the son of Kenaz, the younger brother of Caleb'. In
describing the Midianite raids that were the occasion of Gideon's election (Judg.
6.3-4) the opening clause is formulaic and paratactic (and), and the conditional
clauses are paratactic, but the main clauses are consecutive and their sequence
stops by changing from *qatal* to *yiqtol*: '<u>And</u> it was, if Israel had planted, <u>and</u> if
Midian had come up...<u>and</u> had raided it, *and* they camped against them, *and* they
ruined the produce of the land all the way to Gaza, *and* they left (w^elo' *yiqtol*) no
sustenance in Israel, or sheep or ox or ass'. The aside on Obadiah's concern for
the prophets (1 Kgs 18.4) consists of three consecutive clauses and then stops in
a paratactic verbal clause: '*And* it was, when Jezebel cut off the prophets of
Yhwh, *and* Obadiah took a hundred prophets, *and* he hid them...: <u>and</u> supply
them he did (וכלכלם) with food and water'. How Moab fell into the trap laid for
them (2 Kgs 3.22b-24) is told in a sequence of consecutive clauses whose ending
is marked by a paratactic nominal (infinitival) clause: '*And* Moab saw the water
opposite them as red as blood, *and* they said..., *and* they came to the Israelite
camp, *and* the Israelites stood up, *and* they attacked Moab, *and* they fled before
them, *and* they attacked it—<u>and</u> beaten was (והכות) Moab'. When Elisha sends a
prophet to anoint Jehu (2 Kgs 9.1-5a) most of the text consists of his instructions,
but the narrative framework, introduced by an asyndetic clause, moves through
three consecutive clauses and stops suddenly with a disjunctive (AND) participial clause: 'Elisha the prophet summoned one of the sons of the prophets, *and* he
said to him..., *and* the young man went..., *and* he went in—AND behold the
commanders [were] in session'. The account of the first Babylonian siege of
Jerusalem begins asyndetically, becomes a consecutive sequence, and ends with
a disjunctive nominal clause (2 Kgs 25.10-11): 'At this time the servants of
Nebuchadnezzar, king of Babylon, went up against Jerusalem, *and* the city came
under siege, *and* Nebuchadnezzar, king of Babylon, arrived at the city—AND his
servants [were] besieging it'.

b. *Non-Consecutive Sequences*

Disjunctive sequences, which are explanatory, and sometimes subordinate in translation, can end consecutively, asyndetically or paratactically. After his escapade in Moab, Ehud's escape (Judg. 3.26) is first explained in two disjunctive clauses and then affirmed in a consecutive clause that ends the sequence: 'AND Ehud had escaped while they were dithering, AND he had gone past the sculptured stones, *and* he escaped to Seirah'. The first meeting between Saul and Samuel (1 Sam. 9.15-17) takes place in a consecutive clause that follows a sequence of three disjunctive clauses: 'AND *Yhwh* had opened Samuel's ear the day before Saul arrived..., AND Samuel had seen Saul, AND *Yhwh* had answered him...*and* Saul approached Samuel in the gate'. When *Yhwh* meets Elijah on Mt Horeb (1 Kgs 19.11a), the encounter is explained in a nominal sequence consisting of two disjunctive participial clauses, and ending with an asyndetic nominal clause: 'AND, behold, *Yhwh* passing by, AND a mighty strong wind splitting the mountains and shattering the rocks in front of *Yhwh*—not in the wind [was] *Yhwh*'. Details of the destruction of Jerusalem and the despoiling of the temple are recorded in two disjunctive sequences. The first (2 Kgs 25.8-13) begins with a disjunctive clause ('AND in the fifth month... Nebuzaradan...came to Jerusalem'), shifts to a consecutive clause to record the consequences ('*and* he burned the house of *Yhwh* and the palace'), but then continues in a disjunctive series which stops in a consecutive clause: 'AND all the houses of Jerusalem he burned down..., AND the walls of Jerusalem all around, the Chaldaean army under the command of the captain of the guard broke down, AND the rest of the people left in the city...Nebuzaradan...exiled, AND of the poor of the land some he left..., AND the pillars of bronze...and the bronze sea...the Chaldaeans broke, *and* they carried their bronze to Babylon'. The second sequence (2 Kgs 25.14-17) is composed of disjunctive clauses, but it stops in an asyndetic verbal clause (with a detailed extraposed subject): 'AND... all the bronze vessels which were used in the services they took, AND the firepans and the bowls...the captain of the guard took, those of gold for their gold and those of silver for their silver—the two pillars, the one sea, and the stands which Solomon had made for the house of *Yhwh*, there was just no weighing the bronze of all these vessels'.

Asyndetic sequences tend to be descriptive. They are punctuated by any clause beginning with *waw* or by a clause in a different tense or mood. The invasion of Judah by a legendary foe (Jer. 8.16) is described in two asyndetic clauses, and the sequence ends with consecutive clauses, the second completed by a parallel (coordinate) nominal phrase: 'From Dan is heard the snorting of his horses, at the sound of the neighing of his horses all the land trembles, *and* they come, *and* they devour the land and its fullness, the city and its inhabitants'. The punishment of Samaria (Hos. 14.1) is expressed in asyndetic *yiqtol* clauses, and the end of the sequence is marked by a disjunctive clause: 'Samaria will bear her guilt..., they will fall by the sword, their infants will be dashed, AND his pregnant women will be ripped open'. A sentence on the vanity of success (Qoh. 2.4) consists of four asyndetic clauses and a paratactic clause that stops the sequence: 'I did great deeds, I built myself houses, I planted for myself vineyards, I made myself gardens and parks, <u>and</u> I planted in them all kinds of fruit trees'. Isaiah described the initial advance of the Assyrians (Isa. 10.28) in two asyndetic *qatal* clauses, and ended the sequence by changing to an asyndetic *yiqtol* clause: 'He arrives at Aiath, he passes Migron, at Michmash he is storing his baggage'. Similarly, the cosmic response to *Yhwh*'s enthronement (Ps. 93.3) moves in a crescendo from *qatal* clauses to a final *yiqtol* clause that stops the sequence: 'Lord, the rivers raise, the rivers raise their voice, the rivers are raising their roar'. These asyndetic sequences are sentences extracted from continuous texts and their punctuation, their place in the organization of the text, is syntactic and deliberate and clearly meant to be noticed. The punctuation even draws attention to itself—in a change of cadence, a nuance of meaning, a different tense or aspect.

Paratactic sequences are enumerative. They are punctuated by any other type of clause. The southern boundary of Benjamin (Josh. 18.15-19) is drawn in a series of paratactic verbal (*weqatal*) clauses, introduced by a paratactic nominal clause, and ends without *waw* in an asyndetic nominal clause: '<u>And</u> the southern side from the edge of Kiriath-jearim…, <u>and</u> the boundary continues…, <u>and</u> continues…, <u>and</u> goes down…, <u>and</u> goes down…, <u>and</u> goes down…, <u>and</u> turns…, <u>and</u> continues…, <u>and</u> continues…, <u>and</u> goes down…, <u>and</u> crosses—this [is] the southern boundary'. *Yhwh*'s summons to the Assyrians (Isa. 5.26), similarly, is expressed in two paratactic *qatal* clauses, and its place in the complete poem is marked by a disjunctive *yiqtol* clause that ends the sequence: '<u>And</u> he raised a signal for the nations, <u>and</u> he whistled to him at the ends of the earth, AND behold swiftly, quickly, he comes'. A condemnation of Manasseh (2 Kgs 21.5-6) is expressed in a series of paratactic clauses, introduced by a consecutive clause and concluded by an asyndetic clause: '*And* he built altars to all the host of heaven…<u>and</u> passed his son through fire, <u>and</u> practiced soothsaying, <u>and</u> practiced divination, <u>and</u> made mediums and necromancers—he multiplied the evils he did in the sight of *Yhwh* to provoke him'.

2. *Sequences with Compound and Complex Stops*

Sequences of any kind do not necessarily end abruptly in one clause of a different type, but can end more diffusely in compound or complex stops. Compound stops consist of a different type of clause that ends the sequence—this much is routine—but this different type is continued by one or more clauses that are related to it through sequence or coordination: a consecutive sequence, for instance, can end in a sequence of paratactic or disjunctive clauses, or in a disjunctive clause that is continued by an asyndetic clause or by a consecutive series. A complex stop is a clause of a different type that ends the sequence but is modified by one of more subordinate clauses: it is not the subordinate clause that stops the sequence, but the different type of clause which it modifies. The ending is clearly marked by the different type of clause, but the clause that ends the sequence is not necessarily last in the sequence.

For example, a paragraph in the story of the manna (Exod. 16.17-18) is a consecutive sequence which is punctuated by a disjunctive clause and a following asyndetic clause: '*And* the people of Israel did so, *and* they gathered some more and some less, *and* they measured it with an omer, *and* the more was not too much, AND the less was not too little, each in the measure of their appetite had gathered'. Israel's progress through the wilderness under the guidance of God (Num. 9.17-18) is explained in a disjunctive *yiqtol* sequence that stops in an asyndetic *yiqtol* clause and a coordinate (or, parallel) disjunctive *yiqtol* clause: 'AND at the lifting of the cloud from over the tent the people of Israel set out, AND in the place where the cloud settled there the people of Israel camped—at the command of *Yhwh* the people of Israel set out, AND at the command of *Yhwh* they camped'. The story of how Sisera met his fate in the arms of Jael (Judg. 4.17-21) is a consecutive sequence that opens with a disjunctive clause and stops with a disjunctive clause which is continued in two consecutive clauses: 'AND Sisera had fled on foot to the tent of Jael..., *and* he turned into her tent, *and* she covered him..., *and* she took a tent peg, *and* took a hammer in her hand, *and* came to him stealthily, *and* drove the peg through his temple, *and* it broke into the ground, AND he was sound asleep, *and* he was exhausted, *and* he died'. The summary of the crimes of Bethel (2 Kgs 17.40-41) consists of two consecutive clauses, the first modified by an adversative participial clause, and the sequence ends with a disjunctive clause, which is followed by coordinate asyndetic nominal clauses and a subordinate verbal clause: '*And* they did not listen, but they kept acting in accordance with their old habits, *and* these nations were worshipers of *Yhwh*, AND of their idols they were servants, their children too and their children's children, as their fathers acted, they have been acting until this day'. Josiah's reform (2 Kgs 23.4-5) begins with the cleansing of the temple and the removal of the idolatrous priests, which is recorded in two consecutive clauses with multiple objects and modifiers, and in two paratactic clauses—the second with extended subordinate modifiers—that end the sequence:

> *And* the king ordered Hilkiah the high priest and the priests of the second rank and the keepers of the threshold to take from the temple of *Yhwh* the vessels made for Baal and for Asherah and the whole host of heaven, *and* they burned them outside Jerusalem on the terraces of the Kidron, <u>and</u> he carried their ashes to Bethel, <u>and</u> he arrested the idolatrous priests whom the kings of Judah had appointed and who offered incense in the towns of Judah and in the vicinity of Jerusalem and those offering incense to Baal and the Sun and the Moon and the Constellations and to all the host of heaven.

The rulers are castigated by Micah (Mic. 3.3) in a series of disjunctive clauses which ends with a paratactic clause and a parallel nominal phrase: 'AND who ate the flesh of my people, AND their skin they stripped off them, AND their bones they cracked, <u>and</u> they separated them as in a pot, and like meat in a cauldron'.

3. *Sequences without Stops—New Beginnings*

When the end of a sequence is not marked, the punctuation, that is, the separation of the sequence from the next, occurs at the beginning of the next sequence. It is the same principle which applies—that series depends on sameness and that punctuation, or separation, depends on difference. An absolute beginning, a feature which always marks the start of a new sequence, is the formula *wayhi* + a temporal phrase or clause + a *qatal* sequence, or the alternative *wᵉhayah* + a temporal phrase or clause + a *qatal* or a *yiqtol* sequence. Relative beginnings, which satisfy the principle because they differ from the clause types in the preceding sequence, are usually asyndetic or disjunctive clauses, either nominal or verbal, and which of these is chosen depends on whether the preceding sequence is consecutive, disjunctive, paratactic, or asyndetic.

For example, Josiah's reaction to the tombs he saw in Bethel (2 Kgs 23.16-18) is recounted in a completely consecutive sequence: the preceding sequence (23.15) ends in a compound stop consisting of an asyndetic and a paratactic clause ('he crushed it to powder, <u>and</u> burned the Asherah'), and the following sequence (23.19-23) begins with a disjunctive clause ('AND all the houses of the high places...did Josiah remove...'). Josiah's perfect observance of the law (23.24-25) is summarized in a disjunctive sequence: 'AND furthermore the mediums and the wizards and the teraphim and the idols...did Josiah abolish, in order to confirm the words of the Law..., AND before him there was not a king like him,..., AND after him there did not arise another like him'. It is distinguished from the preceding sequence (23.19-23) that ends consecutively, and from the next sequence (23.26-28) that begins asyndetically. The early years of Jehoiakim's reign (24.1-2) are recorded in a consecutive sequence without a marked ending: 'In his days Nebuchadnezzar...came up, *and* Jehoiakim became his subject..., *and* he turned *and* he rebelled against him, *and* Yhwh sent gangs...against him, *and* he sent them against Judah to destroy him...' The sequence begins with an asyndetic clause to distinguish it from the preceding sequence of *waw*-clauses (23.36-37) and the next sequence (24.3-4) is separated from it by its asyndetic beginning: 'Surely, this happened to Judah by the word of *Yhwh*...' The first paragraph on the siege of Jerusalem in the time of Zedekiah (25.1-2) consists of a consecutive sequence beginning with *wayhi* + a temporal clause: '*And* it happened, in the ninth year of his reign...Nebuchadnezzar...came against Jerusalem, *and* camped against it, *and* they built a siege wall against it, *and* the city came under siege...' The absolute beginning separates it from the preceding consecutive sequence (24.18-20) and, because it lacks final punctuation, the next sequence (25.3-5) begins asyndetically ('On the ninth of the month...'). Gedaliah's reception of Ishmael and the military commanders (25.24) is recounted in a consecutive sequence that consists of two clauses and lacks a marked ending: '*And* Gedaliah swore to them and their men, *and* he said to them...' The next sequence (25.25-26) begins absolutely with formulaic *wayhi* + a temporal phrase: '*And* it happened that, in the seventh month, Ishmael... came, *and* he struck Gedaliah, *and* he died..., *and* all the people rose..., *and* they went to Egypt...' The end of the sequence is unmarked, but the next paragraph (25.27-28) also begins absolutely: '*And* it happened that, in the thirty-seventh year of the exile of Jehoiachin..., Evil Merodach pardoned Jehoiachin..., *and* he spoke kindly to him, *and* he placed his throne...' This sequence also is not stopped, but the following sequence, the last paragraph in the history, is a series of paratactic clauses ending in a disjunctive clause (25.29-30): 'And he changed his prison garb, and he ate food…, AND as for his allowance, a regular allowance was given to him…'

4. *Mixed Sequences*

Sequences sometimes begin with a mixture of nominal and verbal clauses whose consistency or sameness is either in their use or omission of *waw* or in the lack of a series of any kind which might be stopped by a clause of a different type. These mixed sequences almost always develop into a series of some kind whose ending can be marked in one of the usual ways.

For example, the introduction to the reign of Manasseh (2 Kgs 21.1-3), like many such introductions, begins with a nominal asyndetic clause, a verbal disjunctive clause, and a nominal paratactic clause, before developing into a series of consecutive clauses: 'Manasseh [was] twelve years old at his accession, AND for fifty-five years he reigned in Jerusalem, and his mother's name [was] Hephzibah, *and* he did evil…, *and* he rebuilt…, *and* he erected altars for Baal, *and* he made an Asherah…, *and* he worshiped the whole host of heaven, *and* he served them'. The destruction of the cult places in Jerusalem which were associated with named persons (23.10-12a), is recounted in a series of clauses beginning with *waw*, paratactic and consecutive, which develops into a disjunctive sequence: 'And he defiled the Tophet, which [was] in the Valley of the sons of Hinnom…, *and* he removed the horses…from the entrance to the house of *Yhwh* by the quarters of Nathanmelech…, AND the chariots of the sun he burned up, AND the altars on the roof of the upper chamber of Ahaz the king tore down'. The next sequence (23.12b-14) deals with the cult places in the vicinity of Jerusalem destroyed by Josiah, and consists of an alternation of *waw* clauses (consecutive, paratactic, disjunctive, paratactic) that develops into a consecutive sequence: '*And* he hurried from there, and he threw their ashes into the Kidron stream, AND the high places east of Jerusalem…the king defiled, and he smashed the pillars, *and* he cut down the Asherim, *and* he filled their sanctuaries with the bones of men'. The next sequence (23.15), recounting his reforms at Bethel, is also a mixture of *waw*-clauses (disjunctive and consecutive) which ends without *waw* in an asyndetic clause and a coordinate paratactic clause: 'AND the altar which [was] at Bethel, the high place which Jeroboam the son of Nebat made…, that altar and that high place he tore down, *and* he burned the high place—he crushed it to powder, and he burned the Asherah'. The introduction to the reign of Jehoiachin (24.8-9) follows the general pattern of these regnal introductions but does not develop into a series of clauses of the same type, its cohesion consisting only in the use of *waw*-clauses after the initial asyndetic clause: 'Jehoiachin [was] eighteen at his accession, AND three months he ruled in Jerusalem, AND his mother's name [was] Nehushta, the daughter of Elnatan of Jerusalem, *and* he did evil in the sight of *Yhwh*…'

5. Subordinate Sequences

Subordinate clauses modify main clause sequences but do not punctuate them. Like main clause sequences, however, they also consist of series of clauses which can be punctuated in one of the usual ways—by a different type of clause—or can be left without final punctuation.

One example makes the point. The Deuteronomist describes the rejection of all Israel, including Judah, because of the sins of Jeroboam, and pursues the matter past the fall of Samaria, the capital city, to the ruin of Samaria, the Assyrian province (2 Kgs 17.19-24). The main clause sequence (17.19-20, 24) has the facts in a series of consecutive clauses, beginning asyndetically:

> Judah too did not keep the commandments of *Yhwh* their God, *and* they went in the ways of Israel…, *and Yhwh* rejected all the descendants of Israel, *and* he afflicted them, *and* he gave them into the hands of despoilers…, *and* the king of Assyria brought [people]…, *and* he settled them in the cities of Samaria instead of the people of Israel, *and* they took possession of Samaria, *and* they lived in its cities.

The end of the sequence is not marked, but the next (17.25-29) begins with formulaic *wayhi*. The subordinate clauses (17.21-23) give the reasons for this turn of events in two separate sequences. The first (17.21) blames Jeroboam, and consists of a conjunctive and two consecutive clauses punctuated by a paratactic clause: 'Because he tore Israel from the House of David, *and* they made Jeroboam son of Nebat king, *and* Jeroboam drove Israel away from *Yhwh*, <u>and</u> he made them commit a great sin'. The second subordinate series (17.22-23) is directed against the people, and consists of a consecutive and an asyndetic clause, with no final punctuation, both of which are modified by subordinate clauses ('which…, until…, [until he]'), one of which is further modified ('as'), and all of these lack final punctuation: '*And* the people of Israel went along with all the sin of Jeroboam, which he committed, they did not turn away from it, until *Yhwh* turned Israel out of his sight, as he had spoken through his servants the prophets, and [until he] exiled Israel from its land to Assyria until this day'. Both the subordinate sequences are governed by the conjunction 'because' (17.21). They retard the consecutive flow of the main clause sequence but do not punctuate it and are integral to its logic.

6. Punctuation in Dialogue, Discourse, and Soliloquy

Punctuation follows the principles of sequence in all literary styles and genres. Although direct discourse, besides being different in its rhythms and cadences, and in its tense and mood preferences, also interrupts the flow of its prosaic context, it does not punctuate this context. A conversation, for instance, does not stop the narrator's train of thought. A speech, similarly, may delay the prose passage in which it is presented, and will certainly have its own punctuation, but it is syntactically independent and not part of the main clause sequence. A soliloquy, an oracle, a poem also has its own particularity, and does not affect the setting in which it occurs. Direct discourse, like coordination, specifies its surrounding sequence, but unlike coordination does not belong to it. It is punctuated, however, exactly like any other text, either with clear stops, or with the continuation of the text in which it is embedded. Some examples follow.

a. *Quotation*

In the Deuteronomistic explanation of the fall of Samaria (2 Kgs 17.6-18), specifically in the consecutive subordinate sequence (17.7-17) which is set within a main clause consecutive sequence (17.6, 18), there are two quotations. The first (17.12) consists of one modal clause and the second (17.13) consists of two modal clauses and their subordinate modifiers, and neither quotation is punctuated, but their boundaries are simply marked by the continuing text:

> ...and they served the idols of which *Yhwh* had said to them, '*Do not do such a thing*', and *Yhwh* warned Israel and Judah through all his prophets and seers who said, '*Turn from your evil ways, and keep my commandments, my statutes in accordance with the law, which I commanded your fathers, which I sent to you through my servants the prophets*', and they did not listen...

However, later in the same text (2 Kgs 17.35-41) there is another quotation which is divided into two distinct syntactic segments. It is inserted into a narrative framework (17.35, 40-41) which is composed of consecutive clauses whose sequence ends with a disjunctive clause and coordinate nominal clauses. The first part of the quotation (17.35-37) is a consecutive sequence (17.35) that is modified by a subordinate disjunctive sequence (17.36-37a) which in turn is punctuated by a concluding consecutive clause (17.37b): 'Do not fear other Gods, *and* do not worship them, *and* do not serve them, *and* do not sacrifice to them, but rather *Yhwh*...you shall fear, AND him you shall worship, AND to him you shall sacrifice, AND the statutes and ordinances and the law and the commandment... you shall observe, *and* you shall not fear other Gods'. The second part of the quotation (17.38-39) is distinguished from the first by beginning with a disjunctive clause ('AND the covenant...you shall not forget'). Like the first, it continues consecutively ('*and* you shall not fear other Gods') and is modified by a subordinate sequence, but this ends by switching, not from disjunction to consecution but from modality to futurity ('but rather *Yhwh* your God you should fear, AND he will save you from the hand of your enemies'). The separation of the segments is marked by the syntax, that is, by sequences of similar clauses terminated by a clause of a different type, but this sequencing and segmentation could also be confirmed by a rhetorical or a literary analysis.

b. *Dialogue*

Isaiah's conversations with Hezekiah (2 Kgs 20) concern the health of the king (20.1-11) and his legacy (20.12-21). They consist of a command, a prayer, quotations within quotations, questions and answers, and a rhetorical aside. The sequencing and punctuation proceed as usual, and the only complication is the development of the argument in narrative and interlocking exchange which becomes especially intricate when, as in the first conversation, it follows a dramatic rather than a chronological order.

The first conversation is quoted in a narrative frame, in consecutive sequence, about his sickness and his prayer for recovery (20.1, 2, 3b): 'In those days Hezekiah was mortally ill, *and* Isaiah came to him..., *and* he turned his face to the wall, *and* he prayed to *Yhwh*,..., *and* Hezekiah wept bitterly'. In this context, Isaiah quotes *Yhwh* (20.1) whose words consist of an asyndetic modal clause, a subordinate clause and its consecutive sequence: '*and* he said to him, thus says *Yhwh*, "Put your house in order, because you are dying, *and* you will not live" '. Hezekiah's response is addressed to *Yhwh* and consists of an asyndetic modal clause (20.3a): 'Now, *Yhwh*, remember...' Before proceeding with Hezekiah's cure (20.7-11), the narrative continues in a sequence of disjunctive clauses (20.4)—the disjunction separates this segment of the narrative from the preceding—but goes back to Isaiah's visit at the beginning of the story: 'AND Isaiah had not left the lower city, AND the word of *Yhwh* had come to him as follows'. This introduces a quotation of *Yhwh*'s answer, in two parts, to Hezekiah's prayer (20.5-6). The first part (20.5) consists of an address to Isaiah—an asyndetic and a consecutive modal clause—which contains words for Hezekiah in a sequence of asyndetic *qatal* and participial clauses which is punctuated by a change to an asyndetic *yiqtol* future clause: 'Return, *and* say to Hezekiah..., thus says *Yhwh*..., "I have heard your prayer, I have seen your tears, behold I am going to heal you, on the third day you will go up to the house of *Yhwh*" '. The second part (20.6) of *Yhwh*'s answer continues the words meant for Hezekiah and is a consecutive, disjunctive and consecutive clause sequence: '*and* I will add fifteen years to your life, AND from the hand of the king of Assyria I will save you and this city, *and* I will defend this city...' This conversation ends with Hezekiah's cure (20.7) and with the exchange between Isaiah and Hezekiah which logically or chronologically had preceded it (20.8-11). The narrative context consists mostly of staccato segues between the exchanges ('*And* Isaiah said..., *and* they took it, *and* they laid it on the boil, *and* he recovered, *and* Hezekiah said..., *and* Isaiah said..., *and* Hezekiah said...') and a final summation ('*and* Isaiah the prophet called out to *Yhwh*, *and* the shadow returned...'). Two of the quotations are unpunctuated: an imperative (20.7, 'take a fig cake'); a nominal clause with coordinate conjunctive and consecutive clauses (20.8, 'what is the sign that *Yhwh* will heal me, *and* that I will go up to the temple of *Yhwh* on the third day'). Two are punctuated by changing from an indicative to a modal clause: a nominal clause, with modifiers, a coordinate *qatal* indicative clause, and a modal interrogative clause (20.9, 'this is the sign for you from *Yhwh*...: the shadow advanced ten steps, can it return ten steps?'); an asyndetic *qatal* clause and a modal asyndetic clause that ends the sequence (20.10, 'it is easy for the shadow to lengthen ten steps, so let the shadow return ten steps'). The syntax marks the progress of the argument which would be difficult to follow without it.

The second conversation (20.14-19) is set between two annalistic segments: the first (20.12-13) begins asyndetically to separate it from the preceding consecutive sequence (20.7-11) and consists of a consecutive sequence that ends with an asyndetic clause ('there was nothing that Hezekiah had not shown them...'); the second (20.20-21) consists of a disjunctive nominal clause ('and the rest of the deeds of Hezekiah…are they not written…') and two consecutive clauses ('*and* Hezekiah slept…, *and* Manasseh his son reigned…'). Hezekiah's part in the conversation (20.14-19) consists of laconic statements and an aside: an asyndetic clause (20.14, 'from a distant land they came, from Babylon'); two asyndetic clauses (20.15, 'everything in my house they saw, there was nothing I did not show them in my treasuries'); a nominal clause and a subordinate modifier (20.19, 'the word of *Yhwh*, which you have spoken, is good'); a modal and incomplete rhetorical aside (20.19, 'provided there might be peace and stability in my days'). Isaiah is wordier and his contributions can be punctuated: two questions, one *qatal*, the other modal, the latter a stop (20.14, 'what did these men say, and whence might they have come'); an asyndetic interrogative clause (20.15, 'what did they see in your house?'); a quotation within a quotation consisting of a mixed sequence—a nominal asyndetic clause, a consecutive clause, a verbal asyndetic clause, a disjunctive clause, and a consecutive clause (20.16-18, 'Hear the word of *Yhwh*: "Behold the days are coming, *and* there will be carried to Babylon…, nothing will be left, says *Yhwh*, AND some of your sons…will be taken away, *and* they will become…"'). The setting of the conversation is a series of consecutive clauses, again mostly segues into the quotations, and these consecutive clauses set it apart from the preceding segment which ends asyndetically and from the following segment that begins disjunctively. The conversations, even when they are punctuated, barely disrupt the narrative flow.

c. *Soliloquy*

Hezekiah's piety and dependence on the prophet Isaiah is expressed in his prayers and in the responses he receives. When he is cowered by the Rabshakeh's harangue, Isaiah encourages him with a prosaic message (2 Kgs 19.6-7), but when he is incensed by the tone of the Rabshakeh's letter, the response is an oracle that combines Isaiah's narration, the defiance of personified Zion, the bravado claims of the king of Assyria, and a divine soliloquy (19.21b-28). The oracle has a rhythmic, or poetic, cadence, and advances in clear syntactic steps.

The first sequence (19.21b-22) contains Isaiah's introduction and the words of Zion. His speech is composed of asyndetic *qatal* clauses, and his quotation of Zion's words consists of an asyndetic, a disjunctive and a consecutive *qatal* clause, and a concluding coordinate prepositional clause. The end of the segment is marked by the change from asyndetic to *waw*-clauses, and the additional coordinate clause illustrates that what ends a sequence is not necessarily the last in the sequence:

> She despises you, she scoffs at you,
>> the maiden daughter of Zion,
> she shakes her head at you,
>> the daughter of Jerusalem:
> 'Whom have you mocked and contemned,
>> AND against whom have you raised your voice,
> *and* lifted up your eyes?
>> against the Holy One of Israel!'

The second sequence (19.23) quotes the words of the king of Assyria which Zion considered to be mockery and contempt. They are introduced by Isaiah in an asyndetic *qatal* and consecutive clause and consist of an asyndetic *qatal* clause, a coordinate (that is, parallel) asyndetic nominal phrase, and two paratactic clauses (*weqatal* and *weyiqtol*) with a coordinate clause parallel to each. It is the switch from asyndesis to *waw*-clauses that ends the sequence:

> By the hand of your messengers you mocked the Lord,
> > *and* you said: 'With my many chariots
> I ascended the heights of the mountains,
> > the recesses of Lebanon,
> <u>and</u> I cut down its lofty cedars,
> > its finest cypresses,
> <u>and</u> I entered the lair of its denizen,
> > the forest of its fertile highlands'.

The third sequence (19.24) is the continuation of the Assyrian boast. It consists of an asyndetic *qatal* clause, a paratactic *qatal* clause, and a paratactic *yiqtol* clause. This change of conjugation marks the end of the sequence:

> I, I dug,
> > <u>and</u> I drank the water of foreigners,
> <u>and</u> I dried with the soles of my feet
> > all the rivers of Egypt.

The fourth sequence (19.25a), the beginning of *Yhwh*'s rebuke, starts with two asyndetic clauses and ends with a paratactic clause:

> Have you not heard
> > long ago I acted
> <u>and</u> I designed it from distant days.

The fifth sequence (19.25b-26) opens with an asyndetic clause, continues with a consecutive and a disjunctive clause, and this *waw*-series ends in an asyndetic sequence consisting of a verbal clause and an asyndetic nominal clause coordinate (parallel) to it:

> Now I am bringing it about,
> > *and* it is you, sending fortified cities
> crashing into ruined heaps,
> > AND their inhabitants, helpless,
> have become dismayed and ashamed:
> > they were grass in the field,
> growing green,
> > they have become hay on the rooftops,
> scorched before ripe.

The sixth sequence (19.27-28), the grand finale, begins with two disjunctive clauses, one verbal and the other nominal, and continues with a subordinate series—comprising a conjunctive and a disjunctive clause—and then two consecutive clauses. The sequence is punctuated by the change from *qatal* in the opening disjunctive clauses to *yiqtol* (*weqatal*) in the last consecutive clauses:

AND your sitting,
  and your going out, and your coming in, I know,
  AND your ranting against me
—since you have ranted against me
  AND your complacency has come into my hearing—
and I will put my ring in your nose,
  and my bit in your mouth,
and I will send you back
  the same way you came

The structure of the oracle is determined by the syntax, but the selection and the succession of clauses also corresponds to the varied rhythms and cadences and the changing moods of each spoken part.

d. *Discourse*

The Rabshakeh's speech (2 Kgs 18.19-35) is set in a narrative framework composed of a consecutive sequence which introduces it (18.17-19), divides it into two parts (18.26-28a), and is stopped by a final paratactic clause (18.36):

> *And* the king of Assyria sent the Tartan, the Rabsaris and the Rabshakeh from Lachish…, *and* they went up *and* came to Jerusalem, *and* they went up, *and* arrived, *and* stood…, *and* they summoned the king, *and* Eliakim…and Shebnah…and Joah… came out to them, *and* he said to them…, *and* Eliakim…and Shebnah and Joah said…, *and* the Rabshakeh said to them…, *and* the Rabshakeh stood, *and* called out in a loud voice in Hebrew, *and* addressed them, *and* said…, <u>and</u> the people were silent…

The first part of the speech (18.19-25) is divided into four sequences which deal alternately with Hezekiah's reliance on Egypt (18.19-21, 23-24) and on *Yhwh* (18.22, 25). The second part of the speech consists of two sequences, one (18.28b-32) urging the people to make a treaty with Assyria and give up relying on Hezekiah or their covenant with *Yhwh*, the other (18.33-34) describing the universal futility of relying on God.

    The first sequence (18.19-21) begins with a consecutive clause ('*And* the Rabshakeh said to them'), and an asyndetic imperative and an asyndetic indicative clause which are the object of the verb in the first clause ('Say to Hezekiah, "Thus says the great king, the king of Assyria"'). The Rabshakeh's discourse begins with a nominal clause and its modifier, and continues with asyndetic indicative (*qatal*) clauses, the last of which is modified by a subordinate modal and nominal sequence. The staccato rhythm suits the challenge, but it dissolves into empty rhetoric in the final subordinate clause:

> What is this reliance of yours on which you have relied?
> You think that a mere word off the lips is counsel and strength for war?
> Now, on whom have you relied that you have rebelled against me?
> Now, behold, you have relied on Egypt, this broken reed of a staff
> which, if a man should lean on it, it would go through his hand and pierce it.
> Such is Pharaoh, the king of Egypt, to all who rely on him.

The second sequence (18.22) begins with *waw*, which separates it from the preceding asyndetic series, and a subordinate clause. The reply of the Judaeans is quoted in an asyndetic verbal clause, and the retort of the Rabshakeh is an asyndetic nominal clause ('Is it not he?') modified by a relative clause and its consecutive development:

> And if you say to me, 'In *Yhwh* our God we have trusted,
> is it not he whose high places and altars Hezekiah has removed and said
> to Judah and Jerusalem, "Before this altar you shall worship, in Jerusalem" '.

The third sequence (18.23-24) is composed of a disjunctive, a paratactic, a disjunctive and a consecutive clause and is separated from the previous sequence by this exclusive use of clauses that begin with *waw*. The disjunctive and para-tactic clauses are modal—as is the conditional clause—but the consecutive clause is indicative and ends the sequence:

> AND now, make a bet with my lord, with the king of Assyria,
> <u>and</u> were I to give you two thousand horses, if you were able to put riders on them,
> AND how could you repulse one governor among the least of my master's servants,
> *and* yet you have relied on Egypt for chariots and horsemen.

The fourth sequence (18.25) is composed of asyndetic clauses, interrogative and affirmative, and this asyndesis distinguishes it from the preceding. The ending is not marked, but what follows is the continuation of the consecutive frame:

> Now, have I come up against this place to destroy it despite *Yhwh*?
> *Yhwh* said to me, 'Go up against this land and destroy it'.

The fifth sequence (18.28b-32), the first in the second part of the discourse, consists principally of an exhortation to listen to the king of Assyria (18.28b), followed by two warnings not to listen to Hezekiah (18.31, 32b): the exhortation ('listen') and the first warning ('do not listen') are asyndetic, but the second warning is consecutive ('*and* do not listen') and this change to a clause with *waw* ends the sequence. Both warnings contain a quotation. The first (18.31-32a) quotes the advice of the king of Assyria in a series of imperatives: it begins asyndetically but the rest are paratactic, and the series ends by changing to consecutive clauses. The second (18.32b) quotes Hezekiah's assurance to the people. The exhortation (18.29-30) quotes the king of Assyria who advises them to beware of Hezekiah: the first clause is jussive and asyndetic and is modified by a subordinate clause; the second is jussive and consecutive and quotes Hezekiah who assures the people in an asyndetic and a consecutive clause. The king of Assyria, in effect, tries to persuade the people of Jerusalem to abandon their covenant with *Yhwh* and make a treaty with him, by emphasizing the ineffective-ness of theirs and the blessings accruing from his:

> Listen to the word of the great king, the king of Assyria. Thus says the king:
> 'Do not let Hezekiah deceive you,
> because he will not be able to deliver you out of my hand,
> *and* do not let Hezekiah make you rely on *Yhwh* saying:
> "*Yhwh* will surely deliver us,
> *and* this city will not be given into the hand of the king of Assyria" '.
> Do not listen to Hezekiah,
> for the king of Assyria has said as follows:

'Make with me a blessing,
  <u>and</u> come out to me,
<u>and</u> eat from you own vine and fig tree,
  <u>and</u> drink the waters of your own well,
until I come and take you to a land like your land,
  a land of grain and wine,
a land of bread and vineyards,
  a land of olive oil and honey,
and live, *and* do not die'.
And do not listen to Hezekiah,
because he would mislead you by saying:
  '*Yhwh* will save us'.

The sixth sequence (18.33-34), the second address to the people, the last part of the discourse, is composed entirely of asyndetic interrogative clauses, with coordinate and subordinate modifiers:

Has any God of the nations saved his land from the hand of the king of Assyria?
Where are the Gods of Hamath and Arpad,
where are the Gods of Sepharvaim, Hena and Ivvah,
for did they not save Samaria from my hand!
Who is there among all the Gods of the earth who have saved their land from my hand,
that *Yhwh* should save Jerusalem from my hand?

The syntax of the discourse establishes its rhetorical structure. It does not differ from the syntax of any other text, but the discourse does differ from quotations, dialogue and poetry. These most often consist of individual clauses, one or two or more clauses related to one another by sequence, subordination or coordination, in compound or complex sentences. The Rabshakeh's speech, by contrast, is composed of sentences in the same sequence, each with its peculiar clausal structure, grouped together into paragraphs. In this the discourse diverges from the spoken word and resembles a literary work.

7. *Punctuation and Composition*

Individual texts are composed of sequences and sequences tend to be grouped in pairs. The texts are distinguished from one another by their kinds of sequence and punctuation and by the pairing of similar or of different kinds. Homogeneity is unusual. Diversity and variation are characteristic of most literary forms, styles of writing, and particular texts.

In the explanation of the fall of Samaria (2 Kgs 17) there are eight sequences. The first four (17.1-5, 6-18, 19-24, 25-29) are sequences of consecutive clauses, the first three beginning asyndetically and the fourth absolutely (*wayhi* + temporal clause), none with final punctuation but clearly distinguished from the next sequence which begins with a different, non-consecutive, type of clause. The first two match because, among other reasons, their main consecutive clauses are in chronological order, but they differ totally in their use of quotation and subordination. The third and fourth follow a dischronologized narrative order and also agree on other matters, but the third is logical prose and the fourth is mostly quotation. Of the last four sequences (17.30-31, 32, 33-34, 35-41) only two

(17.32, 35-41) are consecutive, and these are paired with a disjunctive (17.30-31) or asyndetic (17.33-34) sequence. The pairing of sequences, whose significance is open to literary analysis, gives the text a certain ebb and flow, but the variety of sequences, and the diversity of clause types and punctuation, add a jagged edge and produce a dense and studied argument.

The Rabshakeh's speech is preceded by eight sequences or paragraphs (2 Kgs 18.1-16) on the highlights of Hezekiah's reign. They are of varying length, composed of a variety of clause types, punctuated in different ways, and structurally and stylistically unlike the paragraphs in the preceding history of Samaria (2 Kgs 17). The first sequence (18.1-3), with Hezekiah's genealogy, chronology, and evaluation, opens with *wayhi* and a temporal clause—which always marks a new beginning—but it contains a mixture of clause types (asyndetic, disjunctive, paratactic, and consecutive) before becoming a series of clauses beginning with *waw*. The next paragraph (18.4) is distinguished from it, therefore, by beginning without *waw*: this asyndetic clause describes Hezekiah ('He is the one who removed the high places'), and leads into a sequence of paratactic clauses ('<u>and</u> broke the pillars, <u>and</u> cut down the Asherah, <u>and</u> smashed the bronze serpent') the last of which is modified by a subordinate sequence ('which Moses had made—for the people of Israel until those days had been offering incense to it—and had called Nehushtan'). The next sequence (18.5-6a) emphasizes Hezekiah's trust in God: it too begins with an asyndetic clause ('In *Yhwh* the God of Israel he trusted'), which distinguishes it from the preceding clauses that begin with *waw*, but then it turns into a series of *waw*-clauses ('AND after him there was none like him…, *and* he clung to *Yhwh*…'), and ends asyndetically ('—he did not turn away from him'). The next paragraph (18.6b-7a) comprises a consecutive and a paratactic clause, and ends by shifting to an asyndetic imperfect (*yiqtol*) clause, which is also modified by an imperfect clause: '*And* he kept the commandments which *Yhwh* commanded Moses, <u>and</u> *Yhwh* was with him—he was successful in every battle that he undertook'.

The fifth sequence (18.7b-8) consists of consecutive clauses and ends in an asyndetic clause: '*And* he rebelled against the king of Assyria, *and* he did not serve him: he defeated the Philistines as far as Gaza and its territory, including watchtowers and fortified cities'. The sixth paragraph (18.9-10) begins with formulaic *wayhi* and temporal clauses and continues with consecutive clauses: '*And* it happened, in the fourth year of king Hezekiah, this was the seventh year of Hoshea son of Elah king of Israel, that Shalmaneser, king of Assyria, came up against Samaria, *and* besieged it, *and* he captured it at the end of three years'. The next paragraph (18.10-12) begins asyndetically to distinguish it from the last and then continues with consecutive clauses and subordinate modifiers: 'In the sixth year of Hezekiah, this being the ninth year of Hoshea king of Israel, Samaria was captured, *and* the king of Assyria exiled Israel to Assyria, *and* he settled them…, because they had not listened to the voice of *Yhwh* their God, *and* they had transgressed his covenant—everything that Moses the servant of *Yhwh* had commanded them—*and* had not listened, *and* had not acted upon it'. The last paragraph (18.13-16) begins asyndetically to distinguish it from the preceding sequence, then continues with consecutive clauses, and ends in an asyndetic clause with a consecutive clause as its complement: the third clause also contains a quotation which begins in the indicative and ends by changing to modal clauses: 'In the fourteenth year of king Hezekiah Sennacherib came up against the fortified cities of Judah, *and* he captured them, *and* Hezekiah king of Judah sent a message to the king of Assyria at Lachish saying, "I have sinned, withdraw from me, whatever you might impose on me I shall bear", *and* the king imposed…, *and* Hezekiah gave…—at that time Hezekiah stripped the gold…, *and* he gave it to the king of Assyria'. All the sequences differ from each other and the varied syntax measures the account.

The pairing of the sequences, more evident in some instances than in others, contributes to its solemnity: the first says he did right, the second gives the details; the third describes his attitude, and the fourth has the specifics; the fifth has his rebellion, the sixth has what happened to Samaria for rebelling; and the seventh and eighth contrast the results of Assyrian attacks on Samaria and Judah.

Syntax is primary and the arbiter of meaning, with sometimes surprising or unexpected results. The poem recited by Isaiah (2 Kgs 18.21b-28) has six sequences, arranged as strophe and antistrophe, no two alike in their agglomeration of clause types and punctuation, and it is perhaps surprising that, although there is some coordination or parallelism, it is sequence that defines the structure and flow of the recitation. The speech of the Rabshakeh (2 Kgs 18.19-35) follows the standard rules of syntax, but its rhetorical structure, its paragraphing and climactic progression, its surge into sophisticated blasphemy, are unexpected in an extemporaneous harangue, or even in battlefield diplomacy. Translation, however, follows other rules, and the punctuation of such ancient discourse may fall on deaf ears.

8. *Conclusion*

Punctuation is tracked by reading a biblical text from the beginning. Sequence is the guide, but it is accompanied by sight and sound and a sense of direction, by observing word order, by distinguishing the rhythms and cadences of clause types individually and in series, by expecting sameness and noting difference. It worked once with study, with listening, with reading aloud. It may be lost now in Masoretic systems of accentuation and topicalization, and in the incompatible grammar, syntax and punctuation of contemporary translation. But syntax was the punctuation of the language and, even if arcane or too busy or out of date, is still a critical point.

The system works not just because there are simple rules derived from plain principles, but also because there is significance and sound, meaning attached to word orders, to clause type and to sequences, to tempo and stress in the starts, concatenations and stops of sentences, and to the structure of paragraphs, strophes, stanzas and whole texts. Clauses are of different types, and sentences of different length, paragraphs and strophes of varying complexity, whole texts of more or less creative inspiration, and their punctuation makes the point.

Some Readings

Buth, R.
   1990   'Word Order Differences between Narrative and Non-Narrative Material in
                Biblical Hebrew', in *Tenth World Congress of Jewish Studies, Division D*. I.
                The Hebrew Language, Jewish Languages (Jerusalem: World Union of Jewish
                Studies): 9-16.

Gross, W.
   1994   'Zur syntaktischen Struktur des Vorfeldes im hebraischen Verbalsatz', *ZAH* 7:
                203-14.
   1996   *Die Satzteilfolge im Verbalsatz alttestamentlicher Prosa* (Tübingen: J.C.B.
                Mohr [Paul Siebeck]).
   1999   'Is there Really a Compound Nominal Clause in Biblical Hebrew?', in C.L.
                Miller (ed.), *The Verbless Clause in Biblical Hebrew: Linguistic Approaches*
                (Winona Lake, IN: Eisenbrauns): 19-49.

Hatav, G.
   2000   '(Free) Direct Discourse in Biblical Hebrew', *HS* 41: 7-30.

Heller, R.L.
   2004   *Narrative Structure and Discourse Constellations: An Analysis of Clause
                Function in Biblical Hebrew* (HSS, 55; Winona Lake, IN: Eisenbrauns).

Khan, G.
   1988   *Studies in Semitic Syntax* (London Oriental Studies, 38; Oxford: Oxford
                University Press).

Korpel, M.C.A., and J.M. Oesch
   2000   *Delimitation Criticism: A New Tool in Biblical Scholarship* (Pericope: Scrip-
                ture as Written and Read in Antiquity, 1; Assen: Van Gorcum).
   2002   *Studies in Scriptural Unit Division* (Pericope: Scripture as Written and Read in
                Antiquity, 3; Assen: Van Gorcum).

Mirsky, A.
   1977   'Stylistic Device for Conclusion in Hebrew', *Semitics* 5: 9-23.

Myhill, J.
   1992   'Word Order and Temporal Sequencing', in D.L. Payne (ed.), *Pragmatics of
                Word Order Flexibility* (Philadelphia: Jon Benjamins): 265-78.
   1995   'Non-Emphatic Fronting in Biblical Hebrew', *Theoretical Linguistics* 21:
                93-144.

Niccacci, A.
   1994   'The Style of Mesha and the Bible: Verbal System and Narrativity', *Or* 63:
                226-48.

Polak, F.H.
   1998   'The Oral and the Written: Syntax, Stylistics and the Development of Biblical
                Prose Narrative', *JANESCU* 26: 59-105.
   2001   'The Style of the Dialogue in Biblical Prose Narrative', *JANESCU* 28: 53-95.

Revell, E.J.
   1989   'The Conditioning of Word Order in Verbless Clauses in Biblical Hebrew', *JSS*
                34: 1-24.
   2000   'The Interpretive Value of the Masoretic Punctuation', in M. Sæbø (ed.),
                Hebrew Bible/Old Testament—The History of its Interpretation. I. *From the
                Beginnings to the Middle Ages (Until 1300)* (Göttingen: Vandenhoeck &
                Ruprecht): 64-73.

Sailhamer, J.H.

    1990   'A Database Approach to the Analysis of Hebrew Narrative', *Maarav* 5-6: 319-35.

Sivan, D., and S. Yona

    1994   'Style and Syntax: Pivotal Use of Extrapositional Syntagms in Biblical Hebrew', *UF* 26: 443-54.

Talstra, E.

    1987   'Towards a Distributional Definition of Clauses in Classical Hebrew', *ETL* 63: 95-105.

    1997   'Tense, Mood, Aspect and Clause Connections in Biblical Hebrew: A Textual Approach', *JNSL* 23: 81-103.

    1999   'Reading Biblical Hebrew Poetry—Linguistic Structure or Rhetorical Device?', *JNSL* 25: 101-26.

Van der Merwe, C.H.J.

    1999   'The Elusive Biblical Hebrew Term *wyhy*: A Perspective in Terms of its Syntax, Semantics, and Pragmatics in 1 Samuel', *HS* 40: 83-114.

Walsh, J.T.

    2001   *Style and Structure in Biblical Hebrew Narrative* (Collegeville, MN: Liturgical Press).

Wendland, E.R. (ed.)

    1994   *Discourse Perspectives on Hebrew Poetry in the Scriptures* (New York: United Bible Societies).

Zewi, T.

    1994   'The Nominal Sentence in Biblical Hebrew', in G. Goldenberg and S. Raz (eds.), *Semitic and Cushitic Studies* (Wiesbaden: Otto Harrassowitz): 145-67.

CANONICAL SIGNALS IN THE ADDITIONS IN DEUTERONOMY 1.39*

Norbert Lohfink

At the beginning of Deuteronomy, Moses, in the course of his first speech, suddenly begins to elaborate. It happens at the point where he describes God's reaction to Israel's lack of faith in the Kadesh-barnea episode. This reaction, consisting of two utterances and their introductions, makes up no less than seven verses: Deut. 1.34-40.

Taken as a whole the utterances are framed by two declarations that, even from a formal point of view, belong together. On the one hand there is God's angry oath that none of these 'men' will see the land promised to the ancestors (v. 35), and on the other there is the command to return to the wilderness (v. 40).[1] Nevertheless, their coherence has been disrupted by the deity's plans for a future that is about to change. From a narratological point of view, these are suspense-producing prolepses from Moses as narrator. God's anger will not strike Caleb and his family (v. 36). Instead, God's anger falls on another, although one would never expect it: Moses himself (v. 37). Joshua, not Moses, will apportion the land to Israel (v. 38). Furthermore, the Israelites who will eventually take possession of the land are as yet only children (v. 39).

The following reflections will be concerned with this last statement. In M[2] it has a measured form:

וטפכם   But your baggage-train[3]
אשר אמרתם לבז יהיה   of which you said: 'it shall become booty!'

---

*   I learned to value Antony F. Campbell during the 1960s in Rome at the Pontifical Biblical Institute as a brilliant student and a very pleasant house-mate. Since then, I have never quite lost contact with him and have always enjoyed his contributions to Old Testament studies. It is with pleasure that I dedicate this brief essay to him on his 70th birthday.

1.   This is in effect a common pattern of speech in Deuteronomy: statement + directive for action. This pattern appears in texts preceding Deut. 1.39, namely 1.6b, 7, 8, 9b, 13, 21. It is already evident from Deut. 1.9b-13 how this kind of pattern can include an elaboration.

2.   Within the context of text criticism, I use the abbreviation proposed by *Biblia Hebraica Quinta* (*BHQ*): M (Masoretic Text), Smr (Samaritan Pentateuch), G (Septuagint), La (Vetus Latina), V (Vulgate). It is not necessary in my analysis to go into textual questions within the Masoretic, Greek or Samaritan texts. I am using *BHS*, G (Göttingen edition) and Tal 1994 as my base texts.

3.   I translate 'baggage-train' in the singular because of the singular in the relative clause as well. The meaning and reference of the word טף can be determined in a particular case only by taking the context into account. For the best investigation of the word, see Locher 1982. Based on this, one could perhaps also translate the phrase as 'your little ones'.

ובניכם	And your sons,
אשר לא־ידעו היום טוב ורע	who today do not yet know good and evil:
המה יבאו שמה	they will arrive there,
ולהם אתננה	and to them I shall grant it,[4]
והם יירשוה	and they will take possession of it.

The basic syntactic structure is as follows: the children, the subject of the sentence (*topic* would be a better term—grammatically the children appear both as subject and as object), are located before the verb. They do not occur in their normal position in the sentence, that is, after the verb (המה, ולהם, והם). In this way they are made the focus of attention. At the same time, they occur here only as pronouns. These pronouns in their turn refer back to a double occurrence of a *nominative absolute* (ובניכם, וטפכם) which is further expanded by a relative clause. This amounts to a threefold sharpening of focus on the subject matter of the passage. Could it possibly be given greater emphasis? Indeed it is—it is even more strongly emphasized when one realizes that both the *nominative absolute* and the clauses themselves form parallels. The *nominative absolute* occurs twice and the principal clause three times. In the former we find a synonymous parallelism. In the latter, successive actions are arranged in a synthetic parallelism corresponding to consecutive phases of the occupation of the land. The whole is clearly designed down to the last detail and its thrust is further enhanced by assonance and rhyme. If the text is felt to be over-full, this is a matter of taste. In antiquity, people presumably saw things differently. There is no doubt the text is highly rhetorical, but each of its elements fits and nothing is amiss. It looks as if it all came from a single hand.

Nevertheless, it is not from a single hand. The sentence is the result of several 'expansions'. In contrast to the situation with many other Old Testament texts where we also, quite justifiably, reconstruct earlier historical stages, here we do not have to rely solely on our analytical skills. Instead, we possess textual evidence which documents for us at least some stages of the history of the text. This situation, which is not a very common one, is of course recognized to some extent in the literature on Deut. 1.39. But have the proper conclusions been drawn from it—for textual criticism and the reconstruction of earlier stages? Two great scholars of the nineteenth century, Abraham Kuenen and Julius Wellhausen, were almost the only ones who saw matters correctly—and with only G in view.[5] For this reason I have sought, in the first part of this essay, to provide a fresh reconstruction of the earlier versions of Deut. 1.39, and to indicate the consequences of this for textual criticism and the reconstruction of stages in the growth of Deuteronomy itself.[6]

4. 'It' refers back to the promised land. It is at the centre of attention since 1.19, and again in 1.35 it is thrust right into the foreground of God's word. Therefore it is the real subject of Moses' story. For a similar resumption made at a considerable remove, cf. אתה in 1.24.

5. Cf. Kuenen 1877: 557-58. Wellhausen (1889: 338) reviews Kuenen's thesis favourably and calls this case 'an example of how text criticism meshes with literary criticism'.

6. In this study I confine myself strictly to the problems of Deut. 1.39. Actually, the problems for text criticism of Num. 14.23 and 32.11 should be dealt with at the same time. The expansions to these texts, usually regarded as additions of the Septuagint, are systematically connected to

One result is that we will not be led back into obscure antiquity. Deuteronomy 1.39 reached its present form only in a late phase of the history of the text. For this reason it is worth asking about the motives that led to such expansions of the text. As will be shown, *canonical* reading guides were, to some extent, built in. In this way at least, a small contribution can be made to the problems, much discussed today, of a *canonical exegesis*. The second, shorter part of my essay is devoted to this issue.

1. *Interlocking Between Textual Criticism and the Reconstruction of Earlier Stages*

The first thing to consider is the evidence of the two decisive and complete text witnesses besides M, namely G and Smr.

The text of G is as follows:

καὶ πᾶν παιδίον νέον	but every child,
ὅστις οὐκ οἶδεν σήμερον ἀγαθὸν ἢ κακόν	that today does not yet know good and evil—
οὗτοι εἰσελεύσονται ἐκεῖ	(all) these will settle there,
καὶ τούτοις δώσω αὐτήν	and to these I will grant it,
καὶ αὐτοὶ κληρονομήσουσιν αὐτήν	and these will take possession of it.

In G an equivalent is lacking for at least the first אשר-clause of M: אשר אמרתם לבז יהיה. Whether καὶ πᾶν παιδίον νέον translated the word וטפכם or the word ובניכם must remain open, because παιδίον is available for both Hebrew words:

- for בן, *Hatch–Redpath* gives 17 occurrences: after ילד (36 occurrences) and נער/נערה (29 occurrences), it is the third most frequent word translated by παιδίον.
- for טף, cf. Gen. 45.19; Num. 14.3, 31; Deut. 1.39(?); 3.6; Josh. 1.14; 8.35 (= G 9.2^f Rahlfs); 2 Chron. 20.13. The number of occurrences is fewer but it is still sufficient for us to reckon here also with a normal enough usage.

The אשר-clause, which is missing in G, is found in Smr. The text of Smr runs:

וטפכם	But your baggage-train
אשר אמרתם לבז יהיה	of which you said: 'it shall become booty!'
ובניכם	And your sons,
הם יבאו שמה	they will arrive there,
ולהם אתננה	and to them I shall grant it,
והם יירשוה	and they will take possession of it.

In Smr, therefore, the second relative clause from M is missing: היום טוב ורע אשר לא־ידעו. Rather, ובניכם (as a parallel to וטפכם) is immediately followed by הם. One must presumably translate the *waw* in ובניכם by 'namely' or 'that is', and understand this new word as an explication of וטפכם which leads on to the main clause.

Deut. 1.39. The thesis presented here could, in a synoptic presentation of these texts, be given an even more persuasive basis than is possible here. Kuenen (1877) has done this in exemplary fashion.

In M both ‏אשר‎-clauses are found—as already described above. In the more recent literature the evidence of Smr is hardly mentioned; as for G, an *abbreviation* or *more concise* form of the translation into Greek is usually assumed. However, the theory of an abbreviation of the text by a Greek translator can scarcely be maintained any longer. It is much more likely that we possess, even if only in fragmentary form, a Hebrew text corresponding to G in the manuscript 4QDeut[h].[7] It runs as follows:

‏...] א ידע היום טוב]...‎

That Deut. 1.39 is the text in question is quite clear from its position in the manuscript. Two factors indicate that we are dealing with a Hebrew parallel to G, as the editor Julie A. Duncan points out clearly:

- One is the requirement of space. The normal number of characters in a line of 4QDeut[h] is 85-95 or 75-85. If one assumes the full text of M, this line of the manuscript would, on the basis of what survives in the preceding lines, have to contain 112 characters. The first relative clause of M may therefore have been missing—as in G.
- The other is that the singular ‏ידע‎ (also corresponding to G) indicates that ‏וטפכם‎, not ‏ובניכם‎, stood at the beginning. Admittedly, there is the possibility in Hebrew of incongruence between subject and predicate. But what is there to compel one to assume any such thing when a (collective) singular is available in ‏וטפכם‎? Given the tendency of the Septuagint of Deuteronomy in particular to align itself as closely as possible to the Hebrew model, one should take the Greek singular seriously.

On the whole therefore, these observations indicate that 4QDeut[h] is to be completed as follows:

‏וטפכם אשר ל] א ידע היום טוב]ורע‎[8]

One may of course still ask whether πᾶν παιδίον νέον can actually be a translation of ‏טף‎. I have already shown that παιδίον can stand for ‏טף‎. The word πᾶν may have been placed in front in order to set the following verb in the singular. The pleonasm παιδίον νέον is unique in G (Gen. 44.20 is only remotely comparable) whereas the expression νέος παῖς is attested in Greek literature since the time of Homer. παιδίον νέον is a diminutive form of it and so the fuller expression may reflect the translator's intention to make the statement in v. 39 stand out as clearly as possible from what precedes it. In any case, it seems to me unnecessary

7. Cf. DJD XIV, 64-65 (Duncan). The manuscript has been known since Duncan (1989). Neither Smr nor 4QDeut[h] is even mentioned by Wevers (1995: 23). He decrees 'LXX simply has καὶ πᾶν παιδίον νέον. This free rendering does rid the text of a troublesome doublet.' Shortly afterwards he speaks of an 'umbrella term'. That G had the text of M in front of him does not seem open to discussion.

8. This is also the reconstruction of Duncan, whom I have followed in the argumentation (DJD XIV, 65).

to postulate a special Hebrew equivalent for νέον when it is not attested elsewhere. Even though it was not a simple matter for the Septuagint translators, the term טף evidently provided a sufficient Hebrew basis for the whole expression.[9]

Given the level of certainty attainable in such matters, one can conclude that there were (at least) three different versions of Deut. 1.39 among Hebrew manuscripts in pre-Christian times. The question is, what is their genetic relationship? Do the shorter versions precede the longer one of M, or are they secondary abbreviations of M?

For a long time it was assumed that G (or the G *Vorlage*) had, at the beginning, 'compressed' the 'over-full' clause contained in M.[10] If anyone even noticed Smr, it was to assume, without further ado, that it too represented a 'deliberate contraction'.[11]

There is a problem with this explanatory model with its notion of secondary contractions of the text. In a first step based on literary and redactional analysis of M alone, the theory is formulated that various expansions were introduced over a long period of time into an originally very short text. This is how M came about. Then, in a second step, the full text (of M) is presupposed, other witnesses are invoked and textual criticism commences. However, such a procedure obliges one to assume that at least some of the early expansions were subsequently shortened or compressed by G or Smr in a late phase of the history of the text. There seems to be no awareness of the possibility that G or Smr might not have been dependent on M at all. In short, we have a thoroughly complicated hypothesis: a short text was *expanded* into an over-full text and this was subsequently relieved of the burden of these *expansions* by being abbreviated.

If, however, we can now dismiss a slimming cure by the Greek translator, a much simpler—and therefore preferable—hypothesis presents itself. It takes the available forms of the text themselves as evidence of a thoroughly plausible process of revision. This can be presented in tabular form as follows:

Deut. 1.39*	Deut. 1.39 Smr	Deut. 1.39 G	Deut. 1.39 M
וטפכם	וטפכם	καὶ πᾶν παιδίον νέον	וטפכם
—	אשר אמרתם	—	אשר אמרתם
—	לבז יהיה	—	לבז יהיה
—	ובניכם	—	ובניכם
—	—	ὅστις οὐκ οἶδεν σήμερον	אשר לא־ידעו היום
—	—	ἀγαθὸν ἢ κακόν	טוב ורע
הם יבאו שמה	הם יבאו שמה	οὗτοι εἰσελεύσονται ἐκεῖ	הם יבאו שמה
ולהם אתננה	ולהם אתננה	καὶ τούτοις δώσω αὐτήν	ולהם אתננה
והם יירשוה	והם יירשוה	καὶ αὐτοι κληρονομήσουσιν αὐτήν	והם יירשוה

9.   It is at least possible that πᾶς νεώτερος ἄπειρος in Num. 14.23 G is likewise an attempt to render טף.

10.   Thus, initially, König (1917: 70). The fullest attempt at justification is Mittmann (1975: 37 nn. 15 and 16). Mittmann could not yet have known 4QDeut[h]. The formulations quoted, including the one in the following sentence, are from König and Mittmann.

11.   So already Dillmann (1886: 240), for the second אשר-clause 'omitted in *Sam.*'.

The second and third columns show simultaneous expansions of the text in the first column that are independent of each other. The first column is inferred from the other two as the text that preceded them both. For its part, the fourth column *conflates* the developments of the text in the second and third columns.

Admittedly, the *expansions* all occur in a late phase of the history of the text. In any case, as is often argued, there are clear indications in the two relative clauses that late additions are involved:

- אשר אמרתם לבז יהיה is a quotation that has no point of reference in the preceding text of Deuteronomy. It is identical, word for word, with a relative clause attached to וטפכם in the parallel account in Num. 14.31. There it refers to 14.3. All this indicates that Deut. 1.39 is an example of quite late assimilation work within the Pentateuch. Smr bears witness to this harmonizing addition, whereas G at this point represents a stage in the history of the text when it had not yet taken place.

- On the other hand, the relative clause אשר לא־ידעו(ן) היום טוב ורע reflects the additional need at this point in Moses' discourse to spell out more precisely who will and who will not enter the land, and to indicate why. The same concern is present in the addition הדור הרע הזה in v. 35.[12] Note that both expressions employ the word pair רע–טוב. One of the expansions is missing in G while the other is not yet present in Smr. Hence, they cannot come from the same hand. At that time, something like the word pair רע–טוב must have been around. Whatever the case, in v. 39 G bears witness to a clarifying addition אשר לא־ידעו(ן) היום טוב ורע while Smr for its part reflects a stage in the history of the text when the addition did not yet exist.

Two additions were therefore made to v. 39 deriving from characteristically late interests. By comparing Smr and G, a still earlier stage of the text can be inferred that was as yet unaware of either expansion. It is to be found in the first column of the table. It is evident from 4QDeut[h] that this stage contained only the noun טף as a *nominative absolute*. Hence, the earliest form of v. 39a that can still be retrieved by textual criticism is:

וטפכם | הם יבאו שמה

The additions were incorporated and transmitted in two different branches of the manuscript tradition.[13] Our M therefore represents a family of manuscripts that has combined both additions in a very elegant fashion in the form of a *conflation*. In a sense, this amounts to a third stage of *revisional development*.

The assumption that an earlier multi-faceted and multi-phase expansion was subsequently shortened becomes unnecessary. The alternative hypothesis outlined here is much simpler and therefore preferable. It can only be falsified if new evidence were to emerge to complicate the picture even more.

---

12. This apposition is missing in G*.
13. The second addition is connected with similar additions in Num. 14.23 G and 32.11 G.

The case of Deut. 1.39 demonstrates once more in exemplary fashion that we cannot simply separate textual criticism and the reconstruction of earlier stages of the text. To be sure, the available evidence provides us with information only about the final stages of the history of the text: for the earlier stages we have to rely almost entirely on internal textual analysis. But the external evidence does provide a much greater degree of certainty for these final stages.

On the basis of the well attested stages, one can rule out from the start a number of ways in which earlier stages of the text might be conceived. I do not intend to take the matter further in this study—beyond offering this particular example: one can no longer simply say that the whole of 1.36 up to and including 1.39aα (as far as יהיה) is a single block of material inserted at a second stage in the history of the text.[14]

It is crucial that one should not covertly and tacitly assume the existence of a textual genealogy in which all other witnesses presuppose M and that they are all to be inferred from it. For example, in the case of G this is what happens with John William Wevers, to whom we owe the critical reconstruction of the Septuagint text of Deuteronomy.[15]

To become even more specific: it is common knowledge that, during as well as after the redaction of the Pentateuch, harmonizing work was performed time and again on parallel yet divergent texts. Deuteronomy 1–3 has been affected in particular by such activity. Many elements from these chapters have been interpolated in an anticipatory manner into Exodus and Numbers. The harmonizing is most noticeable in Smr. Often Smr inserts whole passages from parallel places into a text. When compared to M, many textual redundancies in G can likewise be explained in this way. By way of contrast, we tend to hesitate with this kind of explanation where M is more expansive in relation to G or Smr, or in relation to both G and Smr. In such cases, we opt for a deliberate abbreviation in G and Smr. So too in the case of the text under consideration here, Deut. 1.39. The tacit assumption that M is the text on which all other forms depend lurks in the background. But once this is abandoned, there is no obstacle to reckoning with harmonizations in the Pentateuch, even in cases where M is more expansive. Just to take some examples from Deuteronomy 1, I suspect there are harmonizing expansions in the following cases, besides the one in v. 39:

- In 1.8b, Smr has the shorter reading לזרעם אחריהם which is characteristically deuteronomistic. The broader formulations of M and G are harmonizations with a longer priestly expression from the earlier books of the Pentateuch (similar in 11.9; cf. Lohfink 1991: 28-30).
- In 1.25, G and V have nothing corresponding to M and Smr וישבו אתנו דבר. The introduction of this clause is a harmonization with Num. 13.6.

14. So Mittmann (1975: 37) and most recently, especially, Otto (2000: 22-25). In the same year, Campbell and O'Brien (2000: 45 with nn. 9 and 10) were much more cautious. They even consider it possible that G follows another Hebrew text although they do not mention 4QDeut[h].

15. This is expressed again and again by Wevers (1995). One fears that it also frequently influenced his critical reconstruction of the text in G (Göttingen edition) III,2. At some stage, it will probably be necessary to reassess his whole work from the point of view of this theoretical assumption stemming from the pre-Qumran period.

- In 1.30, G has no equivalent for לעיניכם in M and Smr. In this case, Deut. 4.34 could have provided the stimulus for an expansion in M and Smr.
- In 1.35, G has no equivalent for הדור הרע הזה in M and Smr, as mentioned above. A harmonization with Num. 14.27, 35 is involved. However, the entirely un-Deuteronomic word עדה ('community') is replaced by דור ('generation'), found in two other parallel places—one in Deut. 2.14, the other in Num. 32.13. I will return to this case.
- In 1.35, the infinitive לתת, or its translation, is missing from Smr, G* and V. This addition served to underline the connection with Josh. 21.43-45.

At least some of these cases may be important for the interpretation of the text and for the reconstruction of its history.

2. *Revisional Development as a Canonical Reading Guide*

I have used the term *harmonization* several times already. With Deut. 1.39, it was in relation to at least the first of the two relative clauses in M: '(your baggage-train) of which you said: "it shall become booty"!' This clause is taken over word for word from Num. 14.31. In this way a word of God in Deuteronomy 1 is matched with a word of God in Num. 14.31; in other words, *harmonized* with it. The effect is to highlight more clearly that, at the level of the course of action, it is one and the same activity that is involved in both texts. Perhaps an important detail also needed to be spelled out.

Closer inspection however, reveals something more. In both places, the addition is itself a reference back to a previous utterance by the Israelites. However, it is not to be found in the preceding text of Deuteronomy 1 but in the story that is told in Numbers 14 (v. 3). The reference works in Num. 14.31 but not in Deut. 1.39. To be more precise, it works here too but in a more roundabout way. Moses is after all not telling his listeners anything new in Deut. 1.6–3.29, except for a few details. He is only reminding them of the events they have experienced together. From the reader's point of view, Moses' account rehearses those events which the Pentateuchal narrator had already related at various points in the book of Numbers. The mention of facts which only someone familiar with the broader accounts given there can understand, is entirely possible at the level of the Pentateuch. In Deut. 1.39, Moses would have even been able to have God refer loosely to Num. 14.3 without the need to repeat 14.31 word for word. In Deut. 1.36 too, things are assumed about Caleb which are not mentioned beforehand in Deuteronomy 1. Hence in Deut. 1.39 a relationship between the two events *as a whole* is forged via a reference to something that one can only look up by turning to Numbers 14. It goes without saying that, at the level of this discussion, we are not concerned with an earlier stage of Numbers 13–14 but more or less with the present text. The amount of *harmonization* is therefore more than was initially thought. Whole areas of text are brought into a relationship with one another.

The term *harmonization* can be understood even more radically. Two versions of the same thing can differ markedly or slightly from one another. If elements are added from the competing version, the differences are eased or eliminated completely. The goal of such a harmonization would be the removal of contradictions in favour of a unified statement.

It is a fair assumption that most late additions of this kind have such an aim. One may doubt that the goal was historical reconstruction in the modern sense, but at least it was a clear *fabula* of the Pentateuch. The Pentateuchal *fabula* was to contain no contradictions. This surely must have been the goal too of the first אשר-clause in Deut. 1.39.

Nevertheless, it came about in a very flexible way. The first thing to be established was no doubt a simple *intertextuality*. The reader needed to be aware that he or she should not read one text without at the same time hearing the other. Where the two texts were in tension with one another, the reader was not explicitly told how to arrive at a definitive (and unified) understanding. Rather, the initial aim was simply to engage the reader in the task of understanding. The outcome was the reader's business. We therefore have an identifiable intertextuality that served as a kind of reading guide. One can speak of a *canonical* intertextuality because the need to harmonize is prompted by the perception that contradictory accounts are present within a literary *canon*. At that time the *canon* was possibly still only the Pentateuch. Although the idea of a *canon* may not yet have been appropriate, the Pentateuch already possessed something of a canonical character. Hence it was the locus of a qualified intertextuality which the reader was encouraged to notice.

The proposal can be made even more concrete than this. If we assume that 'this evil generation' in Deut. 1.35 is also a late addition, then it was presumably not at all clear in the pre-Pentateuchal version of Deuteronomy against whom God's anger was directed in 1.34-35. Was it against all Israel; against the spies; against Israel's warriors? The preceding text provided grounds for at least the first two possibilities. In the following text, the word טף in Deut. 1.39* must have been perceived instinctively as a counter-concept to the warriors capable of bearing arms who, in 1.41-45, become the centre of attention. From the context, therefore, all three interpretations are possible. Presumably, Moses originally left it deliberately unclear against whom the anger of God was directed. Within both utterances, therefore, God was able to address any individuals who were or were not the target of divine anger. Only later in the account did Moses become more precise. In a retrospective note in 2.14-16, he makes it clear that all אנשי המלחמה are meant; that is, all the warriors.

Once the text became part of the Pentateuch, such a conscious openness of the narrative was not so easy to sustain. After all, Num. 14.27-35 in particular had been much more precise. Hence Smr introduces the expansion ובניכם ('that is, your sons'). The expansion must be understood as an interpretation of טף that introduces the notion of different generations. This corresponds to the fact that the quotation from Numbers in the first relative clause of 1.39 refers not only to the warriors but to all the people—for, in Num. 14.3, כל־העדה ,העם and

כל בני ישראל (cf. 14.1-2) weep and revolt. Basically, the reader is directed to take into consideration everything that was described as God's punishment, especially in Num. 14.27-35. The word *generation* had already been deployed in the same context in Deut. 2.14, an older text (כל־הדור אנשי המלחמה). It is also introduced in ch. 1 in a revision of 1.35 (הדור הרע הזה, see above) with the same goal. But, as a result of the diverse statements in Numbers 14 and 32.8-13, the concept of generations is no longer restricted in these additions to the warriors as it was in Deut. 2.14—although they continue to be central. It is clear how these revisions encourage the formation of a kind of synthesis of the various reports, without determining the outcome itself.

The second relative clause in 1.39, first attested in 4QDeut[h] and G, is of a different character. One can hardly designate the statement about the children who 'today still do not know good and evil' as a harmonization with the narrative in Numbers. Of course, the motif of the knowledge of good and evil occurs in the Septuagint of Num. 14.23 and 32.11. But the motif of knowledge of good and evil in Num. 14.23 and 32.11 does not seem to belong to the Hebrew *Vorlage* of the Septuagint. It is to be considered as an addition within the Septuagint, most likely in association with Num. 14.29. Hence, in this particular case, any indication of a harmonization by the use of the same words is missing. Besides, the assertion made by the expansion goes well beyond the concept of the generations. There are quite different intertextual references as well.

It is not really satisfactory to see the addition of the second אשר-clause in v. 39 simply as an enrichment of a more narrow context, although it no doubt served that purpose too. As a result of all the revisions that occurred, an elegant keyword connection developed in the standardized Masoretic text. The 'evil' generation may not enter the 'good land' (v. 35), only the next generation which is not yet able to 'discern good and evil' will arrive there (v. 39). This may or may not have been a chance outcome. We cannot clarify it any further because we do not have sufficient documentation to reconstruct the sequence and interrelationship between the various expansions. In any case, further enquiry is needed beyond this particular observation about the intertextual references of the second אשר-clause.

If one takes the revision in v. 39 on its own, a related text in Deuteronomy immediately comes to mind—Deut. 30.15. In 30.15-20, Israel is challenged to decide between life and death, good and evil. Whether Israel will or will not remain in the land depends on this decision. It is at one and the same time a decision for or against the Deuteronomic law. That it concerns the law and remaining in the land, not entering it, creates a certain distance in relation to the revision in 1.39. Deuteronomy 30.15 can be taken to mean that those who will enter the land later must also make a decision, one that has not yet been made by the children in 1.39. But the law is not brought into play in any sense in 1.39 and the issue there is entering the land, not remaining in it. As a result, one may presume that the second expansion in 1.39 was not made in order to gain clarity from Deut. 30.15. Rather, another concern could have played a role in this pairing of keywords, related, perhaps incidentally, to one of the other main concerns of the addition. It may be that, due to the occurrence here of a word-pair from Deut. 30.15, an additional framework of keywords needed to be added to other ones in Deuteronomy.

Whatever the case, more needs to be said about the main topic. One must first deal with the fact that, in the second relative clause of v. 39, not only does the word-pair 'good and evil' occur—whatever it may mean—but it is also a question of the *knowledge of good and evil*. This is a very rare biblical expression and directs us to another area of text.

Except for Deut. 1.39, the verbal phrase ידע טוב ורע ('to know good and evil') and its noun equivalent דעת טוב ורע ('knowledge of good and evil') are found together only once in the whole Hebrew Bible. This is in the narrative of Paradise and the Fall in Genesis 2–3 where, undeniably, they play a decisive role. Here the 'tree of the knowledge of good and evil' (Gen. 2.9, 17) and the 'knowledge of good and evil' are crucial factors in the temptation by the serpent (3.5) and in what motivates the expulsion from paradise (3.22). We have no evidence that the simple expression *to know good and evil/knowledge of good and evil* belonged to the standard vocabulary of normal speech. Comparable expressions exist but they are looser and occur in ever-changing variations.[16] The precise expression in Genesis 2–3 is found elsewhere only in Deut. 1.39. This suggests that it was coined for the story of Genesis 2–3 and introduced there deliberately as a *leitmotif*. When it is subsequently picked up by the addition in Deut. 1.39, it is by way of allusion to Genesis 2–3.[17]

Judging from the context, the expression 'do not (yet) know good and evil' in Deut. 1.39 should be understood principally in relation to the similar, but by no means identical, expression in Isa. 7.15, 16; that is: 'not yet having reached the age for the proper use of reason or perhaps the capacity for making proper decisions'. In Genesis 2–3 however, the expression 'to know good and evil' most likely has a meaning that does not refer to childhood development. Nevertheless, the reference is there and, as often happens, it is not just a matter of the terms employed to denote the reference. Once again one may presume that whole texts or indeed complexes of texts are linked to one another.

Within the context of Deut. 1.39, the question is: Who will enter the promised land and take possession of it? This theme permeates the whole of Deuteronomy and Joshua. From a purely formal point of view therefore, the small intertextual signal in Deut. 1.39 forges a relationship between this leading theme of Deuteronomy—Joshua and the story of Paradise and the Fall, a story that embraces the whole of humanity.

---

16. Another verb can depend on ידע, whose direct object is טוב ורע (Isa. 7.15-16). Alternatively, another similar verb is employed in place of ידע (1 Kgs 3.9). It may not even be a question of a direct object construction (2 Sam. 19.36; 1 Kgs 3.9).

17. In contrast to what I assumed above, the Hebrew original of the Septuagint could also have contained the phrase in Num. 14.23 and 32.11. In that case, they are additions that were connected to the one in Deut. 1.39 and that speak of the same topic—permission to enter the land after the sin of Kadesh.

It is suggested that the initial situation for the generation that is to reach the promised land may be compared with that of the first human couple. The entry into the promised land becomes the mirror image of their placement in paradise and the obverse of their expulsion from paradise. A thematic parallel, in part synonymous, in part antithetical, is established between the story of Paradise and the Fall on the one hand and the whole complex of Deuteronomy—Joshua on the other. It can be pursued in every possible direction by the reader. The author of the gloss does not relieve the reader of the effort required, he merely signals what is possible via the intertextual markers.

This is a quite peculiar kind of reading guide. It offers no definite outcome; it simply urges one to embark upon a consideration of the parallels. I will not try at this point to plumb every insight that could be found here. My only concern is to establish the fact that here, in a textual expansion from a late stage when the Pentateuch at least formed something like a *canon*, a *canonical reading guide* is provided that takes the canon as a single text. As such, it opens up new dimensions of meaning that are proper to the text in its canonical form. The author who once put the account in Deuteronomy 1–3 in the mouth of Moses was surely not thinking of anything of the kind. Perhaps, at that time, Genesis 2–3 did not yet exist.[18]

I am not arguing that we should consider the correspondence between Genesis 2–3 and Deuteronomy–Joshua only because the second relative clause of Deut. 1.39 is present in a part of our manuscripts. Nor should all inquiry cease if, after having done the work of textual criticism, the author of a commentary supposes an original text in Deut. 1.39 which does not contain the two relative clauses in question. The canonical texts as a whole already contain the cues for reading that are signalled by the second gloss of this verse. There is no need for any special authorial intention. The general intention of those who put the existing biblical books together into a canon is sufficient—provided readers recognize certain connections in the text itself. The authors of the Pentateuchal glosses were such readers, and they in turn help other readers.

Because of such views, Walter Gross (2001: 130) has accused me of 'hypostatizing the canon'. His complaint, if I understand him correctly, is that I ascribe authorial intention to the canon whereas in fact only human beings can have authorial intentions. He expresses it as a rhetorical question: 'Whoever intended a sense ascertained this way, generated these references of everything to everything, or ever really thought these theological thoughts?' (Gross 2001: 129). I am not arguing that there is no such thing as *intention*. But the intention that is there is simply the quite general one of those who produced the canon and those who accept it—and this is sufficient. The intention is as follows: there needs to be something like a canon made up of particular books which, taken *together*, Israel

---

18. This is quite apart from a further question, namely, whether Gen. 2–3 may represent a late text (to be located earlier, however, than the completed Pentateuch), and that when it was created it may have known the Deuteronomy of that time and had it in mind. In recent times, Otto especially (1996) has argued for this view. If it is correct, then the small expansion in Deut. 1.39, perhaps without knowing it, reminds us of a part of the prehistory of the Pentateuch.

can use to orient itself. If small glosses creep in here and there which make this general intention concrete in a particular case, then they already presume it and could just as well not be there.

Umberto Eco once stated—about the authors of books and certainly not about the producers of canons: 'The author should die once he has finished writing. So as not to trouble the path of the text' (Eco 1985: 7). It is the original impetus of the text itself which led to the revisions with which this brief contribution has been concerned.

BIBLIOGRAPHY

Campbell, A.F., and M.A. O'Brien
    2000   *Unfolding the Deuteronomistic History: Origins, Upgrades, Present Text* (Minneapolis: Fortress Press).
Dillmann, A.
    1886   *Die Bücher Numeri, Deuteronomium und Josua* (Kurzgefasstes Exegetisches Handbuch zum Alten Testament; Leipzig: Hirzel, 2nd edn).
Duncan, J.A.
    1989   'A Critical Edition of Deuteronomy Manuscripts from Qumran, Cave IV' (unpublished doctoral dissertation, Harvard University, Cambridge, MA).
Eco, U.
    1985   *Reflections on the Name of the Rose* (trans. William Weaver; London: Minerva Paperbacks).
Gross, W.
    2001   'Ist biblisch-theologische Auslegung ein integrierender Methodenschritt?', in F.-L. Hossfeld (ed.), *Wieviel Systematik erlaubt die Schrift? Auf der Suche nach einer gesamtbiblischen Theologie* (QD, 185; Freiburg: Herder): 110-49.
König, E.
    1917   *Das Deuteronomium* (KAT; Leipzig: Deichert).
Kuenen, A.
    1877   'Bijdragen to de critiek van Pentateuch en Jozua: III. De uitzending der verspieders', *Theologisch Tijdschrift* 11: 545-66.
Locher, Cl.
    1982   'Art שׂטר', in *ThWAT*, III: 372-75.
Lohfink, N.
    1991   *Die Väter Israels in Deuteronomium* (OBO, 111; Freiburg: Universitätsverlag; Göttingen: Vandenhoeck & Ruprecht).
Mittmann, S.
    1975   *Deuteronomium 1.1–6.3 literarkritisch und traditionsgeschichtlich untersucht* (BZAW, 139; Berlin: W. de Gruyter).
Otto, E.
    1996   'Die Paradieserzählung Genesis 2–3: Eine nachpriesterschriftliche Lehrer-zählung in ihrem religionshistorischen Kontext', in A.A. Diesel *et al.* (eds.), *'Jedes Ding hat seine Zeit...': Studien zur israelitischen und altorientalischen Weisheit Diethelm Michel zum 65. Geburtstag* (BZAW, 241; Berlin: W. de Gruyter): 167-92.
    2000   *Das Deuteronomium im Pentateuch und Hexateuch: Studien zur Literatur-geschichte von Pentateuch und Hexateuch im Lichte des Deuteronomiums-rahmens* (FAT, 30; Tübingen: Mohr Siebeck).

Tal, A.
　　1994　　*The Samaritan Pentateuch Edited According to MS 6 (C) of the Shekhem Synagogue* (Tel Aviv: Tel Aviv University).

Wellhausen, J.
　　1889　　*Die Composition des Hexateuchs und der historischen Bücher des Alten Testaments* (Berlin: Reimer, 3rd edn).

Wevers, J.W.
　　1995　　*Notes on the Greek Text of Deuteronomy* (SBLSCS, 39; Atlanta: Scholars Press).

Part II

IN THE PENTATEUCH AND FORMER PROPHETS

The 'Paradigmatic' and 'Historiographical' Nature of the Priestly Material as a Key to its Interpretation[*]

Suzanne Boorer

Although many scholars, notably Noth (1972: 8-19), Nicholson (1988) and Campbell (1993) among others, have argued convincingly for an originally independent Priestly document (P), it seems to me that less progress has been made with regard to the issue of its overall meaning. The various attempts that have been made tend to focus only on part of the sweep of the P material and fluctuate between seeing it as legitimating the past or looking to the future.[1] Thus the focus is either on the tabernacle and its cult in the Sinai material, seeing P as validating existing institutions (Schmidt 1993: 259), or as constituting a programme for the future restoration of the community (Noth 1972: 243; Cross 1973: 325; Klein 1981), or the framework surrounding the Sinai material with respect to the (potential) fulfilment of the promise of the land (Elliger 1952; Brueggemann 1982: 101-13 nn. 159-67).[2]

My aim here is a more modest one. I do not wish to revisit this issue directly, but to take a step back and lay the groundwork for tackling the issue of the overall meaning of P anew by asking the question of the nature (or genre) of this P material, and, thus, how it might be seen to function for the reader.[3] By doing this I hope to provide a means by which the interpretation of this material as a whole may be approached so as to do it justice. As a preliminary step it will be helpful to outline some important observations with regard to the overall shape of P and features of the text.[4]

[*] My first major essay, which was published in article form nearly thirty years ago (Boorer 1977), was on the Priestly material under Tony Campbell's supervision. It seems, then, a fitting tribute to him, for not only all that I learnt from him about the Old Testament and how to interpret the text but even more importantly for the enthusiasm and passion for the Old Testament text that he instilled in me, that I should return once more to this rather enigmatic P material. I therefore offer this article with much gratitude.

1. I am basing my discussion on the material outlined as Pg by Noth (1972: 17-19), and will refer to it throughout what follows simply as P. See Campbell and O'Brien (1993: 22-90) for the setting out of Noth's text.

2. Clements (1965: 109, 111, 113, 121-22) and Blenkinsopp (1976: 289) link the re-establishment of the cult with the possession of the land.

3. I am thinking primarily of the exilic/early post-exilic audience, but the implications of the approach that will be argued here can extend beyond this original audience to future generations.

4. This will of necessity be brief and selective, but will provide a sufficient basis for illuminating the current debate regarding the nature of P to be outlined shortly and for the ensuing argument arising out of this.

The shape of P comprises both a linear sequence and a repeated parallel pattern. The linear sequence of 'events' spans from creation to the death of Moses. The story of the cosmos where God is known as *Elohim* (Gen. 1–10*[5]) and of the ancestors where God is known as *El Shaddai* (Gen. 11–Exod. 1.7*) moves forward by means of genealogies; the subsequent story of the nation where God is known as *Yhwh* (Exod. 1–Deut. 34*) moves forward by means of itineraries, unfolding the promises of the Abrahamic covenant (Gen. 17).

A parallel pattern can also be perceived in P between the story of the cosmos (Gen. 1–10*) and the story of the nation (Exod. 1–Deut. 34*). These are linked by the transitional phase of the ancestors (Gen. 1–Exod. 1.7*). In both the stories of the cosmos and the nation the movement is: from creation of the world (Gen. 1.1–2.4a)/nation (Exod. 1–Num. 9*);[6] through destruction of the world (Gen. 6.9–7.24*)/nation (Num. 13–14; 20–Deut. 34*);[7] to a new beginning (realized or potential) for life on or in the land for Noah and his descendants (Gen. 8–10*)/ the next generation of the nation (Num. 13–Deut. 34*) with the associated appearance of the land as cosmos/land of Canaan (Boorer 2001: 20-21, 23).

In the shape of P, in its linear and parallel dimensions, echoes of Mesopotamian creation and flood 'myths' can be found (Blenkinsopp 1976: 285; Lohfink 1994 [1978]: 170-71). For example, the sequential pattern in *Enuma Elish* of 'the cosmogonic victory of the deity resulting in the building of a sanctuary for him' (Blenkinsopp 1976: 285) is echoed in P in its movement from creation of the cosmos through division of the waters to the building of the sanctuary. And the pattern in *Atrahasis* of creation, destruction and fresh start, is the pattern repeated twofold in P in relation to the cosmos and the nation. Such clear parallels would suggest that ancient Near Eastern 'mythic' patterns underlie the shape of P both in its linear sequence and its parallel pattern.

An important feature of the P material is that various scenarios within its sequence combine traditions from the past, reflections of the present experience and concerns of its audience[8] and/or future visions or programmatic elements. Through this combination a series of 'timeless' realities, or realities encompassing in one picture elements across time, is generated within P.

A clear example of this is P's description of the passover/unleavened bread festival of Exod. 12.1-20. The account appears to telescope the originally distinct

---

5. The siglum * denotes the P material contained within the reference.

6. Detailed parallels between these include: the division of the waters symbolizing the creation of the earth (Gen. 1.6-10) and the creation of the nation (Exod. 14.16, 21aαb, 22), and in particular the creation of the cosmos (Gen. 1.1–2.4a) and the construction of the tabernacle and its cult as the pinnacle of the creation of the nation and its identity (Exod. 25–Lev. 9*), seen in the sevenfold nature of the days of creation and the seven speeches of Yhwh to Moses (Exod. 25–31) concluding with the sabbath and the similar language of 'saw', 'finished', 'blessed' at the conclusion of each (Gen. 1.31–2.3; Exod. 39.32, 34, 43). See Boorer 2001: 20-22.

7. Detailed parallels include: the negative way in which all flesh/Israel relate to the land, as corrupting it with violence (Gen. 6.11-13) and slandering it (Num. 13.32), respectively, and the deliverance of individuals—Noah, and Caleb and Joshua, respectively—from the mass destruction the generation. See Boorer 2001: 20-22.

8. Assuming an exilic/early post-exilic audience.

traditions of passover, unleavened bread and the firstborn into one coherent festival which becomes the primary focus for the ongoing celebration of the exodus (Boorer 1992: 143-202). Moreover, this account, which collapses into one the various stages of tradition from the past, is recounted in a form that brings together the description of the rite, as instituted in the past, with its ongoing celebration in the present and into the future. As such the tradition becomes timeless. There is no distinction in time between the narrative event set at the exodus and the ongoing celebration of the ritual: they are one. In contrast to the earlier non-P material in Exodus 12–13 (e.g. 12.29-39; 13.3-16), where narration of the event in the past and its ongoing celebration in the future through rite or law are clearly distinguished in time, there is no such distinction in P's description (Boorer 1992: 159-60): 'The instructions and description of events for the exodus night is the (present and future) cultic celebration…the narrative is the cultic rite/law and the present celebration of passover and unleavened bread is that of the time of the exodus from Egypt' (Boorer 1992: 164-65).

Another example is the description of the tabernacle and its cult (Exod. 25–31; Lev. 8–9). The picture drawn in P of these consists of the combination of distinct past traditions and future ideals. For example, old tent traditions, Jerusalem temple traditions and their corresponding modes of presence, the figure of Aaron and (albeit in relation to the priesthood) royal anointing and clothing traditions[9] are combined with a vision of the leadership of the community by the Aaronide priesthood (Blenkinsopp 1995: 66-97). This gives something unique: a picture that would have been partially recognizable by P's exilic audience in the various past traditions but as conflated together and taken up into a new vision for the future. That is, P's picture of the tabernacle and its cult transcends time, spanning past and future so that past traditions are redeemed, transformed and integrated with programmatic ideals, thus presenting an integrated whole or seemingly 'timeless' vision.

Given all this the question arises: How can P be interpreted as a whole so as to do justice to both its tendency to conflate past traditions with the present and future, and its overall shape with linear sequencing and repeating pattern? I believe that an appropriate way of reading or interpreting P can be found if a clearer understanding of the nature or genre of P, which takes into account these characteristics, can be gained.

There has been some debate about the nature of the P material, prompted largely by N. Lohfink's seminal article, 'The Priestly Narrative and History' (Lohfink 1994 [1978]). The features of the P material of transcending the past in the guise of which it is set, reflecting and addressing the present (i.e. exilic/early post-exilic concerns) and reflecting the movement and framework of ancient Near Eastern 'myths', has led many scholars to describe P as 'paradigmatic'.[10]

---

9. See, e.g., de Vaux 1961: 295-97, 301-302, 347, 450; Haran 1962; Clements 1965: 114; von Rad 1966: 103-104; Cross 1968: 40-67; Fretheim 1968: 315; Mettinger 1982: 81-96; Friedman 1992: 292-300; and Blenkinsopp 1995: 66-97.

10. Or, closely related to this, as 'transparent'. See, e.g., Lohfink 1994 [1978]; Blenkinsopp 1976: 284-86; 1995: 109.

However, based on P's linear sequence of contingent cause and effect 'events', others have seen P as primarily 'historiography' or '*Geschichte*' (e.g. Blum 1990: 330-31; Janowski 1990). Yet others refer to P using both terms (Blenkinsopp 1995: 68, 109; Carr 1996: 129-40; Van Seters 1999: 161-62, 182-83, 188).

Terms such as 'paradigm' and 'historiography' are notoriously slippery. It will be instructive, therefore, to survey selectively this discussion of the nature of P and critique it taking into account each scholar's use of such terms. This may give some clarity with regard to the nature of P, and provide a way forward for interpreting P as a whole while doing justice to all its characteristics.

Lohfink was the first to present an extended discussion of P as 'paradigmatic' (Lohfink 1994 [1978]). He argues against seeing P as 'history' in the sense that it provides information about the past in terms of what might have happened in a cause and effect sequence. What Lohfink means by referring to P as 'paradigmatic' is nuanced in a number of ways. He refers (1994 [1978]: 156) to 'paradigmatic constellations' within P in the sense of being 'the vehicle for some very precisely conceived theological statements'.[11] The material is 'paradigmatic' or 'transparent' in that, although narrated in the guise of the past, it addresses the situations, experiences and problems of the readers (i.e. the exiles) providing guidance through its theological concepts. In order to tease out further the relationship between past and present as embodied in P, Lohfink describes (1994 [1978]: 161) the situations presented as 'paradigmatic' in the sense of repeatedly recurring in the past, present and future:

> Every event is transparently narrated. What once was can also return. The structural congruence illuminates the readers' present—and perhaps every possible present... there is, in a certain sense, a storehouse of paradigmatic world situations, all of which existed at one time and can recur again.

Lohfink (1994 [1978]: 162) goes on to use the terminology of 'myth' to describe the paradigmatic nature of P, seeing the whole of P's narration as telling of happenings in 'the timelessness of primeval time, that are true always and everywhere and therefore can also explain the Now'. In this sense, then, P:

> narrates everything as if it were recounting myths. In a sense it converts history (*Geschichte*) back into myth (*Mythus*). Therefore we get the impression that, in spite of the temporal sequence, we are...looking at a great picture collection assembled on artistic principles. It derives from history and yet its tendency is towards paradigm. (Lohfink 1994 [1978]: 162)

Lohfink's emphasis here has two corollaries. First, the contingent cause–effect sequence as narrated is effectively incidental. What is primarily important is the theological concept or transparency of each 'event' or 'constellation of events' as paradigm in reflecting and addressing the present situation, with the collection of such pictures being along artistic lines only (Lohfink 1994 [1978]: 161-62). Second, the nature of P as 'paradigmatic' or 'transparent' or 'myth' means, according to Lohfink, that it is quite different from the prophetic view of 'history' in

---

11. Lohfink uses here the Jacob material with its concern for the purity of the line by way of example.

that it is not eschatological in the sense that it leads to an expectation of new events or new actions of *Yhwh* in the future that surpass the past and are as yet unknown. Rather, what is offered in P is a vision of a static world that is already known and can be repeatedly returned to.[12] Lohfink states (1994 [1978]: 172): 'The ideal shape of the world is known, it has already existed before. From the point of view of God it is always present, and all that is necessary is to return to it.'[13]

Lohfink has captured a significant perspective regarding the nature of P in describing it in 'paradigmatic' terms, in the sense that, although being expressed in the narration of past events, it reflects and addresses the contemporary situation.[14] This collapsing, or perhaps overcoming, of time, of moving beyond the categories of past, present and/or perhaps future implied in this view, is helpful in attempting to fathom the nature of P and how it can be seen to function. Indeed, the description of P as 'paradigmatic' in this way has, as we shall see, been taken up by most of the recent scholars who have attempted to grapple with this issue: for example, F. Gorman (1990: 106), J. Blenkinsopp (1995: 106-109), D. Carr (1996: 140) and J. Van Seters (1999: 161-62).[15]

What is not helpful is when Lohfink takes his important insight regarding P as paradigmatic in the direction of equating this with 'myth' set over against 'history'. This leads him to downplay the interaction between events described in the narrative sequence and to perceive P in terms of a repeatedly recurring pattern that needs only to be returned to. This seems to assume a cyclical view of 'myth' where time is circular, set over against the linear time of unrepeated, contingent cause and effect events associated with 'history'. This dichotomy cannot be maintained in light of more recent discussions of the development and nature of ancient Near Eastern and Old Testament genres. These show that in both ancient Near Eastern texts and Old Testament texts so-called 'mythic' and 'historiographical' elements are combined and interrelated in various ways, or to use Van Seters' terminology, the 'historicization of myth' or the 'mythologization of history' can be perceived.[16]

In reaction to Lohfink's somewhat outdated view of 'myth' vs. 'history', which leads him to state (1994 [1978]: 162) that P 'converts history back into myth' thus downplaying any 'historical' dimension, E. Blum (1990: 330-31 n. 159) has

12. In this way, P operates like its parallel, the *Atrahasis* myth, where the repeated pattern of movement is from a restless phase to a stable world, see Lohfink 1994 [1978]: 171-72.

13. Note, however, that Lohfink (1994: 145) sees P as concluding in Joshua (Josh. 4.19*; 5.10-12; 14.1, 2*; 18.1...19.51) with the settlement of the land accomplished; cf. Noth (1972: 17-19), whose Pg forms the basis of our discussion, who sees P concluding in Deut. 34* with Israel yet outside the land.

14. Also referred to by Lohfink in terms of 'transparency'.

15. Even Blum (1990: 330-31 n. 159) touches on this when he acknowledges that all biblical presentations (*Geschichte*) tend towards paradigm. The perspective of Damrosch (1987) also lies very close to this view, though different terminology is used; see later discussion.

16. See, e.g., Childs 1960; Cross 1973; Roberts 1976; Van Seters 1983; 1992; Damrosch 1987; Thompson 1992; Clifford 1994; and later discussion.

made a significant contribution to the debate regarding the nature of P.[17] While alluding in passing to the paradigmatic nature of the biblical texts, which he takes for granted, Blum particularly emphasizes P's 'historical' nature (p. 331), in the sense that a central characteristic of the Priestly material is its portrayal of a continuum of a specific cause and effect sequence of 'events'.[18] As such the priestly material is a 'contingent, irreversible history (*Geschichte*)' (p. 330). It presents the creation of the world and the constitution of Israel's institutions within a continuum describing the particularity of human actions and God's specific responses: it is 'a history (*Geschichte*) which fastens the creation and its institutions in a continuum of particular breakings and new beginnings' (p. 330).

Given this, Blum rightly maintains that individual scenarios cannot be taken out of their sequential context and simply applied 'paradigmatically' or 'transparently' to the contemporary situation in isolation, as Lohfink has a tendency to do, but must be interpreted within their narrated sequence. In addition, it means that a cyclical view of time, with its recurring vision of the world already known that needs only to be returned to, as Lohfink maintains, is inappropriate. Rather, in contradiction to Lohfink, Blum rightly maintains (1990: 331 n. 159) that the nature of the Priestly material as 'eschatological', in the sense of looking forward to a future goal (*Yhwh*'s future) beyond that of the contemporary situation, must be taken into account.[19]

To summarize, then, I am maintaining that central to P's nature is that it is: (a) 'paradigmatic' in the sense that, although in the form of a narrative of past events, it collapses time, or circumvents the time categories of past, present and future, in reflecting and addressing the contemporary situation; and (b) 'historiographical' in the sense of portraying a contingent sequence of events interrelated through cause and effect and pointing towards a future goal. However, it needs to be asked how can these perspectives regarding P's nature be held together, and how do they interrelate within P? That is, what does it really mean for the interpretation of P to describe its nature and function as both 'paradigmatic' and 'historical' or 'historiographical' in the senses outlined above?

A helpful direction to follow with regard to this can be found in the recent discussion concerning the nature of ancient Near Eastern (and Greek) genres prior to, or contemporary with, P by J. Van Seters (1983; 1992: 24-44). This also involves 'mythic' and 'historiographical' dimensions and therefore has the potential to shed light on the genre of P.[20]

---

17. Note that Blum denotes the Priestly material as Kp and perceives it as a 'compositional' layer that incorporates non-P material (his KD), expanding it and often correcting it.

18. Blum does not of course use 'history' (*Geschichte*) as Lohfink sets it up initially as the narrating of what actually happened (Lohfink 1994: 149), and therefore questions the dichotomy Lohfink sets up between 'history' and 'paradigm', maintaining that all biblical *Geschichte* tends towards paradigm.

19. Note that Blum, unlike Lohfink, does not see Kp as continuing into Joshua but as ending in Deut. 34*.

20. Van Seters himself focuses on the implications of this primarily in relation to J and does not extend this through to P in a direct, coherent and integrated way, partly because he sees P merely as a supplement to his J; see Van Seters 1999: 160-89; and later discussion.

Van Seters (1992: 105) describes the development of ancient Near Eastern and mid-first-millennium Greek genres in terms of 'the historicization of myth' and/or 'the mythologization of history'. He defines 'myth' as 'a traditional story about events in which the god or gods are the primary actors, and the action takes place outside of historical time' and 'contains some structure of meaning that is concerned with the deep problems of life and offers explanations for the way things are' (p. 25). He defines 'history' as 'written records of past events that celebrate the deeds of public figures and important events of communal interest within a chronological framework' and that 'reflect the problem of historical change and seek to account for it in political terms within "historical" time' (p. 25). There is in many ancient Near Eastern and Greek texts, however, an interrelation of 'myth' and 'history' that reflects the 'historicization of myth' or 'the mythologization of history', depending on whether myth or historical tradition is the primary focus.

'Historicization of myth' often involves the transformation of myths into 'a continuous ordered narration with a larger view of the past' by the imposition of historical categories such as genealogical or chronological succession (Van Seters 1992: 25).[21] 'Mythologization of history' involves the assimilation of mythical elements into historical traditions thus giving 'the particular historiographic form a more universal and paradigmatic character' (p. 25).[22] Van Seters notes (pp. 27-28) that many of the ancient Near Eastern and Greek texts in which 'myth' and 'history' interact in this way focus on the issue of origins. In 'historicizing myth' or 'mythologizing history' in relation to the problem of origins, they assimilate the 'mythic' and 'historical' views of origin, such that they see the portrayal of the beginning as 'timeless', as 'paradigmatic' and as constituting the basis for later corresponding reality at the same time as they portray the beginning as the chronological starting point in a continuous cause and effect series of events (p. 28). Such texts, Van Seters maintains, function to explain, legitimate, or constitute the society, or to present its nature and destiny (Van Seters 1983: 2; 1992: 28, 30-32, 35, 332).[23]

21. For example, the Sumerian king list where the flood is historicized as an event in a sequence of succession of kings (Van Seters 1992: 62-64).

22. See Van Seters 1992: 26-27, 29-30, for examples. This may be done, for example, by the use of absolute references: in time (the beginning); in scope (the world); in ultimate cause (the gods) (Van Seters 1992: 25-26).

23. Damrosch (1987: 39, 50, 59-60, 65, 88-118) presents a similar argument to Van Seters regarding Mesopotamian genre development, albeit using different terminology. Damrosch (pp. 39, 65) maintains that the genres of 'poetic epic', defined as narrative poems concerning mythic stories of interactions of gods and mortals and developing large existential issues within narrative sequences set in early times, and 'prose chronicles' that 'record historical events', usually the exploits of kings (p. 39), influenced each other over time. Hence, there occurred the 'epic expansion of historiography and...a greatly increased historical dimension within poetic epic' (p. 50), to the point where the distinction between epic and chronicles began to collapse. This assimilation of epic and historiography he sees developed in J and 1–2 Samuel. Damrosch's discussion of P (pp. 261-97), which he sees as a supplement to J, is not, however, directly informed by his conclusions regarding the development of the Mesopotamian genres. However, his discussion of P presents some useful insights which will be taken up shortly.

Although Van Seters himself does not apply these observations to his priestly material in an explicit and coherent way,[24] the interrelation of 'myth' and 'history' described by him in relation to ancient Near Eastern and Greek texts is clearly evident in P. The 'historicization of myth' or the 'mythologization of history' is seen in P in that 'myths' or 'mythical elements' such as creation and flood stories have been placed in a 'chronological' sequence as part of a narrative continuum; and indeed, the pattern of creation and flood stories thus established on a cosmic scale is then mirrored in the unfolding sequence of contingent 'events' in the portrait of the nation. In addition, an underlying broad framework for the unfolding of the contingent sequence of historical traditions, as already noted, is provided by the mythic pattern of 'the cosmogonic victory of the deity (reflected in the creation/flood in P) resulting in the building of a sanctuary for him' (Blenkinsopp 1976: 285).[25] Moreover, and most importantly, like the ancient Near Eastern and Greek texts concerned with origins, P assimilates these 'mythic' and 'historical' aspects to give a portrayal of origins (of the world and the nation Israel). As such, taking up Van Seters' conclusions, it is both 'timeless' and 'paradigmatic', constituting the basis for later corresponding reality (the mythical aspect), and, in portraying a continuum of contingent events in narrative sequence, points in the direction of explaining and clarifying present effects and perhaps future goals (the historical aspect). Situating P in relation to the context of genre development in ancient Near Eastern and Greek texts in this way therefore has the potential to advance our understanding of how to interpret P. It sheds light on the nature of the genre of P and how it is possible to describe P as both 'paradigmatic' and 'historical' or 'historiographical'.

We have come some way in explaining and justifying how it is possible that P can be described as both 'paradigmatic' and 'historiographical', but the issue of how exactly these aspects are integrated and are to be interpreted in their interrelation needs further exploration.

J. Blenkinsopp, in his work on P (1976: 284; 1995: 109), reflects something of this recent discussion of genre development when he speaks of P as 'paradigmatic', as 'foundation or charter myth' (1976: 286), and as 'historiographical genre' (1995: 68, 109). In an earlier article, Blenkinsopp (1976: 285-86) refers to P as a 'foundation or charter myth for the rebuilt sanctuary and the cult which was to be carried out in it' on the basis of the mythic pattern underlying its structure, which he sees paralleling ancient Near Eastern creation/flood myths. In his later work he refers (1995: 68-69, 105, 109) to P in 'historiographical' terms, taking the sequential ordering of the setting up of the institutions seriously and interpreting P in the traditions of the Near East and the Levant as presenting the identity, self-understanding and legitimation of the community and its institutions as grounded in the distant past. For Blenkinsopp there is no dichotomy between these descriptions of P in 'mythic' and 'historiographic' terms. These descriptions are both linked in their respective contexts with the assertion that P

24. See n. 27 below.
25. See also Damrosch 1987: 90-91.

is 'paradigmatic' in the sense of being 'transparent', of reflecting and addressing the concerns of the contemporary situation. That is, Blenkinsopp describes P as 'paradigmatic' in a sense that reflects Lohfink's use of the term and is closely related to Van Seters' view of 'mythic' origins, not only in the context of describing P as 'foundation...myth', but also in the context of seeing P as 'historiographical' (Blenkinsopp 1976: 284; 1995: 109).[26] However, although Blenkinsopp freely describes P in both 'mythic/paradigmatic' and 'historiographical' terms, his comments are brief and constitute only allusions. They require further exploration regarding implications for the interpretation of P.[27]

D. Carr (1996) also seeks to describe P in both 'paradigmatic' and 'historiographic' terms, and, although rather brief, his comments are at least an attempt to advance the discussion regarding the implications for how P might be interpreted. Carr (p. 132 n. 33, 140) seeks to integrate Lohfink's insight concerning the nature of P as 'paradigmatic' and Blum's emphasis on P as 'history' (*Geschichte*) by describing P as 'paradigmatic history'. Thus, in line with Blum, cult and other potentialities portrayed in P are 'outgrowths of God's...covenantal responses to human history' (p. 132). However, leaning closer to Lohfink, he maintains (p. 132 n. 33) that P 'reformulates history with a primeval accent'. So, like ancient Near Eastern founding myths, P describes the establishment of the cult and other aspects of human life in a formative 'time', which for P extends over a stretch of 'history' from creation through the death of Moses, and therefore as responses to human history. This is a position close to Van Seters' view of the combination of 'mythical' and 'historiographical' aspects in ancient Near Eastern and Greek texts concerned with origins. Everything, all the basic possibilities of human life, is established by the time Moses dies, that is, in the formative 'time' at the dawn of Israel's 'history', and all Israel can hope for is to actualize these potentialities (Carr 1996: 132). Carr then moves beyond this to explore how this would operate for the exilic audience of P. This involves the way in which 'time' operates in P's 'paradigmatic history'. He does not take up Lohfink's view of recurring or cyclical time, where the 'paradigmatic' situations described in P can repeatedly recur in past, present or future. Rather, although seeing P as 'paradigmatic' in the sense of 'transparent', as do Lohfink and Blenkinsopp, unlike them he sees this working differently in different parts of the text. There is a division in the text in relation to time between the pre-Sinai material and that from Sinai onwards. He sees the pre-Sinai narrative in P as reflecting

26. See also Blenkinsopp (1976: 285 n. 43) where, in the context of describing P as a version of the Mesopotamian deluge myth, he refers to the Greek historiographical tradition as also throwing light on P.

27. Blum (1990: 330-31 n. 26) is also able to describe P as 'history' (*Geschichte*), and like all biblical texts as tending towards 'paradigm'. Van Seters (1992: 5; 1999: 182-83, 188), though describing his P supplement as primarily 'historiography' and thus concerned with the identity of the community—explaining, legitimating and providing programmatic guidance for cultic reform— also describes it in static 'paradigmatic' terms and as 'myth', indeed as the 'mythologization of the earlier historiography (i.e. J)' (Van Seters 1999: 161-62). These are, however, unintegrated allusions. There is no sustained discussion regarding how they are to be integrated in the interpretation of P.

what the audience already knows (i.e. the diaspora practices of circumcision, sab-bath and passover) and thus functioning etiologically, while from Sinai onwards P presents a utopian vision of the future (i.e. the constitution of the nation as a cultic community and their procession into the land) (Carr 1996: 139-40).[28]

Carr's discussion is helpful in that he reintroduces an intentional focus on the issue of the hermeneutics of time, touched on in a different way by Lohfink, in relation to the interpretation of P and how it might have been seen to function in relation to an exilic audience. However, his perception of how time operates in relation to different parts of the text, the pre-Sinai material reflecting past and present and the Sinai material onwards as programmatic future, does not do justice to the nature of the P material. There is, I believe, throughout the whole of P an integration of past, present and/or future elements, such that in each and every part the exilic audience would perceive partial fulfilment and future vision. For example, the material at Sinai combines into one scenario past temple/tent traditions and past royal traditions with future programmatic elements for the order of the priesthood, and so on. This combination of past/present/future tradi-tions and hopes in the scenarios throughout P means that the potentialities described in this 'paradigmatic history' which have been fulfilled should not be relegated to one part of the text and those yet to be realized to another part. They are inseparably integrated with each other throughout the whole.

However, an exploration of P's hermeneutics of 'time', which goes in a differ-ent direction from that of Carr, could provide a helpful way forward in exploring how P as 'paradigmatic history' functions and is to be interpreted while doing justice to both its 'paradigmatic' and 'historiographical' nature. Damrosch's dis-cussion of the nature of P (1987: 262-64, 272-97) provides a more constructive direction for exploring how 'time' might be seen to operate in P. His insights concerning 'time' in P help unfold more precisely and more helpfully what Lohfink and Blenkinsopp seem to be striving after in describing P as 'paradig-matic'. In his discussion he holds together past, present and future dimensions within the nature of every part of P.[29]

Damrosch sees in P the interaction of, and reciprocal influence between, ritual or law and history or narrative. As such, P has 'a deep interest in history' (Dam-rosch 1987: 272), as seen in the presentation of a historical sequence and particu-lar details such as Moses' lineage. Yet this narrative 'history' is transformed by the ritual laws and vice versa. He sees both the narrative and law in their interac-tion in P reflecting ritual time, which has a dimension of timelessness and can incorporate all time. Thus, he observes (p. 281) that in P 'past and present merge in the iterative present of ritual', and he refers (p. 282) to the Priestly writers

28. Carr (1996: 140) sees this division of time in P as in some ways similar to apocalyptic literature, differing only in that 'P is not displacing into the past a prediction of present and future events (so apocalypses), but instead retrojecting legislation shaping the present and the future cultic community of Israel'.

29. Although Damrosch bases much of his analysis on the book of Leviticus, and especially its ritual laws, his discussion suggests some tantalizing directions in which the discussion of P as a whole, comprising narrative and ritual laws and institutions, could go.

taking up past and future 'into a narrative grounded in the ritual present'. Or again, he says (p. 280) that the text 'mixes together past, present and future...', referring to this as the 'interanimation of temporal orders'.[30] In this way he sees throughout the whole of P the reflection of all time, since the distinctions of past, present and future do not apply. Damrosch (pp. 282-84) also uses the analogy of the perfective and imperfective temporalities of Semitic languages to explore how time operates in P.[31] Each part of the text, as the narrative takes on the imperfective time of the ritual law and the ritual law takes on the perfective time of 'historical' narrative, mixes past, present and future, incorporating all time in a kind of 'timelessness'. Thus, for example, rather than speaking of the wilderness/ Sinai material as programmatic in contrast to the pre-Sinai material as etiological as Carr does, Damrosch (pp. 295-97) speaks of the wilderness material as a combination of historical narrative and ritual ordinance reflecting at once a perfective and imperfective mode of discourse—as equating with the present situation of exile, and narrating the past and looking forward to the future all at once.

In my opinion, this discussion of P's hermeneutics of time, implying that throughout P time past, present and/or future is held together inseparably along a trajectory, goes some way toward clarifying the nature of P as both 'paradigmatic' and 'historiographical'.

Finally, F. Gorman (1990; 1993) follows a similar line to Damrosch, although using terminology more akin to Van Seters' 'mythic' view of origins, albeit applied to institutions ordered in 'history'. He perceives 'history' (Gorman 1993: 51) in P in ritual categories, and speaks explicitly about founding rituals in 'paradigmatic' terms. Founding rituals are set in the 'time' of the distant past—they describe a past event, 'a moment of origins'—but constitute the present order of reality, indeed function as 'paradigm' of what is to be (Gorman 1990: 106).[32] Thus in these founding rituals past, present and future are combined and mirrored at once. Over and above this, Gorman adds a further insight, helpful to our discussion, regarding the function of ritual (pp. 18, 227, 232; see also pp. 17, 22, 38, 225). Ritual texts, or we might say P's 'history' viewed in ritual terms, have a 'cognitive' aspect that embodies a world of meaning, and a 'performative' aspect in which the carrying out of the rituals described is the means of enacting, actualizing and realizing this world of meaning. Thus, for Gorman, what is found in P is 'a vision of the world held in conjunction with a means of situating oneself in the world (i.e. ritual)' (p. 232).

This insight into the nature of P is also helpful for working out a way of interpreting P and how, in particular, it might have functioned for its exilic audience. To this task we will now turn, drawing on all the insights regarding the nature of P emerging from the above discussion.

We have seen that P's genre coheres with the development of ancient Near Eastern and Greek genres where the process of 'the historicization of myth'

---

30. This is in the context of discussing Lev. 11–25.

31. Perfective forms are used for singular and one time actions; imperfective forms for ongoing or habitual activities whether past, present or future.

32. See also Gorman 1990: 138; 1997: 58, 61, 62.

and/or 'the mythologization of history', to use Van Seters' terminology, comprises an interrelationship of 'paradigmatic'[33] and 'historiographical' features. Its 'historiographical' quality is seen in its trajectory of contingent 'historical' traditions moving sequentially towards a goal. And yet, it reflects a 'mythic' pattern of the cosmogonic victory of the deity moving to the building of the deity's temple, as well as a repeating pattern on a cosmic and national level of: creation–destruction (chaos)–appearance of land. More importantly the material itself seems to have a 'paradigmatic' quality akin to ritual 'time' that incorporates all time, describing the past, reflecting and addressing the present, and looking to the future all at once. For example, the founding rituals have this quality and yet they are set in a contingent 'historiographical' sequence. What is more, while being paradigmatic, the material incorporates national 'historical' traditions.

So how exactly do these 'paradigmatic' and 'historiographical' qualities interrelate and how can P be seen to function? It does have to do with presenting 'origins', of both the world and the nation Israel, in a way that combines a 'mythical' and 'historiographical' view of such origins. It thus has a constituting and identity-shaping function. But does this get to the heart of the nature of P, and in particular account precisely for the specific way in which 'paradigmatic' and 'historiographical' qualities interrelate and combine in P and thus function for the reader?

The specific genius of the priestly material is that it presents along a contingent traditional 'historiographical' trajectory scenarios composed at least in part of 'historical' traditions, but which are paradigmatic in the sense unfolded above with time past, present, and future incorporated all at once. As such, the 'historical' features of both the scenarios and the trajectory as a whole function 'paradigmatically'; and the 'paradigmatic' scenarios in their 'paradigmatic' trajectory function 'historiographically' in the sense of pointing or moving ('eschatologically') towards a future goal.

Thus, each component scenario in the presentation of the trajectory of the nation comprises a synthesis of past, present and/or future traditions, experiences and hopes into a 'paradigm', so that each section of P can be said to be 'paradigmatic' and to function 'paradigmatically'. But, because they are arranged in a contingent sequential narrative, their paradigmatic meaning must be considered in this context, each in its place in the sequence and in relation to the direction or goal toward which the trajectory as a whole is heading. This not only gives a 'historiographical' dimension to these paradigmatic scenarios, but also gives a 'paradigmatic' dimension to the trajectory. Another 'paradigmatic' dimension to the trajectory of the nation is seen in its repetition or paralleling of the cosmic trajectory of: creation (of world/nation)–destruction (flood as paralleling the death of the Mosaic generation at the edge of the land)–new situation (appearance of the cosmic earth paralleling the land of Canaan). Thus both the trajectory

---

33. As defined in the above survey of views, and standing close to a certain sense of 'myth' emergent in the above discussion.

of the nation, and each of the 'paradigmatic' scenarios of the nation comprising it, must be interpreted in relation to the corresponding cosmic parallel.

Given this, in order to understand how P might function for the reader,[34] it will be helpful to use the terminology and hermeneutics of P. Ricoeur (1967; 1976) to explore P's hermeneutics. Ricoeur refers to texts as secondary symbols with their own narrative, 'geography' and 'history' (though not in the literal sense). The designation of P as a whole as a secondary symbol helps to capture its 'paradigmatic' quality, both in relation to its component elements and as a whole. The 'time' and 'space' dimensions of this secondary symbol (or 'historical' and 'geographical' in Ricoeur's terminology) help to capture something of P's 'historiographical' quality. Although in Ricoeur's hermeneutics (1967) the 'space' and 'time' of a text as secondary symbol need not have any connection with specific historical traditions,[35] this aspect of his hermeneutics can still be applied to, or used to throw light on, P's hermeneutics. We do, however, need to keep in mind that P's 'time' and 'space', while not of course to be taken literally, reflect and incorporate contingent historical traditions. This is the case both in terms of individual traditions and with regard to the whole sequence.[36] The 'time' of P as secondary symbol extends from creation to the end of the Mosaic period; its 'space' extends from the cosmos (creation/flood) to the edge of the land of Canaan.

In Ricoeur's hermeneutics the reader, using critical analysis, must move through the literal sense (or primary intentionality) of the secondary symbol or text in order to reach its analogical reference (or secondary intentionality), that is, 'the world of the text'. This 'world of the text'[37] is reached only by moving through the sense of the text as a whole, that is, through its 'space' and 'time'. The reader, then, appropriates this 'world of the text' opened up in this way by allowing its mode-of-being-in-the-world to inform his/her self-understanding. In this way the reader reaches full understanding, or authentic self-understanding, in that he/she has entered into the way of orienting him/herself within the world opened up by moving through the text and its world.[38]

Applying this to P, then, a reader—for example, in the early post-exilic period[39]—moves through the sense of the whole text, the portrayal of past events in 'space' and 'time', to enter into the world of the text. In moving through the sense of the text, in the various scenarios that make up the trajectory and within the trajectory as a whole, he/she will at each point constantly and continuously

34. I am thinking primarily here of the original exilic audience, but P also has the potential to function in relation to other and later generations of readers.

35. Ricoeur applies this to Gen. 2–3.

36. In that it follows the broad sequence of J or non-P material.

37. Or 'surplus of meaning'; see Ricoeur 1976.

38. This is similar to what Gorman seems to be pointing to when he speaks in terms of world view having a 'cognitive aspect' and ritual texts, or P's 'history' viewed in ritual terms, having a 'cognitive' aspect that embodies a world of meaning, except that Ricoeur speaks in more existential terms.

39. Although it need not be restricted to this.

recognize and relate to what is known from past tradition and/or present experience and tradition. But this will be only a partial recognition since these past traditions and/or present aspects are combined and synthesized and thus reshaped in each element or scenario encountered in a paradigmatic way with future elements and goals (God's future). The trajectory itself also heads towards an as yet unrealized future goal (that God is yet to bring about). Thus, the world of the text will comprise an accumulation of these constant partial recognitions of reshaped traditions and present experience integrated with an accumulation of future elements—visions of goals encountered in combination with past and present aspects. This world of the text then represents the full vision of the complex paradigm that, at each stage and in its pattern and trajectory as a whole, contains past/present and future.

The embodiment of this world of the text, or fulfilment of this complex paradigm, involves the reader (or reading/listening community) appropriating it by allowing it to inform his/her/their self-understanding or identity.[40] But over and above this, given that central to the 'paradigmatic' scenarios and trajectory of the nation as a whole is the institution of rituals (or in Gorman's terminology, 'founding rituals') as commanded by *Yhwh*, the reader will know that part of entering into the fulfilment of this complex paradigm involves not only appropriating the world of the text existentially but also carrying out the divinely constituted rituals that enable the embodying of that 'world'. In Gorman's words (1990: 232), the performing of the rituals is 'the means of enacting, actualizing, and realizing...world view', or we might say in Ricoeur's terminology 'the world of the text'.

The reader, then, in moving through P, may constantly experience 'the now... but not yet', glimpses of the known combined with visions of the future not yet experienced, both at each point and as a consequence of reading the whole. At the same time, however, the reader is provided with the means of entering into, and embodying, the world of the text, the fulfilment of this complex 'eschatological' paradigm with its future, which according to P is ultimately brought about by God.

The groundwork has now been laid for approaching the interpretation of P so as to do justice to both its 'paradigmatic' and 'historiographical' nature and the particular way in which these aspects are integrated within it. The actual task of interpretation can now, therefore, begin.

BIBLIOGRAPHY

Blenkinsopp, J.
    1976   'The Structure of P', *CBQ* 38: 275-92.
    1995   *Sage, Priest, Prophet: Religious and Intellectual Leadership in Ancient Israel* (Louisville, KY: Westminster/John Knox Press).
Blum, E.
    1990   *Studien zur Komposition des Pentateuch* (BZAW, 189; Berlin: W. de Gruyter).

---

40. Approximating to Gorman's cognitive aspect of world view; see n. 38 above.

Boorer, S.
    1977   'The Kerygmatic Intention of the Priestly Material', *AusBR* 25, pp. 12-20.
    1992   *The Promise of the Land as Oath: A Key to the Formation of the Pentateuch* (BZAW, 205; Berlin: W. de Gruyter).
    2001   'The Earth/Land (*erets*) in the Priestly Material: The Preservation of the "Good" Earth and the Promised Land of Canaan Throughout the Generations', *ABR* 49: 19-33.
Brueggemann, W.
    1982   'The Kerygma of the Priestly Writers', in W. Brueggemann and H.W. Wolff (eds.), *The Vitality of Old Testament Traditions* (Atlanta: John Knox Press): 101-13.
Campbell, A.F.
    1993   'The Priestly Text: Redaction or Source?', in G. Braulik *et al.* (eds.), *Biblische Theologie und gesellschaftlicher Wandel* (Freiburg: Herder): 32-47.
Campbell, A.F., and M.A. O'Brien
    1993   *Sources of the Pentateuch: Texts, Introductions, Annotations* (Minneapolis: Fortress Press).
Carr, D.
    1996   *Reading the Fractures of Genesis: Historical and Literary Approaches* (Louisville, KY: Westminster/John Knox Press).
Childs, B.S.
    1960   *Myth and Reality in the Old Testament* (London: SCM Press).
Clements, R.E.
    1965   *God and Temple: The Idea of the Divine in Ancient Israel* (Oxford: Basil Blackwell).
Clifford, R.J.
    1994   *Creation Accounts in the Ancient Near East and the Bible* (Washington: Catholic Biblical Association of America).
Cross, F.M.
    1968   'The Priestly Tabernacle', in S. Sandmel (ed.), *Old Testament Issues* (London: SCM Press).
    1973   *Canaanite Myth and Hebrew Epic* (Cambridge, MA: Harvard University Press).
Damrosch, D.
    1987   *The Narrative Covenant: Transformations of Genre in the Growth of Biblical Literature* (San Francisco: Harper & Row).
Elliger, K.
    1952   'Sinn und Ursprung der Priesterlichen Geschichtserzahlung', *ZTK* 49: 121-42.
Freidman, R.E.
    1992   'Tabernacle', in *ABD*, VI: 292-300.
Fretheim, T.E.
    1968   'The Priestly Document: Anti-Temple?', *VT* 18: 313-29.
Gorman, F.
    1990   *The Ideology of Ritual: Space, Time and Status in the Priestly Theology* (JSOTSup, 91; Sheffield: JSOT Press).
    1993   'Priestly Rituals of Founding: Time, Space and Status', in M.P. Graham *et al.* (eds.), *History and Interpretation: Essays in Honor of John H. Hayes* (JSOTSup, 173; Sheffield: Sheffield Academic Press): 47-64.
    1997   *Divine Presence and Community: A Commentary on the Book of Leviticus* (ITC; Grand Rapids: Eerdmans).
Haran, M.
    1962   'Shiloh and Jerusalem: The Origin of the Priestly Tradition in the Pentateuch', *JBL* 81: 14-24.

Janowski, B.
　　1990　　'Tempel und Schopfung: Schopfungstheologischer Aspeckte der priester-
　　　　　　schriftliche Heiligtums Konzeption', in L. Alonso Schockel *et al.* (eds.),
　　　　　　Schopfung und Neuschopfung (Jahrbuch für biblische Theologie, 5; Neu-
　　　　　　kirchen–Vluyn: Neukirchener Verlag): 37-70.

Klein, R.W.
　　1981　　'The Message of P', in J. Jeremias and L. Perlitt (eds.), *Die Botschaft und die
　　　　　　Boten* (Neukirchen–Vluyn: Neukirchener Verlag): 57-66.

Lohfink, N.
　1994 [1978]　'The Priestly Narrative and History', in *idem*, *The Theology of the Pentateuch:
　　　　　　Themes of the Priestly Narrative and Deuteronomy* (Edinburgh: T. & T.
　　　　　　Clark): 136-72 (first published in 1978 in German as 'Die Priesterschrift und
　　　　　　die Geschichte', in W. Zimmerli [ed.], *Congress Volume, Göttingen 1977*
　　　　　　[VTSup, 29; Leiden: E.J. Brill]: 189-225).

Mettinger, T.N.D.
　　1982　　*The Dethronement of Sabaoth: Studies in the Shem and Kabod Theologies*
　　　　　　(ConBOT, 18; C.W.K. Gleerup).

Nicholson, E.W.
　　1988　　'P as an Originally Independent Source in the Pentateuch', *Irish Biblical
　　　　　　Studies* 10: 192-206.

Noth, M.
　　1972　　*A History of Pentateuchal Traditions* (Englewood Cliffs, NJ: Prentice–Hall
　　　　　　[1948]).

Rad, G. von
　　1966　　'The Tent and the Ark', in *idem*, *The Problem of the Hexateuch and Other
　　　　　　Essays* (Edinburgh: Oliver & Boyd): 103-24.

Ricoeur, P.
　　1967　　*The Symbolism of Evil* (Boston: Beacon Press).
　　1976　　*Interpretation Theory: Discourse and the Surplus of Meaning* (Fort Worth, TX:
　　　　　　Texas Christian University).

Roberts, J.J.M.
　　1976　　'Myth versus History: Relaying the Comparative Foundations', *CBQ* 38: 1-13.

Schmidt, L.
　　1993　　*Studien zur Priesterschrift* (BZAW, 214; Berlin: W. de Gruyter).

Thompson, T.L.
　　1992　　'Historiography', in *ABD*, III: 206-12.

Van Seters, J.
　　1983　　*In Search of History: Historiography in the Ancient World and the Origins of
　　　　　　Biblical History* (New Haven: Yale University Press).
　　1992　　*Prologue to History: The Yahwist as Historian in Genesis* (Louisville, KY:
　　　　　　Westminster/John Knox Press).
　　1999　　*The Pentateuch: A Social-Science Commentary* (Trajectories, 1; Sheffield:
　　　　　　Sheffield Academic Press).

Vaux, R. de
　　1961　　*Ancient Israel: Its Life and Institutions* (London: Darton, Longman & Todd).

AT 'SIXES AND SEVENS' IN EXODUS 6–7?

Mark A. O'Brien

It is every traveller's nightmare to be in a strange city, map in hand, surrounded by traffic signals and signs, yet quite confused: to be, as they say, at 'sixes and sevens'. One begins to doubt the accuracy of the map, the city's signal system, one's ability to read signs. But a crisis can also be an opportunity, a chance to step out, armed with a map or two, and see what there is to discover. One may even come across things en route that make the journey more interesting and exciting than the actual arrival.

Reading Exodus 6–7 can be a frustrating experience, a bit like trying to negotiate a labyrinth: it appears to be a complex, repetitive and uneven text.[1] One of the many benefits of working with Tony Campbell is observing how well he is able to turn frustration into fascination and discovery when dealing with a complex text. He has a unique feel for the elements of the 'art of exegesis'—an ability to read the signals in the text and the 'maps' provided by scholars who have gone before. He engages the text with a sense of adventure and the anticipation of discovery. Our efforts may not always yield what we expect, but the venture invariably proves challenging and informative.

This volume provides a welcome opportunity to celebrate his mastery of the art of exegesis and to explore the meaning of a complex but fascinating text. The passages within Exodus 6–7 that I will focus on are the dialogues between God and Moses. Exodus 5.22-23 will be included because it is the complaint of Moses that prompts God's reply in 6.1. Even though 6.2-8 follows immediately on God's speech in 6.1, it has its own introduction and no reply by Moses. Nevertheless, its location and content invite one to consider how it might relate to the preceding dialogue in 5.22–6.1. Exodus 6.10-12 reverses the order of the preceding dialogue, commencing with an instruction from God followed by Moses' objection: it recurs with some changes in 6.28-30. Exodus 7.1-5 is God's answer to Moses' objection in 6.30 and so constitutes part of the dialogue of 6.28-30. These dialogues, in particular 5.22–6.1(2-8) and 6.28–7.5, have attracted considerable scholarly attention; regrettably, it can only be acknowledged selectively in this essay.

---

1. Awareness of the complexity of this material is not new. For an appreciation of how rabbinic scholarship saw it, see Houtman 1993: 498-500.

1. *The Dialogue in Exodus 5.22–6.1*

In Exod. 5.22–6.1 Moses upbraids God after he and Aaron have been rebuffed by Pharaoh and rebuked by the Israelite supervisors. Aaron, who is at Moses' side throughout the initial encounter with Pharaoh, disappears abruptly from the text until 6.13, where he reappears just as abruptly. His disappearance does not seem to trouble literary-critical analysis, which generally attributes 5.22–6.1 to the same hand as ch. 5. Presumably, this is because the dialogue provides a suitable sequel to the encounter with Pharaoh. Moreover, Moses is the one commissioned in ch. 3 and it is appropriate for him, rather than both characters, to address God in 5.22-23. In contrast, Aaron's reappearance in 6.13 is regarded as a significant literary-critical feature. It will be considered below.

Moses' speech opens with two questions similar to those found in the lament or complaint type of psalm (e.g. Pss. 10.1; 22.1).[2] The formal similarity is clear enough. Not so clear is the meaning and function of Moses' questions or complaints in the context of the exodus narrative. The two questions can be read like a synonymous parallelism in Hebrew poetry: the second ('Why did you ever send me?') develops the thought of the first ('Why have you done evil to this people?'). Taken together, the questions function as implied accusations, identifying the 'evil' as God's choice of Moses. Exodus 5.23a provides evidence to back this up. From the moment that Moses encountered Pharaoh, matters have gone from bad to worse for the people: he is clearly the wrong man for the job. The accusation implied in 5.22 becomes explicit in v. 23b and may be paraphrased as follows: your sending me has certainly not meant deliverance for your people! On this reading, 5.22-23 is about Moses and his vocation. It has support within the larger present text, in particular Moses' repeated objections to his commission in Exodus 3–4. These chapters portray him as a reluctant and uncertain figure.

A rather different understanding emerges if one gives equal weight to the people in the first question and to Moses in the second question. Two related yet distinct accusations are implied. The first is that God has not delivered the people as promised. This accusation becomes explicit in 5.23b. The second is that God has not supported Moses in his mission despite the promise to do so. In contrast to the first reading, the problem here is not that Moses believes he is the wrong man for the job. He may have objected at first but, according to 4.18-20, he eventually accepted his commission and returned to Egypt ready to confront Pharaoh. His complaints are an expression of his solidarity with the people and concern about their fate (Aurelius 1988: 160). The problem here is that God has not helped him in his struggle with Pharaoh (cf. 5.1-19 and 23a). The accusation of lack of support lurks behind his question, 'Why did you ever send me?'

Each of these readings depends on the way one understands the signals in 5.22-23 and their relationship to the preceding context. The subsequent context

---

2.   Cf. Schmidt 1988: 263-64. Ahuis (1982: 46) sees links not only with lament psalms but also the 'confessions' of Jeremiah (cf. 20.7-9). There is also Moses' complaint in Num. 11.11-15.

may incline one in a particular direction, but this will, as with consideration of the preceding context, depend on how a reader sees the signals and reads the signs. Before moving on to the subsequent context, there is another, third, way of reading 5.22-23 that deserves mention.

Some recent studies argue that Moses (and Aaron) bungle their initial encounter with Pharaoh (e.g. Fretheim 1991: 86; Propp 1998: 258-59). In 5.1 they go well beyond what God commissions Moses to say in 3.18 and 4.22-23a. Moses does not work any wonders before Pharaoh as he is instructed to do in 4.21 and, when rebuffed by Pharaoh, he does not threaten him with the death of his firstborn son (cf. 4.22-23). He also seems to have forgotten that God forewarned him twice (3.19; 4.21) that Pharaoh would be stubborn. Finally, in 5.21 there are the ominous words of the Israelite supervisors: 'The Lord look upon you and judge!'

On the strength of this evidence, one could argue that Moses' complaints in 5.22 and his accusation in 5.23b are ill-founded and wrong. In short, Moses shows the same lack of perception in 5.22-23 that he showed in his dealings with Pharaoh earlier in the chapter. This reading assumes a highly coherent present text. One way of testing this is to see whether and in what way the divinity's speeches in ch. 6 are a response to Moses' questions and accusation. If 5.22-23 is to be understood as a blunder by Moses, one would expect the subsequent text to instruct Moses so that he does not bungle matters a second time. Those who see the present text as an amalgam of sources/traditions and editing would not be troubled by such variety. For them the text contains different, even conflicting portraits of Moses by different hands and they have not been harmonized. The biblical text is not only a story but a repository of Israel's varied traditions.

Whichever reading one opts for, there are three elements in 5.22-23 that seem to be common to each. These are: God's relationship to the people of Israel; the nature of Moses' commission or role; the overthrow of Pharaoh (and the Egyptians). How the subsequent text takes up these elements may provide some clues as to how the text is meant to be read.

On initial inspection, 6.1 does not appear to be an explanation or *apologia* for God's activity so far. It is a promise or assurance about the future (Aurelius 1988: 161; Childs 1974: 107). One could compare 5.22–6.1 with some other passages where a complaint or objection is followed by an assurance from God.[3] However, closer inspection suggests there may be more to it than a straight complaint–assurance sequence. To begin with, the opening word of the speech by *Yhwh* ('now') suggests a contrast between what has happened or not happened up to this point and what is about to happen.[4] Does the proclamation of what God is about to do to Pharaoh imply that Israel's God has done nothing so far? A positive response would lend support to the second reading of 5.22-23 outlined above: God has failed to help Moses or deliver the people. This is a possible

---

3. For example, God's assurances in reply to Moses' objections in Exod. 3–4; at a further remove, there is Gen. 15.

4. The Samaritan Pentateuch alone reads 'you' singular (אתה); this evidence is hardly sufficient to challenge the MT.

reading if 5.22–6.1 is taken on its own, but it is clearly in conflict with the larger context of Exodus.

This obliges one to turn to the two other interpretations of 5.22-23. According to one (the first one outlined above), Moses believes that God made a bad choice in sending him. According to the other (the third one outlined above), Moses is to blame because he bungled his mission. The first provides a plausible reading. Even though Moses may think he was a bad choice, God's answer in 6.1 assures him that his mission has provided the moment that God, as it were, has been waiting for. The moment of Moses' perceived failure—and, by implication, of God's mistake—is the 'now' of Pharaoh's downfall. Exodus 3.19 lends support to this reading. There God tells Moses 'the king of Egypt will not let you go unless compelled by a mighty hand'. In 4.21, Moses is told that God will harden Pharaoh's heart. Pharaoh's rebuff in ch. 5 can be seen as the first touch of this 'mighty hand' that will compel him to release Israel. According to 6.1, Moses shall 'now' see the impact of this mighty hand on Pharaoh.[5] The unspoken conclusion: as a result, Moses will see the wisdom of God's choice.

The third reading is also possible, at least when taken in relation to ch. 5. Moses was wrong to complain and accuse God in 5.22-23. The account of his negotiations with Pharaoh indicates that he failed to follow God's instructions. So, in 6.1, God takes charge: 'now you will see what I will do to Pharaoh'. Moses is relegated to the role of spectator. The problem with this interpretation is that it does not mesh easily with what follows. God seems just as concerned as before to have Moses play a leading role in the liberation of Israel (cf. 6.6, 11, 29; 7.1). It would amount to a surprisingly rapid rehabilitation from spectator to key player—as in some games where a player is sidelined for poor play, given a pep talk by the coach and sent on again, all in the space of a few minutes. Exodus 6.2-8 would serve as the coach's 'pep talk', setting Moses straight about the 'game plan' and his part in it. Possible, but hardly compelling.

There is one further question that needs to be asked of 6.1. In what sense does it respond to the three elements that were identified in 5.22-23: God's relationship to Israel ('your people'), Moses' role, and the triumph over Pharaoh (and the Egyptians)? The answer seems fairly clear. Only one element is highlighted—the overpowering of Pharaoh. The other two elements play a subsidiary role: Moses gets to see it while the people get to benefit from it. In these two areas at least, 6.1 allows for or invites elaboration.

2. *Exodus 6.2-8 and its Relationship to the First Dialogue*

This extensive speech requires some comment on its internal organization before exploring its relationship to the surrounding context. Fortunately, a number of

---

5. There is some question whether the 'mighty hand' in 6.1 refers to God or to Pharaoh. Schmidt (1988: 244) prefers God and appeals to Deut. 6.21; Propp (1998: 258) prefers Pharaoh and appeals to Exod. 12.33 and the presence of the verb ותחזק in 'and the Egyptians urged the people'. This is further evidence of the subtlety and at times ambiguity of the signals in the text. Given that, as Propp himself notes (p. 207) '3.19 is most naturally taken as referring to Yahweh's arm', it may be best to follow Schmidt on 6.1.

studies have done this admirably and, despite differences over a few points, they agree that it is a carefully structured piece.[6] The following comments draw on these more detailed analyses.

The speech unfolds in two main parts: what God tells Moses in vv. 2-5 and what Moses is to tell Israel in vv. 6-8. A signal that reverberates throughout the speech and binds its parts together is the proclamation of the divine name *Yhwh*. It begins and ends the speech; it differentiates the epoch of the ancestors from the epoch of Moses and Israel; it occurs in the transition from the first to the second part of the speech where Moses is instructed to proclaim the name to the people (v. 6); and it also occurs at the end of v. 7. A series of verbs in vv. 6-7 details what God plans to do to deliver Israel from Egyptian bondage, all of it in order that Israel will be God's people and *know* that *Yhwh* is their God. The final statement in v. 7 about being freed from the burden of the Egyptians finds a matching statement near the beginning of v. 6—an indication that the two verses are to be read as a section within the speech.

The two parts of the speech are further linked by the references to the ancestors in v. 3 and v. 8a, and by the promise of the land in v. 4 and v. 8a. But, whereas the promise in v. 4 uses the relatively common phrase 'I established my covenant', v. 8a has the unusual 'I lifted up my hand' (NRSV 'I swore'). As an expression of God's promise or oath, this phrase is found, apart from Num. 14.30; Ps. 106.26; Neh. 9.15, only in Ezekiel (cf. 20.5-6, 15, 23, 28, 42; 44.12; 47.14). The phrase may be a sign of different authorship: if so, the hand responsible has deftly enhanced the link between v. 8 and the earlier verses of the speech.[7]

Within the first part of the speech, the references to the covenant/oath at the beginning of v. 4 and the end of v. 5 frame the material in between. Verses 4-5 thus form a section within the first part of the speech, rather like vv. 6-7 in the second part. Closer inspection reveals the two sections are linked. Verses 4-5 forge a bond between the ancestors in Canaan and Israel in Egypt. God established a covenant with the ancestors; on hearing the groans of the Israelites, God remembers that covenant and instructs Moses to give the Israelites a message. The message in vv. 6-7 spells out in a series of verbs how God will act—presumably in accord with the covenant. A further link between vv. 4-5 and vv. 6-7 is provided by the reference to Israel's plight, in particular the use of the root עבד ('slavery') in vv. 5a and 6a.

According to vv. 3-4, the ancestors came to know God as '*El Shaddai*', the one who made a solemn promise in the form of a covenant to give them the land of Canaan.[8] According to vv. 7-8, Israel will come to know that they are *Yhwh*'s

6.   See especially the studies (and bibliography cited) by Auffret 1983a and b, and Magonet 1983a and b; also Ska 1982; 1989: 97-105 (and the bibliography listed in n. 6), and Lust 1996.

7.   Kohata (1986: 28-34) thinks v. 8 reflects Dtr terminology. He also identifies בזרוע נטויה in v. 6 as an expansion. For a discussion of the relationship between the phrase 'I lifted up my hand' and its use in Ezekiel, see Lust (1996: 218-23), who disagrees with Kohata's identification of v. 8 as Dtr.

8.   The repeated occurrence of וגם ('and also') in vv. 4-5 may be a sign of later editing but it seems unlikely. A quite abrupt transition from v. 3 to v. 5 would result. Rather than add, its function here is to emphasize (cf. Labuschagne 1966: 197).

people and that *Yhwh* is their God, the one who will fulfil the promise by leading
them to freedom from Egypt. Overall, one can say of vv. 4-5 and 6-7 that each
has its own structure, each is related to the other, and each forms an integral part
of the larger whole that is vv. 2-8. It is difficult to do justice to such a rich array
of textual signals. Any reading is likely to overlook something or distort the intricate connection between the various signals in some way. In commenting on
such a text, one treads warily in the hope of not doing too much damage.

As noted above, a predominant element in 6.2-8 is the proclamation 'I am
Yhwh'. Closely linked to it are three other elements or signals in the text. One is
what may be called the change of epochs, from that of the ancestors to that of the
people of Israel in Egypt. The second is knowledge of the divine name. It was
part of the divine plan that the ancestors knew God as *El Shaddai*, the one who
made a covenant commitment to give them the land. It is part of the same plan
that the oppressed people of Israel now know this same God by the name *Yhwh*,
the one who will deliver them from oppression and fulfil the ancestral promise.
The third is that the identity of the people of Israel is inextricably linked to this
knowledge ('I will take you as my people and I will be your God', v. 7a)[9]. Israel
becomes God's people by knowing that 'I am *Yhwh*'. How is this knowledge to
come about? According to vv. 6-8, it will be the outcome of all that *Yhwh* will do
for Israel. Knowing fully (as God's people) that 'I am *Yhwh*' is something that
lies in the future.

There is a sense of continuity between the epochs of the ancestors and of
Israel, but also of difference or development. There is continuity and difference
in the knowledge of God and relationship with God: initially this involved the
ancestors knowing God as *El Shaddai*; now it involves Israel knowing God as
Yhwh. There is continuity and difference in the way God has acted on behalf of
the ancestors and will now act on behalf of Israel. There is continuity and development in the portrayal of the ancestors and Moses. As the ancestors were chosen
to be bearers of God's promises in their time, so Moses is now chosen to be the
bearer of God's promise to Israel in Egypt. There is finally the evident continuity
and difference between the *ancestors* of Israel and the *people* of Israel. Particular
points may be debated, but they do not significantly affect this understanding of
the speech.[10]

The tricky step comes next—assessing the relationship of this text to the
preceding dialogue. The new introduction (after 6.1) and the use of the term God
instead of *Yhwh* creates uncertainty as to whether the speech is a reply to Moses'
complaint in 5.22-23 or is about something else. There is also the rather abrupt
shift from what *Yhwh* will do to Pharaoh to what Moses is instructed to do. Yet in

---

9.   Verse 7a ('I will take you as my people and I will be your God') is commonly taken as a
reference to the covenant relationship (so Propp 1998: 273; Schmidt 1988: 285-96; Childs 1974:
115).

10.   One point of debate is whether בְּרִית should be translated as 'covenant' or 'oath'. Propp and
Schmidt opt for 'covenant', Auffret for 'oath'. Another is how to render בְּאֵל שַׁדַּי with the verb
'make known' in v. 3. For a discussion, see Garr 1992. A third is whether in vv. 7-8 knowledge of
God is a prerequisite to occupation of the land or do the two belong together as stages in the
fulfilment of God's promises?

v. 6, Moses is commissioned to bring the Israelites a promise of deliverance, which is the issue voiced in 5.22-23. One way of testing the relationship between 6.2-8 and the preceding dialogue in 5.22–6.1 is to see whether 6.2-8 addresses the three elements or concerns identified in 5.22-23—God's commitment to Israel ('your people'), the role of Moses and the overpowering of Pharaoh. As part of this test, the relationship of 6.2-8 to the earlier chapters of Exodus and the book of Genesis also needs to be taken into account where appropriate.[11] If no favourable evidence is found, then 6.2-8 is either a quite independent piece or the significance I have attributed to the three elements is seriously astray.

Apropos of the first element, it seems clear that 6.2-8 attests God's enduring commitment to the people. It was manifested initially in the establishment of a covenant with the ancestors. It continues in the 'present' of Israel's affliction when God remembers the covenant. It will reach its fulfilment in Israel's deliverance from Egypt, in their privileged status as 'my people' (v. 7), and in the gift of the land. As a result, the people will come to appreciate why God made known to them the name *Yhwh*.

This evidence makes 6.2-8 look like a response to Moses' complaint about God's commitment. There is even a linguistic connection, with the verb 'to deliver' occurring in 5.23 and 6.6.[12] But there is also a gap. The speech does not explain how the rebuff of ch. 5 fits into the scheme of things. There are two possible ways to close this gap. One is to appeal to an earlier reading of 5.22-23—the rebuff was due to Moses bungling things, not a failure by God. The other is that Pharaoh's rebuff falls within God's plan to deliver the people—an option that finds some textual support in the wider context. There is God's foreknowledge in 3.19 that Pharaoh will not let Israel go unless compelled by a 'mighty hand', and there is God's plan in 4.21 to harden Pharaoh's heart. A hardhearted Pharaoh will surely refuse to free Israel and this is precisely what happens in ch. 5. In 6.2-5, Moses is shown how all this falls within the larger horizon of God's purpose for Israel, one that reaches back to the ancestors and the revelation of the name *El Shaddai*.

The second element is the role or commission of Moses. Three interpretations of it were outlined in the discussion of 5.22-23: God has chosen the wrong man for the job; Moses has carried out his commission but God has failed to support him; Moses himself is to blame because he mishandled the negotiations with Pharaoh. None of these is taken up explicitly in Exod. 6.2-8. Nevertheless, in v. 6 *Yhwh* commissions Moses to bear a message to the Israelites. Furthermore, as already noted, vv. 2-5 seem to draw a relationship between the role of the ancestors and that of Moses. God's opening words to Moses in 6.2, 'I am *Yhwh*', appear to parallel God's opening words to Abraham in Gen. 17.1, 'I am *El Shaddai*'. Does the text imply that, within this covenant trajectory, the role of Moses is analogous to that of the great ancestor Abraham? The two figures mark

11. Among recent studies, Ska (1989: 102-105) has explored the relationship between 6.2-8 and ch. 5, while Seitz (1990: 154-59) has done the same for Exod. 3–4 and 6.2-8.

12. Ska (1989: 102-105) notes this and a number of other linguistic similarities between terms in 6.2-8 and the account of Moses' encounter with Pharaoh in ch. 5.

key epochs in the unfolding of God's purpose for Israel. If this is so, 6.2-8 can be seen as addressing Moses' personal crisis in 5.22-23 by elevating him to the status of an Abraham. Like Abraham, Moses is chosen by God to usher in a new epoch, that of the people of Israel and its special relationship to God who it will know as *Yhwh*. Admittedly, one cannot press the relationship between 5.22-23 and 6.2-8 beyond the general level, but 6.2-8 may create the general frame within which more specific matters are explored. As will be shown below, 7.1-5 deals with the specific issues of Moses' mission to Pharaoh and God's plan to overcome Egyptian oppression.

In relation to what one may call the three sketches for the 'portrait' of Moses that have been identified, the interpretation outlined would best fit the second sketch: he has been chosen to play a key role in God's overall plan (despite the setback with Pharaoh) and this plan is now laid out for him in full. However, it may also be just possible to relate our reading to the first and third sketches: apropos of the first, Moses may think he is the wrong choice but God thinks otherwise; apropos of the third, God is committed even to an incompetent like Moses!

Exodus 6.2-8 does not make any direct reference to the third element identified in 5.22-23, the struggle with Pharaoh. The emphasis is on what God will do for Israel rather than on what God will do to Pharaoh, as in 6.1. However, one could say that Pharaoh is 'included' in the promise that God will deliver Israel from the burden of the Egyptians (vv. 6-7).

Of the three concerns raised in 5.22-23, my analysis indicates that the most explicit response of 6.2-8 is to the first one (God's commitment to the people). There is evidence of a general response to the second concern (the role of Moses) but only fleeting evidence of the third concern (the overthrow of Pharaoh). However, it was noted earlier how 6.1 addresses the issue of Pharaoh's overthrow but only touches briefly on the other two concerns. It thereby invites elaboration. In its own way, Exod. 6.2-8 can be seen to take up the invitation.

This reading of 5.22–6.8 allows a brief comment to be made on the relationship between 6.2-8 and chs. 3–4. These two texts have become focal points in the debate about the source hypothesis and whether P (to which is attributed 6.2-8) is a continuous source or one or more stages in the redaction of the Pentateuch.[13] The brief comment concerns the name *Yhwh* and the status of the people. Exodus 6.2-8 claims that what is about to take place will lead the people to *know Yhwh*. The verb 'to know' does not occur in chs. 3–4 in association with the name. Comparison of the two passages reveals a distinction between the revelation of the name *Yhwh* and Israel coming to know the one who bears this name. This *knowing* is an essential ingredient in the identity of Israel as the people of *Yhwh*. Israel

13. The number of studies on the composition of Exodus advocating source and/or redaction theory is legion and need not be listed here; see Propp 1998: 56-115. The difficulty in finding clear signs of the compositional process behind the present text—particularly in the context of a complex and long-standing debate—may be reflected in the work of Erhard Blum. After much careful analysis, he proposes that P is 'neither source nor redaction' (1990: 228); for his discussion of 6.2-8, see pp. 232-42, and for his more recent reflections on the relationship between Exod. 3–4 and 6.2-8, see Blum 2002: 119-56.

will become *Yhwh*'s people in the full sense when it knows (experiences and acknowledges) all that *Yhwh* is to do on Israel's behalf.[14] That such a knowledge can only come about as a result of God's action is supported by 6.9. It reports the people's failure or inability to listen to Moses because of their broken spirit. In their oppressed situation, they are unable to accept the message; that is, they are unable to know *Yhwh* in the manner outlined. Once delivered from oppression however, they will know *Yhwh*. Exodus 6.2-8 may well be from another hand to Exodus 3–4 but the two passages serve a larger purpose within the Torah; namely, that revelation of the divine name does not automatically mean that Israel knows *Yhwh* in the sense of being totally committed to the god who bears that name.[15] The subsequent narrative in Exodus–Numbers returns again and again to this, at times painful, lesson. Israel is reminded that it is a goal yet to be achieved in Deut. 26.16-19.

3. *The Dialogue in Exodus 6.10-12*

The sequence of this dialogue is the reverse of 5.22–6.1(2-8). Here, God instructs Moses to confront Pharaoh and Moses objects. The instruction seems to clash with v. 1 where all Moses has to do is watch God in action. As well, v. 11 does not appear to take into account Moses' setback in ch. 5. It is as if he is to confront Pharaoh for the first time. Once again, however, the text signals can be read in more than one way. Moses really needs to be in Pharaoh's presence to witness God's actions against him, and this is what happens in the plague stories that follow. As for Moses' setback, 6.1 dealt with it and so there is no need to repeat it here. Moses' objection in v. 12 clearly refers to the people's refusal in v. 9 but even so the fit is not neat. Moses complains that he is 'uncircumcised of lips' (NRSV 'poor speaker'). Does this mean that Moses is the wrong person to confront Pharaoh (cf. 6.30), or does it offer a reason why the people refused to listen to Moses? If so, it is not the reason given in v. 9. A reader could ease the tension by noting that v. 9 is the narrator's comment whereas v. 12 expresses the opinion of the character Moses.

Depending on how one sees the signals, this dialogue will, like the preceding one, be judged at home in its context or somewhat at odds with that context. One thing does however seem clear: as a dialogue, it is unresolved, ending with a question. The resolution comes in 6.28–7.5, but in a somewhat repetitive manner and with a lengthy genealogy in between (6.13-27).

4. *The Dialogue in Exodus 6.28–7.5*

This dialogue consists of the narrative introduction in v. 28, God's command in v. 29, Moses' reply in v. 30, and God's response to Moses in 7.1-5. Exodus

14. For a similar view, see Blum 1990: 328. Israel is already called 'my people' in Exod. 3.7. It is quite another thing for Israel to *know* that it is *Yhwh*'s people.

15. This comment does not take into account the conflict between 6.3 and texts in Genesis such as 15.7 and 28.13. The issue is beyond the scope of this essay. For a novel approach, see Moberly 1992.

6.28-30 is normally identified as a resumptive repetition (*Wiederaufnahme*) of
6.10-12, an editorial device for resuming the narrative thread after an insertion—
in this case 6.13-27. There are actually two resumptive repetitions because the
genealogy in 6.14-25 is itself framed by two passages that facilitate its insertion,
v. 13 and vv. 26-27. Prior to these insertions, it is most likely that 6.10-12 was
immediately followed by 7.1.[16]

The arrangement of the text makes it difficult to tell how the narrative is
unfolding. From one angle the genealogy with its framing passages seems to
draw a stage of the narrative to a close, while 6.28 opens a new stage. As already
noted, the dialogues in 5.22–6.1(2-8) and 6.10-12 are between God and Moses:
Aaron does not rate a mention. In contrast, the framing texts assert three times
that God spoke to both Moses and Aaron (vv. 13, 26, 27). Aaron is of course
mentioned with Moses in Exodus 4–5; the references here could therefore have
the earlier chapters in mind. But there is no report in Exodus 4–5 that God gave
instructions to Moses and Aaron together. Exodus 6.13, 26-27 may point more
firmly to what follows: the word 'hosts' in 6.27 (NRSV 'company by company')
occurs in 7.4 while 7.8 and 9.8 report God giving orders to both Moses and
Aaron.

Given that a stage of the narrative is drawing to a close here, it is appropriate
to find some genealogical information about the two Israelites who have domi-
nated the story thus far. In another sign of pause, the genealogy begins by
recalling the first three names in the list with which the book of Exodus begins
(Reuben, Simeon, Levi; cf. 1.1-5). Surprisingly, the genealogy devotes more
attention to Aaron than Moses and traces his descendants as far as Phinehas, a
key player in the story of Israel's apostasy at Shittim in Numbers 25.

Perhaps one should not be surprised that 6.13-27 appears to look back and
forward. After all, it is immediately followed by 6.28-30, which does much the
same: it resumes 6.10-12 after the insertion of vv. 13-27 in order to move the
story on. The phrase 'I am *Yhwh*' in 6.29 recalls v. 2 but can also be seen to
prepare for its occurrence in 7.5. The command in 6.29 to speak to Pharaoh king
of Egypt echoes v. 11 but enlarges the content of its command to 'all that I am
speaking to you'. The participial form of דבר in this phrase is best taken as a
reference to a divine message that is soon to come.[17] Moses' objection in 6.30
recalls, in its turn, v. 12, but without reference to the refusal of the Israelites to
listen to him. The focus is now on Pharaoh, in preparation for the speech in 7.1-5
and the subsequent story of the plagues. One could even suggest that the
presence of the insertion (6.13-27) facilitates the sense of a story arriving at a
point and then moving on by creating some distance between the repetitions in
6.10-12 and 6.28-30.

The one verse not mentioned so far is 6.28. It is somewhat repetitive in relation to v. 29 and there is a paragraph break in the MT between the two verses.
Does this indicate, as Propp suggests, that an editor sought to enhance the sense

---

16. So Childs 1974: 118-19; Schmidt 1988: 296; Propp 1998: 267.
17. Cf. Schmidt 1988: 295. Note also that the phrase כל אשר recurs in 7.2.

of a new stage by introducing v. 28 with its opening ויהי phrase but that another countered this by inserting the paragraph marker 'to emphasize the resumption'?[18] If this was the case, it is some comfort to know that Hebrew editors themselves disagreed at times about how signals in the text were to be read.

Granted a dual role for 6.28-30, what might be the relationship of 7.1-5, which forms part of this dialogue, to the surrounding context? More particularly, what might be its relationship to the three concerns of 5.22-23—God's relationship to the people, Moses' role, and the conquest of Pharaoh? Like 6.2-8, it appears to be a carefully structured piece. Verses 1-2 focus on Moses and Aaron and their respective roles in God's plan. Verses 3-4 focus on how God will deal with Pharaoh and Egypt and how the roles of Moses and Aaron are integral components of God's plan. Verse 5 then spells out the purpose of this divine plan or initiative—that 'The Egyptians shall know that I am *Yhwh*'—and when that purpose is to be achieved.

What 7.1-5 lacks, in comparison with 6.2-8, is an emphasis on God's relationship with Israel. The one explicit reference to it is 'my people' in 7.4. Is this due to the fact that 7.1-5 is the immediate prelude to the story of the plagues and so it is appropriate for the speech to emphasize the other two elements? Or, is it because God's relationship to Israel has been covered in 6.2-8 and so only a brief reference to it is required in 7.4 (cf. 6.7)? Perhaps both.

The focus of 7.1-5 is clearly on the role of Moses (and Aaron) and the details of God's plan for Pharaoh and the Egyptians. In 5.23, Moses complains that he has been a completely ineffectual messenger for God against Pharaoh. Exodus 7.1-2 looks like a reply to this complaint, elevating Moses to a higher god-like status and appointing Aaron his prophet (messenger). But it is not immediately clear what Moses' god-like status means. In 6.12 and 30, Moses objects that he is a 'poor speaker'. Does being made god-like mean that this handicap is now overcome? If so, it would make Aaron's role as prophet superfluous. Perhaps 7.2 can shed some light on Aaron. As a follow-up to v. 1, it establishes a chain of command from God to Moses to Aaron to Pharaoh. This elevates Moses by making him the primary recipient of God's word, which he then passes on to his prophetic spokesman Aaron. Hence, the relationship between Moses and Aaron mirrors that of Exodus 4; the difference is that there it was for the benefit of the people, here it is for the overthrow of Pharaoh.

But this still leaves unresolved Moses' objection that he is a poor speaker/messenger. Verse 3 may help: it states that God will harden Pharaoh's heart. According to v. 4, the outcome of this is that he will not listen to Moses or Aaron. Pharaoh's rejection of Moses and Aaron is thus paradoxically a sign of God's power over Pharaoh. This can be applied to Moses' complaint about the outcome of his first encounter with Pharaoh and his reluctance to try again. Although Moses thinks it is his own ineffectiveness as God's messenger, or even a failure on God's part, it is actually God's doing, part of the divine purpose.

---

18. Cf. Propp 1998: 269. For Weimar, the phrase ויהי is, among other things, a sign of 'ein neuer Hauptteil des Exodus-Buches' in 6.28 (1980: 16-17).

Within the larger story, it is a reminder to Moses about what God had forewarned him in 3.19 and 4.21. This angle also sheds further light on why Aaron is called Moses' prophet. As his prophet, he is an integral part of the divine plan but, for him as for Moses, this means rejection by Pharaoh. [19]

Exodus 7.1-2 is not only a 'reply' to Moses' complaints; one would expect that it also has the subsequent narrative in mind. In the story of the plagues, Moses is certainly the recipient of the divine message and plays a key role in the story but, contrary to 7.1-2, it is he who speaks to Pharaoh, not Aaron. Aaron does not function as a prophetic mediator of Moses' words. An apparently clear signal is not taken up—at least not explicitly—in the subsequent narrative.[20]

What of the third element identified in 5.22-23—the overthrow of Pharaoh? In 7.1-5, Moses is assured that God will triumph but that it will involve further rejection by Pharaoh (v. 4). Paradoxically, the more Pharaoh rejects Moses the more this is a sign of God's power over him—via the hardening of his heart— and a sign that the deliverance of Israel is unfolding according to the divine plan. Does the text invite one to read 6.1 as part of this paradox? From one angle, what Moses will 'see' is his further rejection by Pharaoh. From another angle, he is invited to 'see' this as a sign of 'a mighty hand' at work. Only the mighty hand of God can control the heart of Pharaoh. By the same token, God's assurance that Moses will 'see what I will do to Pharaoh' could also be read as a reference to the coming plagues. But, if the 'signs and wonders' referred to in 7.3 are the plagues, then the parallelism in vv. 3 and 4 associates them more with the Egyptians than with Pharaoh. Verses 3a and 4a refer to Pharaoh while vv. 3b (the signs and wonders) and 4b refer to the Egyptians.

Given that 7.1-5 serves as a preface to the plague stories, the focus on the Egyptians makes good sense for two reasons. First, it is the Egyptians and their land that are most afflicted by the plagues. Second, as a consequence of all that is to happen they will know 'that I am *Yhwh*'. According to 14.25, the Egyptians make this confession just before they are annihilated (cf. 14.18)—the scene provides an ironic contrast to the portrayal of Israel. In 6.7, God promises that Israel will 'know that I am *Yhwh*'. Exodus 14.31 reports that Israel, on seeing the destruction of the Egyptian people, believes in *Yhwh*. In doing so, it grows in its identity as the people of *Yhwh* and in its knowledge of *Yhwh*.

5. *Conclusion*

In the light of the preceding comments, can one say that all the other signals in the texts examined lead, in their various, sometimes elusive ways, to this—the

---

19. For a somewhat different reading of 7.1 in relation to the context, see Propp 1998: 282, 284-86.

20. Campbell (2002) proposes that signals like these may well have served as prompts that an Israelite storyteller could develop in performance. His proposal has important implications for our understanding of how texts were used in ancient Israel: instead of taking a narrative as a canonical text to be expounded, as we do, ancient storytellers used the pre-canonical text as a base to be expanded.

knowledge of *Yhwh* (Eslinger 1991: 57-58)? Is this why God's speeches in 6.2-8 and in 6.29 begin with the proclamation 'I am *Yhwh*'? Or, does this proposal betray a desire for closure vis-à-vis Exodus 6–7, a desire that may lead me to overlook or slip around texts that do not 'fit', texts that may challenge or illuminate my understanding in unexpected ways? Like a traveller too keen to find the city's centre, who can miss many of the fascinating streets and suburbs along the way.

BIBLIOGRAPHY

Ahuis, F.
    1982   *Der klagende Gerichtsprophet: Studien zur Klage in der Überlieferung von den alttestamentlichen Gerichtspropheten* (TM, 12; Stuttgart: Calwer Verlag).
Auffret, P.
    1983a   'The Literary Structure of Exodus 6.2-8', *JSOT* 27: 46-54.
    1983b   'Remarks on J. Magonet's Interpretation of Exodus 6.2-8', *JSOT* 27: 69-71.
Aurelius, E.
    1988   *Der Fürbitte Israels. Eine Studie zum Mosebild im Alten Testament* (ConBOT, 27; Stockholm: Almqvist & Wiksell).
Blum, E.
    1990   *Studien zur Komposition des Pentateuch* (BZAW, 189; Berlin: W. de Gruyter).
    2002   'Die literarische Verbinding von Erzvätern und Exodus. Ein Gespräch mit neureren Endredaktionshypothesen', in J.C. Gertz, K. Schmid and M. Witted (eds.), *Abschied vom Jahwisten. Die Komposition des Hexateuch in der Jüngsten Diskussion* (BZAW, 315; Berlin: W. de Gruyter): 119-56.
Campbell, A.F.
    2002   'The Storyteller's Role: Reported Story and Biblical Text', *CBQ* 64: 427-41.
Childs, B.S.
    1974   *Exodus* (OTL; London: SCM Press).
Eslinger, L.
    1991   'Freedom or Knowledge? Perspective and Purpose in the Exodus Narrative (Exodus 1–15)', *JSOT* 52: 43-60.
Fretheim, T.
    1991   *Exodus* (Interpretation: Louisville, KY: John Knox Press).
Garr, W.R.
    1992   'The Grammar and Interpretation of Exodus 6.3', *JBL* 111: 385-408.
Houtman, C.
    1993   *Exodus*, I (HCOT; Leuven: Peeters; Kampen: Kok).
Kohata, F.
    1986   *Jahwist und Priesterschrift in Exodus 3–14* (BZAW, 166; Berlin: W. de Gruyter).
Labuschagne, C.J.
    1966   'The Emphasizing Particle *gam* and its Connotations', in W.C. van Unnik and A.S. van der Woude (eds.), *Studia Biblica et Semitica* (T.C. Vriezen Festschrift; Wageningen: Weenman).
Lust, J.
    1996   'Exodus 6,2-8 and Ezekiel', in M. Vervenne (ed.), *Studies in the Book of Exodus: Redaction—Reception—Interpretation* (BETL, 126; Leuven: University Press): 209-24.

Magonet, J.
    1983a   'A Response to "The Literary Structure of Exodus 6.2-8" by Pierre Auffret',
             JSOT 27: 73-74.
    1983b   'The Rhetoric of God: Exodus 6.2-8', *JSOT* 27: 56-67.
Moberly, R.W.L.
    1992   *The Old Testament of the Old Testament: Patriarchal Narratives and Mosaic
             Yahwism* (Overtures to Biblical Theology; Minneapolis: Fortress Press).
Propp, W.H.C.
    1998   *Exodus 1–18* (AB, 2; New York: Doubleday).
Schmidt, W.H.
    1988   *Exodus* (BKAT, 2/1; Neukirchener–Vluyn: Neukirchener Verlag).
Seitz, C.R.
    1990   'The Call of Moses and the "Revelation" of the Divine Name: Source-Critical
             Logic and its Legacy', in C.R. Seitz and K. Greene-McCreight (eds.), *Theo-
             logical Exegesis: Essays in Honor of Brevard S. Childs* (Grand Rapids:
             Eerdmans): 145-67.
Ska, J.L.
    1982   'La place d'Ex 6.2-8 dans la narration de l'exode', *ZAW* 94: 530-48.
    1989   'Quelque remarques sur Pg et le dernière redaction du Pentateuque', in A. de
             Pury (ed.), *Le Pentateuque en Question* (Labor et Fides; Geneva: Cerf):
             95-125.
Weimar, P.
    1980   *Die Berufung des Mose. Literaturwissenschaftliche Analyse von Exodus 1,23–
             5,5* (OBO, 32; Göttingen: Vandenhoeck & Ruprecht).

GENOCIDE IN DEUTERONOMY:
POSTCOLONIAL VARIATIONS ON MIMETIC DESIRE

Mark G. Brett

> ...the Hittites, Girgashites, Amorites, Canaanites, Perizzites, Hivites and Jebusites, seven
> nations more numerous and stronger than you: when *Yhwh* your God has delivered them
> over to you and you have defeated them, then you must ban them completely (*herem*).
> Make no treaty with them, and show them no mercy. Do not intermarry with them.
> (Deut. 7.1-3)

> However, in the cities of these peoples *Yhwh* your God gives you as an inheritance, do
> not leave alive anything that breathes. Indeed, you will ban them completely (*herem*).
> (Deut. 20.16-17)

What purposes are served by the biblical discourses that 'ban' the prior inhabitants of Canaan? How are we to understand the intersection between ancient
concepts of *herem* and modern concepts of genocide? There is a range of critical
methods which might be adopted: semantic, literary, historical, psychological,
sociological and theological. To start with, however, it is important to recognize
the different reasons why the question is asked at all. Writing in contexts where
the effects of colonialism on indigenous people[1] are still painfully evident, the
question cannot be approached with an easy neutrality. These biblical discourses
of cultural destruction have had a significant impact, for example, in the colonial
histories of South Africa, South and North America, and in my own country
Australia (e.g. Deist 1994; cf. Niditch 1993: 3-5; Richard 1996). It would not be
enough simply to illuminate the cultural logic of holy war, or to explore the legal
innovations of Deuteronomy, while ignoring this history of reception, or perhaps
denying the relevance of the term 'genocide'.[2]

Not all questions, however, can be addressed at once, and in this paper it will
be suggested that careful historical study of Deuteronomy may actually help us to
deal with contemporary issues of reconciliation with aboriginal groups. I am
pleased to contribute this discussion to a *Festschrift* honoring my colleague Tony
Campbell, whose meticulous work on historical issues has been a model for
Australian scholars over the past three decades.

---

1. The term 'indigenous' raises a number of hermeneutical problems, but it will be used in this
essay as an umbrella category, without presuming any historical claims about the self-descriptions
of the prior inhabitants of Canaan. See further, e.g., Van Seters 1972; Na'aman 1996; and Rainey
1996.
2. As Colin Tatz points out, the United Nations *Convention on the Prevention and Punishment
of the Crime of Genocide* (1948), Article II, does not restrict itself to mass killing, but refers also to
'mental harm' caused by practices of cultural genocide (see Tatz 2003).

1. *The Historical Setting of Deuteronomic Genocide Texts*

For the last two hundred years, critical scholars have suggested that the composition of Deuteronomy (or at least a central core of it) took place in seventh century BCE Judah. The arguments for this hypothesis were based mainly on comparisons internal to the biblical tradition. More recently, a number of studies have reinforced the hypothesis by benchmarking the dating in relation to non-biblical material which, without question, comes from the seventh century. In particular, there are a series of striking comparisons between Deuteronomy and the vassal treaties of the neo-Assyrian king Esarhaddon (VTE).[3] In one of the most comprehensive analyses of these comparisons, Eckart Otto argues for a quite specific dating of Deuteronomic material between 672 and 612 BCE (Otto 1999: 14).[4]

In particular, he argues that Deut. 13.2-10 'subversively' mimics VTE §10 (Otto 1999: 14, 364-65),[5] adapting the source texts to demand exclusive loyalty to *Yhwh*, rather than loyalty to the Assyrian king (see table below).

Vassal Treaty of Esarhaddon §§10, 12	*Deuteronomy 13.2-10 (Eng. 13.1-9)*
If you hear any evil, improper, ugly word which is not seemly nor good to Ashurbanipal, the great crown prince designate, son of Esarhaddon, king of Assyria, your lord, either from the mouth of his *enemy* or from the mouth of his *ally*, or from the mouth of *his brothers, his uncles, his cousins, his family, members of his father's line,* or from the mouth of *your brothers, your sons, your daughters*, or from the mouth of a *prophet, an ecstatic, an enquirer of oracles*, or from the mouth of any human being at all; you shall not conceal it but come and report it to Ashurbanipal, the great crown prince designate, son of Esarhaddon, king of Assyria. … If you are able to seize them and put them to death, then you shall destroy their name and their seed from the land.	If there should arise among you *a prophet or dreamer of dreams* who provides a sign or portent, and if the sign or portent come true—concerning which he had spoken to you, saying, 'Let us go after other gods (whom you have not known) so that we may worship them': Do not listen to the oracles of that *prophet or that dreamer of dreams*; for *Yhwh* your God is testing you, to know whether you love *Yhwh* your God with all your heart and all your being… And that prophet or that dreamer of dreams shall be killed, for he fomented apostasy against *Yhwh* your God, who brought you out of Egypt and redeemed you from slavery… If *your brother, the son of your mother, or your son, or your daughter or the wife of your bosom, or your friend who is as your own self*, entices you secretly, saying, 'Let us go and worship other gods'—whom neither you nor your fathers have known, some of the gods of the peoples who are round about you…—do not assent to him or listen to him! Let your eye not pity him, nor shall you hold back or condone him. You must surely kill him.

In the Assyrian text, the potential sources of threat are listed in an order that begins from the obvious outsider, the 'enemy', then moves to the 'ally', family

---

3.   Influential work from this perspective includes Moran 1963 and Weinfeld 1972: 81-126.

4.   For example, Deut. 28.20-44 appropriates the list of curses in VTE §56. See Parpolo and Watanabe 1988: 49, and the discussion in Steymans 1995: 119-41; cf. Otto 2000.

5.   Additional material is drawn from other vassal treaties, according to Otto, but VTE §10 provides the basic structure. Norbert Lohfink uses the term 'counter-propaganda' (Lohfink 1994: 194). Cf. the idea of 'mimicry' in postcolonial studies—adopting genres from a dominant culture and turning them to native advantage (Bhabha 1994: 102-22).

members, prophets and anyone else. The Deuteronomic author, on the other hand, puts the prophetic threat first, then moves to family members, with much greater focus on the possibility of conflict within the most intimate family relationships, specifying not just 'brother' but 'full brother' ('the son of your mother'), not just wife, but 'the wife of your bosom' (Levinson 2001)

Deuteronomy 13 is particularly relevant to our theme, since immediately following the material adapted from Esarhaddon's treaty, it is said in 13.16 (Eng. 13.15) that even Israelites who are proven disloyal to *Yhwh* shall be punished by having their *entire town*, people and livestock, devoted to the ban (*herem*): 'You shall surely put the inhabitants of that city to the sword, banning it—all who are in it and its cattle—with the edge of the sword'. The reference to capital punishment in 13.10 provides a bridge to this *herem* regulation ('you must surely kill him').[6] The comprehensive version of *herem* in 13.16 is also used in relation to the indigenous peoples in Deut. 20.16-18, and most importantly, this is a relatively rare variation of holy war.[7] This particular concept of the ban appears in the destruction of Jericho (Josh. 6.21), which includes the slaughter of livestock along with the mass killing of men, women and children, but the majority of other conquest narratives are not so comprehensive. Joshua 11.14, for example, describes the taking of livestock without any recognition that this is contrary to the legal requirement of Deut. 20.16-18. We may therefore explore the hypothesis that Deuteronomy 13 belongs to the same stratum of tradition as 20.16-18 and that this stratum was composed in the seventh century, after the older conquest narratives.[8] (An implication of this hypothesis, which will be further analysed below, is that the genocide texts in 7.1-6 and 20.16-18 cannot have been formed according to a conventional ethnocentric logic, since this particular version of *herem* is applied not just against strangers, but it is envisaged as potentially cutting across the most intimate family relationships within Israel.[9])

This is not to deny that Deuteronomy contains material which is both earlier and later than the seventh century. There are good reasons to think, for example, that the laws regarding warfare in Deut. 20.1-14 and 21.10-14 are earlier than the section in 20.16-18 which bans the indigenous peoples of the promised land (Rofé 1985; Fishbane 1985: 199-209). (In 21.10-14, for example, foreign women taken in battle can become wives, without mentioning any exceptions for Canaanite women.) On the other hand, parts of Deuteronomy seem to address an audience in exile, and for example, the message concerning a new exodus in

---

6. Richard Nelson notes that the polar opposite of *herem* was 'to leave survivors or to treat people, animals and objects as plunder... Not to treat as *herem* was to "spare, keep back" (חמל 1 Sam. 15.3, 9, 15; Jer. 51.3)' (Nelson 1997: 45). To this list of examples one could add Deut. 13.9 (Eng. 13.8), where חמל is opposed to *herem* in the immediate context (13.16 [Eng. 13.15]).

7. On the variations of holy war, see Niditch 1993 and Stern 1991.

8. Lohfink (1994: 187-88) comes to the same conclusion for different reasons.

9. A similar observation might be made in reference to the destruction of Achan's family and flocks in Josh. 7.24-26, except that the term *herem* is not used in that context of punishment, and, contrary to Deut. 20.16-18, the flocks of Ai are carried off as plunder in Josh. 8.2, 27. In prophetic traditions, the term *herem* is applied to the destruction of Israel in Isa. 43.28, but in the eschatology of Zech. 14.11 it is envisaged that Jerusalem will never again be subjected to such a *herem*.

Deut. 30.1-10 in no way suggests that returning exiles should engage in some new version of violent conquest. Georg Braulik has demonstrated that 30.5 plays on the vocabulary of 7.1, since in both texts *Yhwh* 'brings' the community to the land to 'possess' it, but in the case of the exiled community addressed in 30.1-10, the call to conquest has been removed.[10]

Deuteronomy 7.1	*Deuteronomy 30.4-5*
When *Yhwh* your God *brings you* into the land you are entering *to possess* and drives out many nations before you—the Hittites, Girgashites, Amorites, Canaanites, Perizzites, Hivites and Jebusites, seven nations more *numerous* and stronger than you...	Even if you have been banished to the extremity of the heavens, from there *Yhwh* your God will gather you and bring you back. And *Yhwh* your God will *bring you* into the land that your ancestors *possessed*, and you will *take possession* of it. He will make you more prosperous and *numerous* than your ancestors.

Following Braulik's work, it does not seem likely that the Deuteronomic genocide texts were composed in the exilic or post-exilic periods.[11] Yair Hoffman's recent proposal to date them in the Persian period, for example, has significant flaws. His argument is partly based on the presumption that the *herem* texts conflict with a key moral principle in Deuteronomy: love for strangers (Hoffman 1999). But Richard Nelson has dealt with precisely this question, showing that the protection of resident aliens (גרים) depends upon their relative openness to cultural assimilation, whereas un-assimilated foreigners are not protected: 'Deuteronomy insists on benevolence and consideration for resident aliens and other needy and marginalized groups, but does so only on the basis of a recognition of some level of community membership and of obligations creation by shared experience' (Nelson 1997: 49).[12] We should note that eighth-century prophetic tradition expressed its concern for the marginalized by focusing on widows, orphans and the poor, without mentioning גרים. Only with Deuteronomy and the later prophets, Jeremiah and Ezekiel, does the concern for aliens become a litmus test of moral concern (e.g. Jer. 7.6; Ezek. 14.7). Frank Crüsemann (1996: 182-85) reasonably concludes that it was the flood of refugees southward, after the fall of the northern kingdom, which was the cause of this heightened awareness. The experience of these refugees displaced by Assyrian expansion was apparently matched with Israel's story of suffering under the power of Egypt. Hence one could say that the shared experience expressed in the

10. For further details, see Braulik 1997: 33-38. Braulik's essay stands against the common presumption encountered in postcolonial studies that exodus themes are ineluctably linked with conquest ideology. See, e.g., Said 1988 and Boer 2001.

11. The only possible exceptions to this would be in the narrative prologue to Deuteronomy, which many scholars date late, but there the *herem* applied to Heshbon and Bashan excludes livestock (Deut. 2.34-35; 3.6-7), so it does not match the requirements of Deut. 20.16-18. Cf. Braulik (1997: 24-27), who stresses that this aspect of the prologue refers to the past, not the return from exile addressed in 30.1-10.

12. For a more comprehensive discussion, see also Sparks 1998, which proposes a similar sharp distinction between the גר and the בן נכר/נכרי, both in Deuteronomy and in other literature of the Hebrew Bible. See especially the summaries in Sparks 1998: 283-84, 314-19.

dictum 'Love the גר, because you were גרים in Egypt' (Deut 10.19) is suffering under imperialism, but this gives rise to solidarity only through assimilation to *Yhwh*'s rule.

One permutation of loyalty to *Yhwh* included the protection of גרים, but the *herem* extrapolates from the demand for exclusive loyalty to *Yhwh* to a specific class of persons or things declared *herem* which belong exclusively to *Yhwh* and therefore cannot be put to human use, except, in some cases, by priests (e.g. Num. 18.14). In non-military contexts, the *herem* status need not include destruction, but in the conquest traditions it customarily does (Nelson 1997: 41-46).[13] In short, the moral conflict, which Hoffman perceives between *herem* and the love of strangers, is more an issue for hermeneutics and biblical theology; the cultural logic of seventh-century Deuteronomy saw *herem* as a mutation of exclusive loyalty to *Yhwh* and did not perceive the conflict. This issue cannot therefore form the basis of arguments for late redaction.

Hoffman's discussion does however raise some interesting questions about how these texts would have been read in the context of post-exilic politics of identity. He suggests that the Deuteronomic genocide texts are post-exilic additions designed to satirize Ezra 9.1-2 by listing peoples who no longer existed, thereby disclosing the call to ethnocentric holiness as hopelessly anachronistic.[14] This paradoxical suggestion might have had some validity except for the fact that the 'detestable practices' mentioned in Ezra 9.1 are only 'like (כ)' those of the prior inhabitants of the land; Ezra's rhetoric would not have been undermined if these inhabitants no longer existed. But if we pursue Hoffman's line as a question of reception, rather than composition, it is interesting to note that Joshua 6 provides the paradigm case in which the full extent of the ban in Deut. 20.16-18 is inserted into a conquest narrative (envisaging the killing of women, children and animals), yet it is precisely the Jericho story which illustrates that a foreign woman—Rahab—may be exempt from *herem* regardless of her cultic or moral history, as long as she demonstrates loyalty to *Yhwh* and to Israel (6.21-25). If Rahab were read in the Persian period as in some way representing the women proscribed by Ezra and Nehemiah, then the story in Joshua 6 does raise a question about why Ezra 9.1-2 fails to mention any exemptions for foreign women who were proselytes.[15]

No single historical setting will provide a privileged framework for understanding the genocide material, but there is much to be learned from Israel's ideological contest with Assyrian imperial power in the seventh century. In what follows, I will make a few form-critical and hermeneutical observations about how these seventh-century comparisons may be understood.

---

13. See also the literature in n. 18 below.

14. Cf. Stern (1991: 102-103) who suggests an analogous idea that, in the seventh-century context, Deuteronomy prevents violence against contemporary enemies by restricting *herem* to peoples who have already vanished.

15. *Contra* Sparks (1998: 295, 318), there is not sufficient reason to suppose that Ezra 6.19-21 allows for proselyte women; the text may simply distinguish between returning exiles and other Jews (presumably non-exiles) who had 'separated themselves from unclean practices'.

2. *Form Criticism and Discursive Hybridity*

However convincing the comparisons between Deuteronomy and Esarhaddon's treaties might be, it does not follow that the genre of Deuteronomy should be seen as a 'treaty' or 'covenant'. One should note that the vassal treaty tradition is much older than the seventh century, and indeed, the blessings in Deuteronomy 28 and the historiographic prologue in chs. 1–3, have more in common with earlier Hittite models than the Assyrian ones (Weinfeld 1972: 67-84; 1992: 170; Mendenhall and Herion 1992: 1180-83). The genre of Deuteronomy might equally be identified as a 'polity' (McBride 1987), or 'catechesis' (torah) (Olsen 1994: 2, 7-14; cf. Braulik 1994), or perhaps more specifically during the monarchic period a 'polity', and in later periods 'catechesis' (Rütersworden 1987; Olsen 1994: 9-10). Moreover, within the genocide texts, there are traces of other literary forms, such as the 'fear not' saying in Deut. 20.1 which was conventionally part of prophetic tradition, not just in Israel but also in neo-Assyrian prophetic oracles addressed primarily to kings (Nissinen 2003). The concept of *herem*, however, was not derived from Assyria; the only non-Israelite example of it can be found in a Moabite inscription from the ninth century (Kang 1989: 80-84).[16] In earlier conquest tradition, the *herem* appears as a vow, and not as a law (Num. 21.2-3) (Weinfeld 1991: 364; cf. Weinfeld 1993).

In short, the book of Deuteronomy is a tissue of quotations drawn from numerous locations of culture, reflecting a series of adaptations in response to political, economic and cultural challenges. It would be quite misleading to cover this generic complexity with a single literary category or *Sitz im Leben*. A tradition such as we find in Deuteronomy can be read as 'an historically extended, socially embodied argument, and an argument precisely in part about the goods which constitute that tradition' (MacIntyre 1981: 207).

In codifying its ideas of what counts as good, the Pentateuch incorporates multiple changes to its laws. Most importantly in this context, Deuteronomy 7 adapts older legal traditions from Exod. 23.20-33, even though the Exodus text has no *herem*, but only the destruction of cultic objects and the gradual expulsion of prior inhabitants. For example, where Exod. 23.29-30 speaks of 'driving out' these people, Deut. 7.22 has 'put an end'. Where Exod. 23.27 has 'make them turn back', Deut. 7.23 has 'until they are wiped out' (see further Weinfeld 1991: 380-84). Moreover, Michael Fishbane (1985: 204-205) has argued that the genocide material in Deuteronomy 20 is an interpretive innovation which resulted from combining Exod. 23.20-33 with 22.19 (Eng. 22.20): the latter verse indicates that anyone sacrificing to other gods is *herem*.[17] The legal hermeneutics of

---

16. K.L. Younger argues, however, that Assyrian, Hittite and Egyptian conquest accounts reveal a common imperialistic ideology which is shared with the biblical conquest narratives. He notes that the ninth-century Assyrian king Assur-nasir-pal II spoke of 'total war', and his conquest accounts included the killing of young boys and girls (see Younger 1990: 95-96, 235-36, 253).

17. Christa Schäfer-Lichtenberger (1994) has, however, suggested that people considered *herem* outside the context of warfare need not have been condemned to death. This might apply to cases like Exod. 22.19 (Eng. 22.20) and Deut. 7.2, where there is no mention of swords or burning (see also Nelson 1997: 42; cf. Moberly 1999: 135-37).

Deuteronomy are therefore a product of intertextual interactions both with older Israelite legal traditions, as well as with the neo-Assyrian treaties and their Hittite precursors.

The mix of genres in Deuteronomy therefore includes elements of treaty, blessings, curses, polity, catechesis, speeches, vows, laws, prophecy and historiography, all overlapping in complex and mutable ways. It is not that these genres are organic wholes, each with their own history of development and 'institutional' locations (*Sitze im Leben*), juxtaposed in Deuteronomy to suit the intentions of its authors and editors. Rather, what we find in Deuteronomy is better described as 'discursive hybridity': a mix of literary conventions and transformations located in a web of mimicry and ideological contestation.

I am not simply recommending here a particular methodological perspective like 'rhetorical criticism', which emphasizes the particularity of texts over against the generalizing tendency in the discipline of 'form criticism'.[18] Nor do I have in mind the versions of postmodernism which endlessly reiterate the gospel of indeterminacy, as if discourse can float free from the constraints of linguistic conventions or socio-economic power, mutable though they may be. My reading of Deuteronomy in this essay has more affinity with the approaches to discourse in postcolonial studies, within which the details of cultural hybridity are related to specific socio-economic struggles.[19] The intention is not to generalize about imperialism as a substitute for analysis, but to study specific ideological effects and heterogeneous strategies of resistance. For example, in line with Edward Said's cautionary remarks about over-generalizing, Mark Hamilton has studied the influences of neo-Assyrian imperialism, distinguishing between the assimilationist royal inscriptions from Sam'al in southern Anatolia, on the one hand, and Deuteronomy's cultural resistance, on the other (Hamilton 1998, citing Said 1993: 3, 74, 162-63).[20]

Nevertheless, it would be quite wrong to conclude that biblical scholars should eschew comparisons or analogies from different periods of history.[21] As long as generalizing theories are not used to fill in historical gaps, there is nothing questionable about the formulation of hypotheses or heuristic models which may be tested in specific contexts. And in the next section, I will investigate the application of one theoretical model to the *herem* texts, particularly in dialogue with Norbert Lohfink's recent overture on the theme of mimetic desire (Lohfink 1995).

18. For a lucid analysis of this shift, and its methodological ambiguities, see Trible 1994: 5-84. Cf. Sweeney and Ben Zvi 2003: *passim*.

19. For theoretical discussions, see especially Ashcroft 2001; Bhabha 1994; and Gandhi 1998. For detailed applications in biblical studies, see Brett 2000 and Smith-Christopher 2002.

20. Contrast Dutcher-Walls (2002), whose use of 'core-periphery' sociological theory to explain the restrictions on wealth in Deut. 17.17 does not account for the celebration of wealth in Sam'al's royal inscriptions.

21. Hence even the anti-relativist champion of induction, Karl Popper, argues that objective knowledge does not progress by collecting atomistic facts but by the testing of hypotheses (Popper 1972).

3. *Mimetic Desire in Postcolonial Perspective*

The theory of mimetic desire has been elaborated especially by René Girard and applied to a wide range of literatures, including the Bible (see especially Lohfink [ed.] 1983; Williams 1991; Swartley [ed.] 2000). We will not be concerned here with the exegesis of Girard's complex and controversial work, but will focus instead on Lohfink's specific application of the theory to Deuteronomy. To begin with, however, a summary of the basic framework of ideas is necessary. Girard adopted the classical Greek term 'mimesis' to indicate that beyond mere imitation, human beings learn *what* to desire by acquisitively desiring what we perceive others to desire. But this leads to a dangerous double-bind in which the model is 'always a potential rival and the rival is always an implicit model' (Williams 1991: 8). The tensions inherent in this double-bind are relieved by collective violence against scapegoats, by means of which social boundaries are established that sustain the group. Religious ritual, for example, can often be seen as a 'mock mimetic crisis', performed in sacred time, reiterating the death or expulsion which constituted the group's unity (Williams 1991: 11).

These ideas have been applied, and revised, in many different ways in biblical studies, but here I want to draw an analogy between mimetic desire and some similar ideas in postcolonial studies. Homi Bhabha has made famous the idea of 'colonial mimicry', a sly mixture of deference and critique which indigenous subjects adopt in exercising cultural resistance. In one of the most influential discussions of this idea, Bhabha described an example of the 'imitation' of biblical discourse in colonial India, in which the sacred text of the dominant culture was appropriated in an anti-colonial mixing of borrowed and local content (Bhabha 1994: 102-22). Other postcolonial critics have described similar phenomena, such as when Elleke Boehmer speaks of the ambivalent process of 'cleaving' away from colonial definitions and, at the same time, 'cleaving to' or appropriating textual forms from the dominant culture (Boehmer 1995: 106-107). Mary Louise Pratt also provides examples of the hybridization of colonial discourse, in selective combination with indigenous themes, as a means of maintaining subordinate cultural identity (Pratt 1994; cf. Hawley 1996; Ashcroft 2001: *passim*). This paradigm of research, then, intersects with Girard's work, but postcolonial studies attend especially to the complexities of socio-economic power in the expression of mimetic desire.

Lohfink has identified a specific terminology in Deuteronomy which he links to the idea of mimetic desire: 'When you come to the land *Yhwh* your God is giving you, do not learn (למד) to imitate (עשה ב), the detestable ways of those nations' (Deut. 18.9). The notion of 'learning' torah is a key motif of Deuteronomic theology, but here it is applied to *Yhwh*'s rivals.[22] The other significant place where this prohibition on mimesis appears is in Deut. 20.17-18: 'you shall

---

22. For the language of 'teaching/learning' (למד) and 'imitating' or 'doing according to' (עשה ב), see especially Deut. 1.5; 4.1, 5, 10, 14; 5.31; 6.1, 7; 11.19; 17.11; 24.8; 31.19, 22; 33.10 (Braulik 1994; Lohfink, 1995: 258).

commit them to the ban—the Hittites and the Amorites, the Canaanites and the Perizzites, the Hivites and the Jebusites—as *Yhwh* your God has commanded, that they may not teach (למד) you to imitate (עשה ב), all their detestable practices'. Lohfink argues that this fear of mimetic desire in Deuteronomy suggests that we look also for the scapegoat process which Girard's model implies. What we find, however, is not an overt ritual which reiterates the founding violence or exclusion, but rather this legal discourse of the *herem* which marks the exclusion of near rivals (Lohfink 1995: 259-60).

This hypothesis can be supplemented from a different direction by some observations made by Gordon Matties, who points out that in Girard's model the ritual victim must be seen to be 'outside' the community, when in practice victims are usually on an ambiguous margin between 'outside' and 'inside'. And in one permutation of this marginalized position, the victim must be made to appear 'more foreign' than they actually are, in order to reconstitute the community's boundaries (Matties 2000: 90). It seems to me that the dynamics of mimetic desire in Deuteronomy are best seen within this framework supplied by both Lohfink and Matties: the legal discourse excluding the indigenous peoples arises precisely from a need—perceived by the Deuteronomic authors—to inscribe new boundaries of exclusive loyalty to *Yhwh* within an Israelite society which over the previous centuries had commonly worshipped other gods alongside *Yhwh*. Thus, Girard comments that 'there is reason to believe that the wars described as "foreign wars" in the mythic narratives were in fact formerly civil strifes' (Girard 1977: 249). One of the functions of the scapegoating process, then, is to obscure such civil conflicts behind the text.

What kind of 'civil strifes', we may ask, would Deuteronomy want to obscure? There is now a significant consensus among archaeologists that early Israel was in fact indigenous to Canaan (Dever 2001: 41, 99; Finkelstein and Silberman 2001: 117-18; McNutt 1999: 57, 63; Smith 2002). Deuteronomy's reformation of Israelite ethnic identity—centering it on a radically exclusive loyalty to *Yhwh*— excluded not so much 'indigenous' peoples but close kin who held different religious views and practices. This is the socio-cultural context of the seventh century which explains the link between the *herem* declared on Israelite towns in Deuteronomy 13 and the same unusual *herem* in Deut. 20.16-18 declared on the prior inhabitants of Canaan. What appears on the surface of Deuteronomy 20 as a programme for genocide is actually part of an internal social and religious reform.

Even on the surface of the text, this ambivalence towards Israel's own indigenous past has left a trace: the 'Most High (*Elyon*)' in Deut. 32.8 is the same Canaanite divine name that is used by the indigenous priest Melchizedek in Gen. 14.19. Even a reader with no interest in the history of the text is left with the problem of how the indigenous divinity *Elyon* can be represented in Deut. 32.9 as allotting the people of Israel to *Yhwh* when *Yhwh* is said to be the only God (32.39). The assimilation of *Yhwh* and *Elyon* has been almost entirely obscured by the text, but not quite. In theological terms, we could say retrospectively that *Yhwh*'s identity is partly indigenous, but that other aspects of 'Canaanite' religion have been represented as more foreign in order to assert a new system of ethnic boundaries.[23]

There is actually no evidence, however, that the Deuteronomic reform led to mass killings. Whatever historical events might lie behind Josiah's reform narrative in 2 Kings 22–23, and leaving aside debates about editing, we may note that although Josiah slaughters the priests of the high places in the north (2 Kgs 23.20; cf. 23.5, 24), the priests from high places in the south escape (2 Kgs 23.8-9). The focus of the reform is on religious objects and practices, and there is no wholesale destruction of towns. It may well be that the most extreme form of the ban in Deut. 13.14-16 and 20.16-18 was never taken literally in the seventh century.[24] The rejection of this form of *herem* in Jewish tradition has clear precedent in biblical narrative (see Weinfeld 1993: 91-92, citing *Lev. R.* 17.6); it is the reception of these texts in Christian tradition which has yielded the most violent consequences, notably when Christian hermeneutics was wedded to colonialism.

4. *A Postscript on Mimesis and Desire*

The theology of Deuteronomy appears markedly ironic, since the quest to formulate an exclusivist worship of *Yhwh* was itself shaped, it seems, by a mimetic logic which is both borrowing from Assyrian culture while resisting foreign influence, appropriating the imperial discourses of loyalty, violence and punishment. And all this is justified by love for a God whose character is revealed in a narrative of liberation from Egyptian imperialism.

It would be too easy to dismiss the antinomies of Deuteronomy as the confused theology of ancient people. It is by no means clear that modernist secularism has provided a better solution to the perennial problems of mimetic desire.[25] A common secularist ideology in the West, consumerism, is based not so much on possessions as such, but on acquisitive desire. It embodies one more permutation of the same mimetic logic, although now it is played out on the stage of globalized capital, and it has a more subtle system of victimization.[26] Zygmunt

23. Cf. Levinson 1997: 148-49. Some might argue that Deuteronomy's reform is more religious than 'ethnic', but here I have in mind a 'constructivist' rather than 'primordial' model of ethnicity. See the emphasis of Brett (1996: 12-14) and Weinfeld (1972: 225-32, especially p. 229): 'the social polarity in Deuteronomy is גר–אח, whereas in P it is גר–אזרח'. Levinson (1997: 149) aptly comments that 'ethnicity, both Israelite and Canaanite, becomes a tendentious literary construct'.

24. Moberly (1999: 137) stresses that the *herem* in Deut. 7.2 could not have meant death, since that would remove the temptation of inter-marriage mentioned in 7.3. In this respect, 7.2 needs to be distinguished from 20.16 where death is the clearly stated implication of *herem* (see above, n. 18). Nevertheless, Moberly's argument for a non-literal interpretation of 20.16-18 has some validity. The same strictures against Israelite towns are articulated in Deut. 13.14-16, and they are not implemented in the narrative of Josiah's reform.

25. See, e.g., Bauman 1998: 23-35; Rose 1990; and McPhee 1992. These studies illustrate how modern societies have frequently victimized religious minorities.

26. 'The structure of the laws of the market that [civilized] society has instituted and controls, because of the mechanism of external debt and other similar inequities, that same society *puts to death* or (failing to help someone in distress accounts for only a minor difference) *allows* to die of hunger and disease tens of millions of children…without any moral or legal tribunal ever being

Bauman provides an acute analysis of consumerist ideology when he writes (1998: 25):

> Ideally, nothing should be embraced by a consumer firmly, nothing should command a commitment forever, no needs should be ever seen as fully satisfied, no desires considered ultimate. There ought to be a proviso 'until further notice' attached to any oath of loyalty and any commitment.

Global capital masquerades as a common good, when even its most thoughtful advocates have identified its inability to deal with 'other social needs, such as the preservation of peace, alleviation of poverty, protection of the environment, labor conditions, or human rights—what are generally called "public goods"' (Soros 2002: 14; cf. Sacks 2003: 105-24).

A key question for those who inherit the tradition of Deuteronomy is how ultimate loyalty to God can be conceived without the constant re-creation of religious or secular scapegoats. In a remarkable recent essay (1990), Steve Charleston has argued that native American Christians need to see the heritage of their own indigenous nation as providing their own 'Old Testament', so that their Christian identity is founded on three Testaments, rather than two. Australian aboriginals have independently begun to argue for the restoration of their own traditional law, along the similar lines (Gondarra 1996; see further Brett 2003). This theological project might be compared with the Deuteronomic authors who resisted the dominant imperial culture of the time, and asserted that they had their *own* treaty. Both these ancient and postmodern projects are driven by an anti-imperial assertion of dignity before God. And a key virtue of Charleston's proposal is that it makes the victims of colonialism visible, rather than erasing them.[27] Perhaps in this respect Deuteronomy can be followed, if not imitated.

BIBLIOGRAPHY

Ashcroft, W.
    2001   *Postcolonial Transformation* (London: Routledge).
Bauman, Z.
    1998   'Parvenu and Pariah: Heroes and Victims of Modernity', in J. Good and I. Velody (eds.), *The Politics of Postmodernity* (Cambridge: Cambridge University Press): 23-35.
    1998   *Work, Consumerism and the New Poor* (Buckingham: Open University).
Bhabha, H.
    1994   *The Location of Culture* (London: Routledge).

considered competent to judge such a sacrifice, the sacrifice of others to avoid being sacrificed oneself' (Derrida 1995: 86).

27. In an unhappy reflex, a recent discussion of Deuteronomy's significant influence on American political thought in the eighteenth century neglects to mention how native Americans were affected (see Connor 2002). Contrast Donaldson 2000 and O'Connell 1992. In the Australian context, the rights of indigenous people have barely begun to be recognized.

Boehmer, E.
    1995   *Colonial and Postcolonial Literature* (Oxford: Oxford University Press).
Boer, R.
    2001   *Last Stop to Antarctica: The Bible and Postcolonialism in Australia* (Bible and
            Postcolonialism, 6; Sheffield: Sheffield Academic Press).
Braulik, G.
    1994   'Deuteronomy and the Commemorative Culture of Israel', in *idem*, *The
            Theology of Deuteronomy* (Richland Hills, TX: BIBAL Press): 183-98.
    1997   'Die Völkervernichtung und die Rückkehr Israels ins Verheissunglsland:
            Hermeneutische Bemerkkungen zum Buch Deuteronomium', in Vervenne and
            Lust (eds.) 1997: 3-38.
Brett, M.G.
    1996   'Interpreting Ethnicity', in *idem* (ed.) 1996: 3-32.
    2000   *Genesis: Procreation and the Politics of Identity* (London: Routledge).
    2003   '*Canto Ergo Sum*: Indigenous Peoples and Postcolonial Theology', *Pacifica*
            16/3: 247-56.
Brett, M.G. (ed.)
    1996   *Ethnicity and the Bible* (Leiden: E.J. Brill).
Charleston, S.
    1990   'The Old Testament of Native America', in S.B. Thistlethwaite and M.B. Engel
            (eds.), *Lift Every Voice: Constructing Christian Theologies from the Underside*
            (San Francisco: HarperCollins): 49-61.
Connor, G.E.
    2002   'Covenants and Criticism', *BTB* 32: 4-10.
Crüsemann, F.
    1996   *The Torah: Theology and Social History of Old Testament Law* (Edinburgh:
            T. & T. Clark).
Deist, F.
    1994   'The Dangers of Deuteronomy: A Page from the Reception History of the
            Book', in F. García Martínez *et al.* (eds.), *Studies in Deuteronomy* (Leiden: E.J.
            Brill): 13-29.
Derrida, J.
    1995   *The Gift of Death* (Chicago: Chicago University Press).
Dever, W.
    2001   *What Did the Biblical Writers Know and When Did They Know it? What*
            Archaeology Can Tell Us about the Reality of Ancient Israel (Grand Rapids:
            Eerdmans).
Donaldson, L.
    2000   'Son of the Forest, Child of God: William Apess and the Scene of Postcolonial
            Nativity', in C.R. King (ed.), *Postcolonial America* (Urbana: University of
            Illinois Press): 201-22.
Dutcher-Walls, P.
    2002   'The Circumscription of the King: Deuteronomy 17.16-17 in its Ancient Social
            Context', *JBL* 121: 601-16.
Finkelstein I., and N. Silberman
    2001   *The Bible Unearthed: Archaeology's New Vision of Ancient Israel and the*
            Origin of its Sacred Texts (New York: Free Press).
Fishbane, M.
    1985   *Biblical Interpretation in Ancient Israel* (Oxford: Clarendon Press).
Gandhi, L.
    1998   *Postcolonial Theory* (St Leonards: Allen & Unwin).

Girard, R.
1977   *Violence and the Sacred* (Baltimore: The Johns Hopkins University Press).
Gondarra, D.
1996   *Series of Reflections on Aboriginal Religion* (Darwin: Bethel Presbytery, Uniting Church in Australia).
Hamilton, M.
1998   'The Past as Destiny: Historical Visions in Sam'al and Judah Under Assyrian Hegemony', *HTR* 91: 215-50.
Hawley, S.
1996   'Does God speak Miskitu? The Bible and Ethnic Identity Among the Miskitu of Nicaragua', in Brett (ed.) 1996: 315-42.
Hoffman, Y.
1999   'The Deuteronomistic Concept of the *Herem*', *ZAW* 111: 196-210.
Kang, S.-M.
1989   *Divine War in the Old Testament and in the Ancient Near East* (BZAW, 177; Berlin: W. de Gruyter).
Levinson, B.
1997   *Deuteronomy and the Hermeneutics of Legal Innovation* (New York: Oxford University Press).
2001   'Textual Criticism, Assyriology, and the History of Interpretation: Deuteronomy 13.7 as a Test Case in Method', *JBL* 120: 238-41.
Lohfink, N.
1994   'The Strata of the Pentateuch and the Question of War', in *idem*, *Theology of the Pentateuch* (Edinburgh: T. & T. Clark): 173-226.
1995   'Opferzentralisation, Säkularisicrungthcsc und mimetische Theorie', in *idem*, *Studien zum Deuteronomium und zur deuteronomistischen Literatur*, III (Stuttgart: Katholisches Bibelwerk): 219-60.
Lohfink, N. (ed.)
1983   *Gewalt und Gewaltlosigkeit im alten Testament* (Freiberg: Herder).
MacIntyre, A.
1981   *After Virtue* (Notre Dame: University of Notre Dame Press).
Matties, G.
2000   'Can Girard Help Us to Read Joshua?', in Swartley (ed.) 2000: 85-102.
McBride, S.D.
1987   'Polity of the Covenant People', *Int* 41: 229-44.
McNutt, P.
1999   *Reconstructing the Society of Ancient Israel* (Louisville, KY: Westminster/ John Knox Press).
McPhee, P.
1992   *A Social History of France 1780–1880* (London: Routledge).
Mendenhall, G., and G. Herion
1992   'Covenant', in *ABD*, I: 1180-83.
Moberly, W.
1999   'Toward an Interpretation of the Shema', in C. Seitz and K. Greene-McCreight (eds.), *Theological Exegesis* (Grand Rapids: Eerdmans): 135-37.
Moran, W.
1963   'The Ancient Near Eastern Background to the Love of God in Deuteronomy', *CBQ* 25: 77-87.
Na'aman, N.
1996   'The Canaanites and their Land: A Rejoinder', *UF* 28: 767-72.

Nelson, R.
1997   '*Herem* and the Deuteronomic Social Conscience', in Vervenne and Lust (eds.), 1997: 39-54.
Niditch, S.
1993   *War in the Hebrew Bible* (Oxford: Oxford University Press).
Nissinen, M.
2003   'Fear Not: A Study on an Ancient Near Eastern Phrase', in M.A. Sweeney and E. Ben Zvi (eds.), *The Changing Face of Form Criticism for the Twenty-First Century* (Grand Rapids: Eerdmans): 122-61.
O'Connell, B. (ed.)
1992   *On Our Own Ground: The Complete Writings of William Apess, A Pequot* (Amherst: University of Massachusetts Press).
Olsen, D.
1994   *Deuteronomy and the Death of Moses* (Minneapolis: Augsburg).
Otto, E.
1999   *Das Deuteronomium: Politische Theologie und Rechtsreform in Juda und Assyrian* (BZAW, 284; Berlin: W. de Gruyter).
2000   'Political Theology in Judah and Assyria', *SEA* 65: 59-76.
Parpola, S., and K. Watanabe (eds.)
1988   *Neo-Assyrian Treaties and Loyalty Oaths* (State Archives of Assyria, 2; Helsinki: Helsinki University Press).
Popper, K.
1972   *Objective Knowledge* (Oxford: Oxford University Press).
Pratt, M.L.
1994   'Transculturation and Autoethnography: Peru 1615–1980', in F. Barker *et al.* (eds.), *Colonial Discourse/Postcolonial Theory* (Manchester: Manchester University Press): 24-47.
Rainey, A.
1996   'Who is a Canaanite? A Review of the Textual Evidence', *BASOR* 304: 1-15.
Richard, P.
1996   'Biblical Interpretation from the Perspective of Indigenous Cultures of Latin America (Mayas, Kunas, and Quechuas)', in Brett (ed.) 1996: 297-314.
Rofé, A.
1985   'The Laws of Warfare in the Book of Deuteronomy: Their Origins, Intent, and Positivity', *JSOT* 22: 23-44.
Rose, P.
1990   *Revolutionary Antisemitism in Germany From Kant to Wagner* (Princeton, NJ: Princeton University Press).
Rüterswörden, U.
1987   *Von der politischen Gemeinschaft zur Gemeinde: Sudien zu Dt. 16,18–18,22* (BBB, 65; Frankfurt: Athenaeum).
Sacks, J.
2003   *The Dignity of Difference: How to Avoid the Clash of Civilizations* (London: Continuum, 2nd edn).
Said, E.
1988   'Michael Walzer's *Exodus and Revolution*: A Canaanite Reading', in E. Said and C. Hitchens (eds.), *Blaming the Victims: Spurious Scholarship and the Palestine Question* (London: Verso): 161-78.
1993   *Culture and Imperialism* (New York: Random House).
Schäfer-Lichtenberger, C.
1994   'Bedeutung und Funktion von *Herem* in biblisch-Hebräischen Texten', *BZ* 39: 27-75.

Smith, M.
  2002   *The Early History of God: Yahweh and the Other Deities in Ancient Israel* (Grand Rapids: Eerdmans, 2nd edn).
Smith-Christopher, D.
  2002   *A Biblical Theology of Exile* (Minneapolis: Fortress Press).
Soros, G.
  2002   *On Globalization* (Oxford: Public Affairs).
Sparks, K.
  1998   *Ethnicity and Identity in Ancient Israel* (Winona Lake, IN: Eisenbrauns).
Stern, P.
  1991   *The Biblical Herem: A Window on Israel's Religious Experience* (BJS, 211; Atlanta: Scholars Press).
Steymans, H.U.
  1995   *Deuteronomium 28 und die adê zur thronfolgeregelung Asarhaddons: Segen und Fluch im Alten Orient und in Israel* (OBO, 145; Göttingen: Vandenhoeck & Ruprecht).
Swartley, W. (ed.)
  2000   *Violence Renounced: René Girard, Biblical Studies and Peacemaking* (Scottdale, PA: Pandora).
Sweeney, M., and E. Ben Zvi (eds.)
  2003   *The Changing Face of Form Criticism for the Twenty-First Century* (Grand Rapids: Eerdmans).
Tatz, C.
  2003   *With Intent to Destroy: Reflecting on Genocide* (London: Verso)
Trible, P.
  1994   *Rhetorical Criticism* (Minneapolis: Fortress Press).
Van Seters, J.
  1972   'The Terms "Amorite" and "Hittite" in the Old Testament', *VT* 22: 64-81.
Vervenne M., and J. Lust (eds.)
  1997   *Deuteronomy and Deuteronomic Literature* (Leuven: Leuven University Press).
Weinfeld, M.
  1972   *Deuteronomy and the Deuteronomic School* (Oxford: Clarendon Press).
  1991   *Deuteronomy 1–11* (AB, 5; New York: Doubleday).
  1992   'Deuteronomy, Book of', in *ABD*, II: 168-83.
  1993   'The Ban on the Canaanites in the Biblical Codes and its Historical Development', in A. Lemaire and B. Otzen (eds.), *History and Traditions of Early Israel* (VTSup, 50; Leiden: E.J. Brill): 142-60.
  1993   *The Promise of the Land: The Inheritance of the Land of Canaan by the Israelites* (Berkeley: University of California).
Williams, J.G.
  1991   *The Bible, Violence and the Sacred: Liberation from the Myth of Sanctioned Violence* (New York: HarperCollins).
Younger, K.L.
  1990   *Ancient Conquest Accounts* (JSOTSup, 98; Sheffield: JSOT Press).

THE RHETORIC OF WAR AND THE *BOOK* OF JOSHUA*

Wonil Kim

I

When we consider the subject of war in the Hebrew Bible, we may conjure up an image of a battle being fought on the ground somewhere in ancient Israel or in Canaan: the horses and their neighing, the soldiers and their screams, the chariots, the weapons and their clattering, the dust, the blood, the moaning, the corpses of both the soldiers and the civilians, and a child's cry, and so on. But what relation does that image bear to the actual historical reality of war once fought? At best, only a circuitous one. Even if we are prepared to argue that the text accurately reflects, even describes, a war once fought, we would have to admit from the outset that the reflection or the description is that of a memory of the war distilled into the materiality of the text far removed from the battle ground. And whatever memory may have been etched into the text, the event as an immediate presence has all but disappeared into the irrecoverable time and space of the past, unavailable to the reader. Only an image, a textual image, remains. When we speak of war in the Hebrew Bible our subject is therefore not so much 'war' as the *rhetoric* of war in the *text* of the Hebrew Bible.

II

Some have argued, as has Giovanni Garbini (1988: xv-xvi), that, whether history or religion, the Hebrew Bible texts in the end leave us only with ideology:

> It is often said that the Bible is a religious book and not a history book… [But] in the Old Testament it is difficult, I would say impossible, to draw a dividing line between what is 'history' and what is 'religion'… The 'historical' conception of the Old Testament [is] that political thought which identifies with religious thought…and that religious thought which makes itself historical thought…and creates a fictitious but sacral history come together in a circularity which in our all too knowing language is no longer politics or religion or history—but only ideology.

We can hardly disagree with Garbini that the text is a product of ideology. But one does not have to go as far as to establish the 'fictitiousness' of the historical writing of the Hebrew Bible in order to label it as ideology. It is one thing to

---

* With respect and affection for Tony Campbell. My encounters with this passionate Jesuit scholar have been nothing less than a sheer delight.

argue for a generic distinction and say that biblical 'history' is in reality 'fiction' and not historiography. It is another, however, to say that biblical 'history' is ideological because it is 'fictitious'. Politics, religion, and history, even at their best, 'non-fictitious', moments, are ideological.

Louis Althusser (1969: 234) settled the question for us long ago when he said that 'in ideology the real relation is inevitably invested in the imaginary relation, a relation that *expresses* a *will* (conservative, conformist, reformist or revolutionary), a hope or a nostalgia, rather than describing a reality'. And as Terry Eagleton (1991: 19) notes of the ideological function of language, 'it is fundamentally a matter of fearing and denouncing, reverencing and reviling, all of which then sometimes gets coded into a discourse which looks as though it is describing the way the things actually are'. Eagleton agrees with J.L. Austin's (1962) speech act theory which sees the function of language as belonging to the class of speech acts, and is therefore, performative. Language gets something done. That is its function. As Eagleton observes elsewhere (1983: 205):

> [The heart of literary criticism is]…its concern for the kind of *effects* which discourses produce, and how they produce them… It is in fact, the oldest form of 'literary criticism' in the world, known as rhetoric. Rhetoric, which was the received form of critical analysis all the way from ancient society to the eighteenth century, examined the way discourses are constructed in order to achieve certain effects. It was not worried about whether its objects of inquiry were speaking or writing, poetry or philosophy, fiction or historiography: its horizon was nothing less than the field of discursive practices in society as a whole, and its particular interest lay in grasping such practices as forms of power and performances.

III

In the last section ('Biblical Theology or Biblical Sociology?') of his monumental and epoch-making work, *The Tribes of Yahweh* (1979),[1] Norman Gottwald offers a challenging methodology: a combination of a functionalist approach to religion and a socio-historical interpretation of Old Testament texts. As a Marxist social historian, he sees the biblical records basically as ideological products that serve as instruments of stratified social formation. Their theological assertions therefore defy any reconciliation with the actual historical data, especially of the pre-monarchic revolutionary times. An exclusive 'Mono-Yahwism', not 'election', served as a religious symbol for the pre-monarchic egalitarian society that had to fight off the stratified and hostile communities that surrounded it. Without appropriating this sociological analysis, any attempt of biblical theology to reflect systematically on biblical faith has failed, and will continue to fail. Thus Gottwald pronounces as beyond redemption the methodological bankruptcy of biblical theology as we have known it. He then calls for a solution that substitutes biblical sociology for biblical theology.

---

1. See also Pixley 1981 and 1987.

IV

Marxist literary criticism has come a long way since its inception in the late nineteenth century.[2] Even throughout a good portion of the twentieth century, Marxist debate pivoted around the 'active' or 'passive' role of literature in social formation. The question was whether a literary work functions as an active agent for social change or it passively reflects the social reality out of which the work emerges. As the Eagleton quotation above shows, however, Marxist literary critics' concern now lies in the *function* of *language* itself. They contend that even seemingly innocent and neutral sign systems have a *rhetorical* function. While we must always explore the relation between literature and its social context in order to better understand the text, we must ultimately encounter the text's more immediate *rhetorical* function.

2.   See Lukacs 1962; 1964; 1974; Jameson 1971; 1972; 1981; Demetz 1959; Williams 1977; Eagleton 1976; 1980; 1983; 1984; 1991; Macherey 1992; 1998; Mulhern 1992. Marxist literary theory has had its share of tortuous history even from before the October Revolution of 1917 (Demetz 1959), as is well testified by the debate between the two opposing critical schools: the Plekhanovites (Plekhanov and his followers) and the Bogdanovites (Bogdanov and his followers). (For a study on the history of these two schools during this period, see Lucid 1972.)

The debate surrounds the nature and function of literary art. Plekhanov, along with Trotsky and others, sees the aesthetics as essentially a passive process. He believes an artist unconsciously intuits the world and expresses it without subjecting it to much conscious volition. He therefore wants to leave the artist with political freedom, in which she would accurately, if passively, render the 'objective' reality as she sees it. Bogdanov, along with Gorky, and others, on the other hand, takes a more activist view. Borrowing from Tolstoy's notion of emotional 'infection', he views literature less as a passive, contemplative reflection of social reality than as a tool for making an impact on society. Thus, he calls upon the artist to play the role of an active agent for social agenda.

The debate continues beyond 1917 and defines the terms of Russian literary disputes for decades to come. Daniel Lucid observes the final outcome of the debate as of the early 1970s, well before the demise of the Soviet Union:

'As a result, Soviet Marxist aesthetics has been left with a Bogdanovite literary theory and a Plekhanovite practical criticism, with the theory harping on the tendentious duties of contemporary art, and the criticism *investigating the social origins of past art*' (Lucid 1972: 435 [emphasis added]).

Gottwald has his own complexities and we cannot place him at a single spot on the map just surveyed without doing him injustice. One can nonetheless detect in Gottwald a trace of certain aspects of the debate. For instance, it is doubtful Gottwald believes the literary agents who produced the Old Testament's extant texts played only a passive, reflective role, especially when he speaks of their 'endeavor to justify Israelite particularism by recourse to various subterfuges and rationalizations' (Gottwald 1979: 702). To be sure, the agents and the brokers of many of the biblical texts played the role opposite to what the Bogdanovites would have prescribed for them. Nevertheless, they were active agents in the fullest sense of the word, and Gottwald recognizes it. On the other hand, however, Gottwald's call for substitution of biblical sociology for biblical theology appears to betray a Plekhanovite sentiment. Like the Plekhanovites, he wants to use the text primarily for the purpose of obtaining clues to the social reality that they depict or fail to depict, that is, to use it mainly as data for sociological understanding of the world behind the text. While recognizing the text as a product of agenda-filled activities of the writers and the redactionists, Gottwald's interest lies ultimately in the text's utility as a clue for ascertaining the social reality and the origins behind the text.

As Francis Mulhern (1992: 19) aptly observes:

> Textual practice is internal to history, which inhabits it. The tradition of rhetoric assumes just this: linguistic practice is discourse, situated and motivated utterance, organized in and organizing specific relations of culture. To explore the historicity of the text is, then, not simply to relate a frail singularity to the broad design of a period; it is also to investigate its direct social relations, the formations of writing and reading—and these not as 'context' or 'background' but as substantive elements of the practice itself.

V

Pierre Macherey (1992), a Marxist philosopher, has a well-developed theory on this approach.[3] Building on, and moving beyond, Althusser's theory of the relationship between literature and ideology, Macherey raises the question of *literary production*. Against the traditional view, he sees the writer not so much as the creator as the producer of the text. This means for Macherey that literature is a *material production*. His immediate interest lies in the materiality of the text itself rather than in some pre-literary status that gives rise to the text. It is therefore for him (Balibar and Macherey 1996: 284):

> …pointless to look in the texts for the 'original' bare discourse of [the] ideological positions, as they were 'before' their 'literary' realization, for these ideological positions can only be formed in the materiality of the literary text. That is, they can only appear in a form which provides their imaginary solution, or better still, which displaces them by substituting imaginary contradictions soluble within the ideological practice of religion, politics, morality, aesthetics and psychology.

What Macherey (Balibar and Macherey 1996: 287) takes most seriously is therefore the immediate reality of the text and its effects:

> Literature is not fiction, a fictive image of the real, because it cannot define itself simply as a figuration, an appearance of reality. Literature is the production, by a complex process, of a certain reality—not…an autonomous reality, but a material reality—and of a certain social effect… Literature is not therefore a fiction, but the production of fictions: or better still, the production of fiction-effects (and in the first place the provider of the material means for the production of fiction-effects).

VI

Gottwald (1990: 40-41) is of course well aware of some of these theories and their ramifications, and it is clear he respects biblical literature as a legitimate genre of its own:

> When we take a stance within a work of fiction—and I would say also within a biblical history-like genre as well—whose relation to the historical is not straightforward, we discover that part of the text's very ideology as text is to present itself, as it were, outside of history or, at best, to be a reference to a general human condition uncluttered by historical specificity.

3. I am immensely grateful to Professor Ted Stolze at California State University at Hayward for helping me walk through some of the difficult aspects of Macherey's theory.

But we note that, while acknowledging literature as literature, Gottwald (1990: 40-41) still uses the text to go after the extra-textual historical referent: 'This feature, which Eagleton calls "the pseudo-real" of the text, is an aspect of its guise as literature and in this act of self-hiding we see the text's ultimate residual connection to history'.

Even as he endeavours to find 'contact points' between his methodology and Brevard Childs's version of canon criticism, Gottwald staunchly remains a social historian for whom the sociology of Israel's literature constitutes the fundamental methodological matrix. He 'takes canonical criticism's concerns seriously... respects what it aims to accomplish' (1985: 312), and is confident that 'canonical criticism is not inconsistent with social scientific criticism' (p. 322). These assertions notwithstanding, however, in the end it is the sociology of Israel's literature, not literature as literary production, that captures his imagination. Even the final canonical shape is a result of the canonical process, 'operative as a basic communal activity...[that] had a social matrix...underscoring the ideological component of Israelite society and religion...[thus providing] a datum of importance' (pp. 313-14). Without this datum provided by social science, 'canonical criticism may obscure the reality that the mere assertion of what has been affirmed as Canon does not tell us precisely enough what the force and thrust of the canonical decision actually was for the canonizing community, and thus derivatively or analogously what its force and thrust might be for us' (p. 315).

Gottwald thus asks persistently, 'what did the canonizing community think it was commending when it singled out this particular literature?' He insists on knowing how 'changing notions of the relation...between actuality and interpretation...[gave] different colorations to what is signified by accepting a canon' (p. 317). Gottwald therefore cannot help but 'choose to locate biblical theology in its metaphorical range of reference to Israelite socioeconomic, political, and cultural life by showing how the basic assertions of that theology correspond to socioeconomic, political, and cultural interests and desiderata in ancient Israel' (p. 318).

Because the canon, the interpreter, and 'the God shown in Scripture' are all 'historically moored', Gottwald cannot take anything less than 'the whole of biblical societies' as 'the object of study' (p. 308). For him, exegesis is an investigation 'for the sake of a social understanding of Israel' (p. 314). He therefore does 'not hesitate to claim that social scientific criticism completes the task...by providing...detailed social referential readings of the biblical texts' (p. 308). So, as we have seen above, even as he refers to Eagleton's notion of literature as 'pseudo-real', his goal is to discover 'the text's ultimate residual connection to history' in '[the text's] act of self-hiding'.

Gottwald has thus chosen not to deal with the text, its theology, and its normative claim on their own terms as literary production. There is of course no doubt that he clearly sees the material effect of the Bible as a literary production.[4]

---

4.   We may ask why Gottwald wants to replace biblical theology with biblical sociology. If we suspect Gottwald has a normative theological interest, he admits as much: '*The Tribes of Yahweh* ends with a theological reflection because it had in fact begun that way and was shaped in part by a

But he attempts to solve the problematic of this literary production and its material effect by exposing the socio-historical reality that the text presumably hides. This approach is markedly different from that of Macherey, his fellow Marxist, who believes it is 'pointless to look in the texts for the "original" bare discourse of [the] ideological positions, as they were "before" their "literary" realization' (see above).

VII

Particularly helpful is Macherey's 'theory of literary *reproduction*' (1998: 42-51). With this further nuanced and refined theory he argues that literature is constituted by its material reproduction, which belongs to the very nature of literature. Relying on, and expanding, Marx's notion of 'the eternal charm of Greek art' (heralded by Hegel's notion of art in *Phenomenology of Spirit*), Macherey establishes a clearly articulated methodological presupposition (p. 43):

> [I]n the very constitution of the work of art in general, and of the literary work in particular, there is something which condemns it to become outdated and no longer to exist except in the form of a relic in the absence of the social content in relation to which it was produced. It no longer subsists except through the mediation of its material envelope, as a 'work' inscribed in the literal body of its own text, but emptied of its living significance and by definition ephemeral, and testifying enigmatically by means of this alteration that its time is gone forever...which means...that these 'works' have not been produced as such, but precisely have become works in completely different conditions which are those of their production.

Extrapolating on Foucault's admonition (1972: 7-8) that the author should resist the temptation to become 'the name, the law, the secret, [and] the measure' of her work, but should let go of her work 'to be recopied, fragmented, repeated, simulated, divided, finally to disappear without the one who has happened to produce it ever being able to claim the right to be its master', Macherey (1998: 46-47) goes as far as to redefine the traditionally established production–reproduction

---

theological matrix' (1991: 12). He is only painfully aware of the *normative theological* nature that constitutes biblical literature, which, as literature, has its material reality and social effects. He in fact speaks emphatically of the text's social function: 'It is insufficient and untenable merely to conceive of the task of religious communities to be the intellectual elaboration and refinement of the received game traditions. Once we are able to understand religious traditions as functions of material conditions of life and the social relations rooted in those conditions, we are obligated precisely as religious persons to subject the received traditions to a thoroughgoing analysis of their social content and to take responsibility for religious reconstruction appropriate to the social content of our own experience' (1979: 703).

His report on how he made the methodological shift also reveals this normative concern: 'In terms of social and ecclesial contexts, I have moved from vague awareness of biblical hermeneutics as the practice of "applying" to my own world certain principles or analogies drawn from the Bible to a recognition of the full hermeneutical circle in which my social structural stance and consciousness correlates with biblical readings' (1991: 10).

The normative claim of biblical theology fails him, and he switches to social sciences—for a theological and normative reason.

relationship of a literary work: '[T]he event [of writing], which is everything but the act of a subject who would be its Author, precedes the work, which is itself only the repetition, in a relationship which is not that of massive identity but of insensible difference'.

Macherey thus maintains that the author is never the absolute Author, but rather 'the reader, critic, translator, editor, even…a simple copyist' (p. 47). Rather than being produced, then, the works actually 'begin to exist only from the moment they are "reproduced"' (p. 47). For him there is 'a poetics of reproduction functioning as a model of writing' (p. 48). Writing by necessity is done on the previous writing: 'One writes on the written' (p. 49). The palimpsest is not so much a literary genre as 'the very essence of the literary, which coincides with the movement of its own reproduction… [T]here is no first writing which is not also a rewriting' (p. 49).[5]

What Macherey has established, then, is a dialectical ontology of the literary work—a dialectical ontology that is self-sustaining and self-deconstructing as a reproduction: not only a reproduction of apparent and coherent meanings, but a reproduction of gaps, silences, contradictions, and their frequent 'misreadings' that open the text up back to the extra-literary world, particularly the reader; an open-ended, unpredictable reproduction, the nature of which is not guaranteed; a reproduction with a distinct materiality of its own far removed from the 'original' extra-literary factors; and, most importantly, a reproduction with an equally distinct *material effect*, a point well articulated by Eagleton as well.

VIII

Gottwald's proposal may force us to ask if we have to choose between a total abandonment of biblical theology, on the one hand, and an uncritical re-absorption of biblical theology, on the other. Were these the only choices, we could perhaps easily sympathize with Gottwald and comply with his invitation to substitute biblical sociology for biblical theology. But before rushing to the decision, it may behove us to examine the biblical texts with the full implications of Macherey's theoretical perspective in view.

IX

The way James Barr addresses the troublesome texts of Joshua gives the impression at first that he is approaching this issue with a premise seemingly close to Macherey's theory. Referring to the issue of חרם ('total, ritual destruction'), he recognizes that the historical question is not the most important point (1993: 209-10):

---

5.   This is of course how the entire Hebrew Bible (in fact, the whole Bible) was written. For one of the best and most recent examples of tradition and redaction criticism at work, see Campbell and O'Brien 2000. For an excellent study on the growth of the book of Joshua toward extermination theology, see Campbell 2000.

Even if the whole tradition of the holy war was 'a fiction', this does not deal with the problem: the problem is not whether the narratives are fact or fiction, the problem is that, whether fact or fiction, the ritual destruction is *commended* [*sic*?]. The total destruction of the Canaanite population is commanded in the texts, and accounts of its being carried out, as at the capture of Jericho, are very emphatically phrased. If it was fiction, it seems it was a fiction of which people approved and one which parts of the Bible sought to inculcate as a good model. And, though there is a wide variety of biblical depictions of warfare, there appears to be no passage that explicitly states disapproval of חרם or denies that it was commanded by God.

As it becomes immediately clear, however, Barr is not ready to argue, as a theologian with a Machereyan bent might, that the theological task is therefore to take on the dialectical material reality of the text as a self-sustaining yet open-ended reproduction. On the contrary, and as we may well expect of Barr, he takes an historicist approach and expends full energy to argue against the notion that חרם was justified in view of the 'child sacrifice' by the Canaanites, a theory that, according to Barr, does not have a sound historical ground. Barr is in fact un-equivocal about his methodology. Accusing biblical interpretation of being 'strongly inclined to restrict its sources of guidance to the *internal* relations per-ceptible within the biblical text itself', he asserts that 'interpretation for modern situation can occur only when you bring to the text other factors, other ideas, other knowledge of situations, which are expressly other than internal content and internal relations of the text' (1993: 206-207).

X

It is obvious that concern about material effect of the text is what prompted Gottwald to turn to sociology. And Barr is correct in observing that the text presents חרם, fact or fiction, to inculcate it as a good model. Their concern is material effect of the reproduced text, and because of this concern they both turn to extra-textual factors.

Macherey's methodological implications would invite us, however, to exam-ine the *rhetoric* of Joshua's war as *material reproduction of the text* with specific material effect without having to depend primarily on the extra-textual referents; to raise the question of theological validity of the text and to seek answers from 'the *internal* relations perceptible within the biblical text itself' (*contra* Barr).

XI

Another scholar, a *theologian* of the Hebrew Bible, equally disturbed by and concerned about material effect of the reproduced texts, turns inward to the text and takes an *intra*-textual approach. We may say that he does so in a remarkably Machereyan way, although he is neither a Marxist nor influenced by Macherey. As early as 1970, Rolf Knierim began to argue that what ultimately matters when we say 'biblical revelation' is the people affected by such 'revelation' *in actu*.[6]

6. Cf. Knierim 1970 (English 1995).

At the height of the debate surrounding von Rad's notion of *Heilsgeschichte*, he responded to the deadlocked exchange between Rendtorff (1962 and 1968) and Zimmerli (1962) regarding the question of revelation as word (Zimmerli) and as historical event (Rendtorff). He entered the debate by suggesting that a question of God and God's revelation is in the end a question of the people affected by the discourse *in actu*. All the competing theological claims of the texts intend, and attempt, to exert the effect of its own material reality on the reader, the ultimate target of the text's intentionality. In other words, biblical texts and their theological claims are a *rhetoric* in the classic sense of the word.

Moving thus beyond the question of the modality of revelation (word or history) to that of substance with rhetorical aims, Knierim looks at the discourse taking place on the textual ground. For it is there where both complementing and contradicting *conceptualities* of the text dance vigorously in competition with each other, wooing and demanding the reader's response and compliance, at the moment when those conceptualities are reproduced with material effect *in actu*.

Knierim's treatment of the rhetoric of war in the Hebrew Bible within this methodological framework offers an alternative to the socio-historical approach examined above, an alternative that has a strong affinity to Macherey's nuanced proposal.[7]

As does Barr, Knierim first of all argues that we must 'not approach the problem of Yahweh's war against the Canaanites by referring to the historical argument'. We must instead 'focus on the concepts of the texts, not on what happened [or did not happen] in history' (1994: 5). If the war against Canaanites did not happen the way it is described, the canon would certainly charge Israel with disobedience ('Is history an excuse for Israel's disobedience?'), because 'the texts and their theology, especially when adopted canonically', expect 'to be actualized when the occasion arrives' (p. 5). The issue is not one of history but of the effect of the text as reproduction.

For the same reason, Knierim does 'not believe that the discussion of war in Old Testament theology can be based on the tradition-history of ancient Israel's theologies' (1994: 7). Tradition-history may reconstruct different stages of the concepts of war throughout the Hebrew Bible and delineate its historical development in order to understand the *Sitz im Leben* of each concept. But 'the Old Testament does not say, at least not in principle, that each of these concepts was only valid for its own time'. On the contrary, by canonically juxtaposing these concepts the Hebrew Bible presents these 'different conceptual legacies as potentials for present and future times' (p. 7). None of the concepts is replaced by another. And all of them are included in the canonical accumulation with due canonical claims of theological validity for all generations. Tradition-historical analysis of sacred war in the Hebrew Bible therefore does not replace or supercede the effects of the canonized text as literary reproduction. But while rejecting historical argument, Knierim, unlike Gottwald or Barr, anchors his analysis within the material substance of the biblical text. Instead of building an argument

---

7. Cf. Knierim 1994. This article is a response to von Waldow 1984.

on extra-literary referents, or lack thereof, he insists that any concept of war in the Hebrew Bible needs to be examined on its textual, canonical, and conceptual levels as reproduction of material effect, 'whether Israel's history honored or violated it' (1994: 8).

XII

Knierim recognizes that the Hebrew Bible assumes the inevitability of war not only among the nations of the world but also in Israel's covenant history (1994: 15). And he agrees with H. Eberhard von Waldow (1984: 33, 45) that any theology of war in the Hebrew Bible must be evaluated by the fundamental criterion of creation theology, as it is articulated, for instance, in Genesis 1. He believes, as does von Waldow, that 'Genesis 1 can provide a basis for the universal validity of the thesis [that] "war is sin"'. But he concurs with von Waldow on these methodological premises 'only with serious qualification' (1994: 12):

> The priestly writers were probably no soldiers. But the assumption that they were pacifist is an illusion. Similarly, the assumption that their theology of creation only had to do with peaceful cultic purity and the social ethos of the community, and had nothing to do with the concept of the epiphanic military conquests of the promised land, is also an illusion. These writers spoke most programmatically about Yahweh's sacred war on behalf of Yahweh's elected people. From a strictly exegetical perspective, the view that the priestly concept of Israel's life in the promised land stands in the service of God's care for creation and all humanity equally remains incomprehensible... God's order of creation and Yahweh's wars in history function for the sake of Israel's election.

While he has no objection to the notion of anyone's election, he asks 'for whose sake election functions' (1994: 12), and in whose service a war is fought by the elected people.

The sacred and the punitive nature of Joshua's wars is also an issue. The text makes it clear that the wars of land occupation are *Yhwh*'s typical sacred wars. The text also sees these wars 'as *Yhwh*'s punitive action against the [depravity] of the Canaanites' (von Waldow 1984: 30). This much is obvious. But Knierim moves beyond the obvious by noting that the text knows the God (of the Deuteronomistic or Priestly theology) is the creator of the entire earth and universal lord of history who uses his military power precisely *as* the creator of the world and universal Lord of history. So he asks if 'Israel's sacred wars [are] examples or paradigms for the creator's protection of the life of all nations equally, in accordance with the principle of the sanctity of life drawn out from the order of creation; ...[if they are] wars in which Yahweh uses Israel for the benefit of all humanity' (1994: 13). In other words, the text's claim of sacredness is not a self-sufficient proof of its sacredness. And if the Canaanites' depravity was the cause of the conquest wars, then this scenario only begs the question: '[W]hy were they alone to be wiped out, or at least to be subjugated, and not all other nations likewise?' (1994: 13).

A *conceptual* exegesis of the *texts* offers an indisputable answer. It is neither Israel's oppression in Egypt nor the sins of the Canaanites that forms the ground for the occupation and its wars. 'The theology of Exodus 3.7-8', argues Knierim, 'is the theology of the land of Israel as Yahweh's own people. All other notions, including the notion of liberation from oppression, stand in the service of this theology.'[8] Regardless of the need to liberate Israel or to punish the Canaanites,

> '[the Canaanites'] expropriation was a foregone conclusion'... They had to be expropriated of their land because Yahweh had promised their land to Yahweh's own people. Yahweh was going to fulfill this promise to make the land Yahweh's own land, but not because of the Canaanites' 'depravity'. Had their 'depravity' been the legitimate and basic reason for their expropriation, all nations existing in the same sinful condition should have been expropriated, and Yahweh's people could have settled anywhere rather than only in the land of Canaan. They could have possessed the earth. (1994: 13-14)

Without referencing the historical reality behind the text, the conceptual analysis of the text as text, as theological expression with its concomitant claims, already reveals the questionable nature, to say the least, of Joshua's (= *Yhwh*'s) wars against the Canaanites. And another textual-conceptual picture of this same *Yhwh* as the life-giving creator of the earth in Genesis 1 brings the contrast between the two images to full view. In the face of this contrast, we now have a *biblical theological* task at hand, especially in view of the *effect* of these *God*-images as reproduction on the readers *in actu*.

XIII

Literature is a projected reality, a discourse with its own material logic. We are not therefore mandated to judge the *book* of Joshua only in reference to what really happened or did not really happen in history outside the *book* of Joshua. The *book* of Joshua produces and reproduces its own world with its own ideological agenda, namely, a specific aim of convincing its reader of a truth claim in the name of God. And that truth claim has less to do with whether or not Joshua's military conquest happened than with whether or not it should ever happen, then, now, or in the future—in historical reality or in an imaginary solution to a perceived historical problem.

After arguing for the possibility that the חרם texts (Josh. 10.28-41; 11.8b-15) are later Deuteronomistic insertions, Antony Campbell wonders 'how a narrative that smacks of standard national boasting about land seizure has been turned into a thoroughgoing theology of extermination by those who must have known it was untrue' (2000: 86). Then he entertains the following possibility of redactional motive (p. 88):

> Are the extermination texts in Joshua another attempt to come to terms with the locals by affirming that none survived? Joshua's generation alone is proclaimed as faithful to the LORD (Josh. 24.31; Judg. 2.7). Deuteronomy 7.1-4 makes clear the LORD's will for locals: extermination. Therefore, despite texts to the contrary, Joshua's generation must have done it and it is to be recorded in the *book* of Joshua. (Emphasis added)

---

8.   Knierim 1995: 133, 309-21; Kim 2000: 292-320.

Campbell does not pretend to offer a conclusive answer to the traditional, redactional questions: 'Early or late, widespread or isolated, these texts pose problems for the history of traditions. Late and isolated looks more likely; even as such the origins of the theology of extermination remain obscure.' Apparently, however, it is not just a tradition-historical question for Campbell. For he ends his article by asking a haunting question: 'Why, for God's sake, are the heights and depths so dangerously close?' Why, indeed? Campbell's suggestive scenario above is not unlikely. And we can ask further if in such a scenario the texts' intention would have been only to revise a history of the past. It would be a rhetorical question. We may have here a prime example of literary reproduction at work, a reproduction with a not-so-subtle political agenda, with a clearly intended, as well as unintended, *effect*.

The *book* of Joshua is a *reproduced literature* with *reproduced God-effect*,[9] not only throughout its traditional, redactional stages but also beyond its final 'writing' stage because, and precisely to the extent which, the *canon* that includes it is a *reproduced literature of reproduced God-effect*. Susan Niditch (1993: 4) rightly observes that 'the particular violence of the Hebrew Scriptures has inspired violence, and served as a model of, and for persecution, subjugation, and extermination for millennia beyond its own reality…' Michael Prior (1998: 11) bemoans the fact that 'the ethnocentric, xenophobic and militaristic character of the biblical narratives of Israelite origins is treated in conventional biblical scholarship as if it were above any questioning on moral grounds, even by criteria derived from other parts of the Bible'. Hopefully, it has been shown that such 'questioning…on moral grounds…by criteria derived from other parts of the Bible' is doable, that it has in fact been done.

Walter Brueggemann rightly cautions us to take 'great care and attentiveness to the "unintended effects" of our reading' of these texts (2003: 119). Indeed we should. But the book of Joshua is a *reproduction*, both in its writing and in our reading, with not only unintended but also *intended God-effects*. Caution is needed there as well. And it just may well be the case that the same canon of the Hebrew Bible that gives us these texts of *intended and unintended God-effects* also offers us a sufficiently diverse resource of *reproduced* texts of *God-effects* with which we can dialectically counter the *God-effect* the *book* of Joshua *reproduces*.

BIBLIOGRAPHY

Althusser, L.
    1969   *For Marx* (New York: Vintage Books).
Austin, J.L.
    1962   *How to Do Things with Words* (Cambridge, MA: Harvard University Press).
Barr, J.
    1993   *Biblical Faith and Natural Theology* (Oxford: Clarendon Press).

9. I owe this expression to Professor Ted Stolze. I believe he coined it.

Balibar, E., and P. Macherey
    1996   'On Literature as an Ideological Form', in T. Eagleton and D. Milne (eds.),
                Marxist Literary Theory (Oxford: Basil Blackwell): 275-95 (first published in
                Oxford Literary Review 3 [1978]: 4-12).
Brueggemann, W.
    2003   *An Introduction to the Old Testament: The Canon and Christian Imagination*
                Louisville, KY: Westminster/John Knox Press).
Campbell, A.F.
    2000   'The Growth of Joshua 1–12 and the Theology of Extermination', in Kim,
                Ellens, Floyd and Sweeney (eds.) 2000: II, 72-88.
Campbell, A.F., and M.A. O'Brien
    2000   *Unfolding the Deuteronomistic History: Origins, Upgrades, Present Text*
                (Minneapolis: Fortress Press).
Demetz, P.
    1959   *Marx, Engels, and the Poets* (Chicago: University of Chicago Press).
Eagleton, T.
    1976   *Marxism and Literary Criticism* (Berkley: University of California Press).
    1980   *Criticism and Ideology: A Study in Marxist Literary Theory* (London: Verso).
    1983   *Literary Theory* (Minneapolis: University of Minnesota Press).
    1984   *The Function of Criticism: From the Spectator to Post-Structuralism* (London:
                Verso).
    1991   *Ideology* (New York: Verso).
Foucault, M.
    1972   *Histoire de la folie à l' âge classique* (Paris: Gallimard).
Garbini, G.
    1988   *History and Ideology in Ancient Israel* (New York: Crossroad).
Gottwald, N.K.
    1979   *The Tribes of Yahweh: A Sociology of the Religion of Liberated Israel, 1250–
                1050 B.C.E.* (Maryknoll, NY: Orbis Books).
    1985   'Social Matrix and Canonical Shape', *Theology Today* 42.3: 307-21.
    1990   'Literary Criticism of the Hebrew Bible: Retrospect and Prospect', in V.L. Tol-
                lers and J. Maier (eds.), *Mappings of the Biblical Terrain: The Bible as Text*
                (Bucknell Review, 33.2; Lewisburg, PA: Bucknell University Press; London:
                Associated University Press): 27-44.
    1991   'How My Mind has Changed or Remained the Same' (unpublished address to
                the Society of Biblical Literature, Annual Meeting, Kansas City, MO, 25
                November [a courtesy of Professor Norman Gottwald]).
Jameson, F.
    1971   *Marxism and Form: Twentieth-Century Dialectical Theory of Literature*
                (Princeton, NJ: Princeton University Press).
    1972   *The Prison-House of Language: A Critical Account of Structuralism and
                Russian Formalism* (Princeton, NJ: Princeton University Press).
    1981   *The Political Unconscious: Narrative as a Socially Symbolic Act* (Ithaca, NY:
                Cornell University Press).
Kim, W.
    1999   'Liberation Theology and the Bible: A Methodological Consideration', in Kim,
                Ellens, Floyd and Sweeney (eds.) 2000: I, 292-320.
Kim, W., D. Ellens, M. Floyd and M. Sweeney (eds.)
    2000   *Reading the Hebrew Bible for a New Millennium: Form, Concept, and Theo-
                logical Perspective* (2 vols.; Harrisburg, PA: Trinity Press International).

Knierim, R.
1970   'Offenbarung im Alten Testament', in H.W. Wolff (ed.), *Probleme Biblischer Theologie: von Rad zum 70. Geburtsag* (Munich: Chr. Kaiser Verlag, 1971): 206-35 (now published as 'Revelation in the Old Testament', in *The Task of Old Testament Theology: Methods and Cases* [trans. H.T.C. Sun and K. Torjesen, assisted by R. Knierim; Grand Rapids: Eerdmans, 1995]: 139-70).
1994   'On the Subject of War in Old Testament and Biblical Theology', *Horizons in Biblical Theology* 16.1: 1-19.
1995   *The Task of Old Testament Theology: Substance, Method, and Cases* (Grand Rapids: Eerdmans).

Lucid, D.P.
1972   'Preface to Revolution: Russian Marxist Literary Criticism, 1883–1917' (unpublished doctoral dissertation, Yale University).

Lukacs, G.
1962   *The Historical Novel* (London: Merlin Press).
1964   *Studies in European Realism* (New York: Grosset & Dunalp).
1974   *The Theory of the Novel* (Cambridge, MA: MIT Press, repr. [1920]).

Macherey, P.
1992   *A Theory of Literary Production* (trans. Geoffrey Wall; London: Routledge).
1998   *In a Materialist Way: Selected Essays* (ed. Warren Montag; trans. Ted Stolze; London: Verso).

Mulhern, F. (ed.)
1992   *Contemporary Marxist Literary Criticism* (New York: Longmans, Green).

Niditch, S.
1993   *War in the Hebrew Bible: A Study in the Ethics of Violence* (Oxford: Oxford University Press).

Pixley, G.V.
1981   *God's Kingdom: A Guide for Bible Study* (Maryknoll, NY: Orbis Books).
1987   *On Exodus: A Liberation Perspective* (Maryknoll, NY: Orbis Books).

Prior, M.
1998   'A Land Flowing with Milk, Honey, and People (The Lattey Lecture 1997)', *Scripture Bulletin* 28: 2-17.

Rendtorff, R.
1962   'Geschichte und Wort im Alten Testament', *EvT* 22: 621-49.
1968   'The Concept of Revelation in Ancient Israel', in W. Pannenberg (ed.), *Revelation as History* (trans. D. Granskou; New York: Macmillan): 25-53.

Waldow, H.E. von
1984   'The Concept of War in the Old Testament', *Horizons in Biblical Theology* 16.2: 27-48.

Williams, R.
1977   *Marxism and Literature* (New York: Oxford University Press).

Zimmerli, W.
1962   ' "Offenbarung" im Alten Testament: Ein Gespräch mit R. Rendtorff', *EvT* 22: 15-31.

ON THE LITERARY FUNCTION OF THE NOTICE CONCERNING HIEL'S RE-ESTABLISHMENT OF JERICHO IN 1 KINGS 16.34

Marvin A. Sweeney

I

Interpreters normally take relatively little notice of 1 Kgs 16.34, which notes Hiel the Bethelite's re-establishment of the city of Jericho at the cost of his two sons. They generally note that the statement fulfills Joshua's oath uttered at the conclusion of the conquest of Jericho in Josh. 6.26 that whoever tried to rebuild the city would do so at the cost of his firstborn and youngest sons. But having done so, they simply leave it at that and consider the verse as little more than an interesting footnote that appears at the conclusion of the introductory regnal account concerning Ahab ben Omri in 1 Kgs 16.29-30.[1]

And yet it is striking that the narrator would take the trouble to mention such a fact, with little thought given to its implications for the immediate literary context or the events that are related therein. Does this notice have any significance in the present context? Or is it mentioned as a seemingly irrelevant historical note simply to satisfy the interests of a pedantic scribe, who wanted his audience to know that Joshua's oath had not gone unfulfilled? Indeed, there are indications that this statement serves more than simply an interest in antiquarian history. Joshua's conquest of Jericho marked the first major victory in Israel's conquest of the land of Canaan, and it therefore marks the first territory after Gilgal that formally functioned as part of the promised, holy land of Israel from the standpoint of the Deuteronomistic History (DH). The oath uttered by Joshua might then be taken as a warning to anyone who might try to compromise the status of that land.[2] Is it any accident, then, that our notice appears at the beginning of the narrative concerning the reign of King Ahab of Israel, easily regarded within the DH as the most notorious of all of northern Israel's monarchs after Jeroboam ben Nebat? Although every northern monarch is judged to be as wicked as Jeroboam

---

1. For representative treatments of this verse, see Montgomery and Gehman 1951: 286-88; Gray 1970: 369-71; Würthwein 1977: 203-204; Long 1984: 173-74; De Vries 1985: 204-205; Fritz 1996: 161-62; Walsh 1996: 219; Cogan 2000: 421-22. Of this group, only De Vries and Walsh hint at any further narrative function. Otherwise, the commentators understand the reference retrospectively in relation to Josh. 6.26, and frequently attempt to comment on the historical circumstances that might prompt reconstruction of Jericho.

2. Compare De Vries (1985: 204), who suggests that Ahab's wickedness prompted Hiel's action, and Walsh (1996: 219), who notes that the action places Ahab's reign 'under the shadow of death'.

(Cross 1973), it is to Ahab that the wicked Judean King Manasseh, whom *Yhwh* holds responsible for the decision to destroy Jerusalem and the Temple, is compared (1 Kgs 21.1-18). Perhaps it is no accident then that Manasseh's great grandson, Zedekiah, was captured by the Babylonians at Jericho (2 Kgs 25.1-7), thereby putting an end to the long line of kings who sat on the throne of David in Jerusalem. Certainly the notice has some significance within the Elijah/Elisha traditions as well, for it is at Jericho that Elijah is taken to heaven in a fiery chariot (2 Kgs 2), leaving Elisha as Elijah's successor to complete the work of removing the house of Omri from the throne.

It is the contention of this paper that the notice in 1 Kgs 16.34 serves a programmatic function, both within the Ahab narrative and within the larger DH. It will attempt to demonstrate this contention by two primary means: (1) a close literary analysis of this verse in relation to the immediate literary context of the Ahab regnal account in 1 Kgs 16.29–22.40; and (2) a broader discussion of the function of the statement as part of the Ahab regnal account within the larger DH from Joshua through the end of Kings.

II

Although most scholars consider 1 Kgs 16.34 to be an appended notice to the introductory regnal account for Ahab ben Omri in 16.29-33, close attention to the literary structure of Ahab's regnal account in 16.29–22.40, particularly the role played by the syntactical features of the account in organizing the presentation of the narrative, indicates that the verse actually serves as a programmatic introduction to the material that follows.

In order to assess the literary structure of Ahab's regnal account in 1 Kgs 16.29–22.40, the formal boundaries of the narrative must first be established. The passage begins with a typically formulated introductory regnal account in 16.29-33.[3] A conjunctive *waw* joined to the proper name 'Ahab', that is, ואחאב, introduces the initial statement of Ahab's regnal information, including his name, the year in which his rule began (calculated in relation to the reign of his Judean counterpart), and the duration of his reign, in v. 29, 'and Ahab ben Omri ruled over Israel in the thirty-eighth year of Asa, king of Judah, and Ahab ben Omri ruled over Samaria for twenty-two years'. And the second part of the introductory regnal account in vv. 30-33 presents a typically formulated evaluation of Ahab's reign. It begins with a *waw*-consecutive imperfect verb, ויעש followed once again by Ahab's proper name, אחאב בן־עמרי, which introduces the *waw*-consecutive verbal chain of statements that provides a negative evaluation of Ahab's reign, namely, 'and Ahab ben Omri did (ויעש אחאב בן־עמרי) more evil in the eyes of *Yhwh* than all who were before him…' The following series of statements formulated with *waw*-consecutive verbs indicates that it was not enough for him to follow in the ways of Jeroboam, but he took the Phoenician princess Jezebel as wife, worshipped Baal, built an altar for Baal, made an Asherah, and generally did more to provoke *Yhwh* than all the kings of Israel who preceded him.

3. See especially Long (1984: 172-73, 158-65) for discussion of the form.

Our statement in 1 Kgs 16.34 stands out in that it is not formulated initially with a *waw*-consecutive verb like the statements of the introductory regnal account. It is linked to the preceding statements by its use of the third masculine singular pronoun in the initial statement, 'in his days (בימיו) Hiel the Bethelite built Jericho; with Abiram, his first born, he founded it, and with Sagub, his youngest, he set up its gates according to the word of *Yhwh*, which he spoke by the agency of Joshua ben Nun'. Although the third masculine singular suffix obviously depends upon the explicit references to Ahab ben Omri in vv. 29-33 for its referent, the following *waw*-consecutive formulation in 1 Kgs 17.1 suggests the possibility of a syntactical relationship with the following material that must be considered.

Before considering that relationship, we must first establish the conclusion of the Ahab regnal account. A typically formulated concluding regnal account for Ahab ben Omri appears in 1 Kgs 22.39-40, immediately following the account of Ahab's death in 22.1-38.[4] Again, the passage begins in typical form with a conjunctive *waw* formulation, 'and the rest (ויתר) of the acts of Ahab and all that he did, and the house of ivory that he built, and all the cities that he built, are they not written in the book of the chronicles of the kings of Israel?' A series of typically formulated *waw*-consecutive statements then conclude the account with the notice that he slept with his fathers and that his son, Ahaziah, succeeded him as king. The typically formulated introductory regnal account form in 1 Kgs 22.41-45 introduces an entirely new unit, the regnal account of Jehoshaphat ben Asa of Judah, in vv. 41-51. Indeed, the entire structure of 1–2 Kings is constituted by the regnal accounts of the kings of Israel and Judah.

This leaves a large body of material in 1 Kgs 17.1–22.38 to account for in the structure of Ahab's regnal account. Although much of this material focuses on the prophet Elijah and his colleagues, it is presented here because it portrays the major events of King Ahab's reign that illustrate the information provided in the introductory and concluding regnal accounts. For the most part, interpreters have read this material diachronically, identifying separate blocks of tradition concerning Elijah in 1 Kings 17–19 and 21, and the Aramean wars in chs. 20 and 22, particularly since the latter focus on different prophets, the anonymous figure in ch. 20 and Micaiah ben Imlah in ch. 22.[5]

Although these texts may have originated as separate traditions, however, they must be read in relation to each other in the synchronic literary form of the text. Whereas most interpreters, based on diachronic presumptions, would assess the narrative as a series of episodes, united at the level of either the Josianic or exilic deuteronomistic (Dtr) or earlier redaction concerning Elijah's confrontation with Ahab (chs. 17–19), Ahab's war with the Arameans (ch. 20), Elijah's condemnation of Ahab for his murder of Naboth (ch. 21), and Ahab's death in battle at Ramoth Gilead (22.1-38), the syntactical features of this narrative provide a very different set of structural guidelines. Indeed, a series of *waw*-conjunctive

4. See especially Long (1984: 240, 158-65) for discussion of the form.
5. See especially Fohrer 1968; Hentschel 1977; White 1997; Beck 1999; Otto 2001: 119-246. For a convenient overview of discussion, McKenzie 1991: 81-100.

formulations, each of which introduces a name or description of a major character in the narrative, introduces each episode following the initial block of material
in chs. 17–19. Thus, the body of Ahab's regnal account begins with the well-
known block of material concerning Elijah's confrontation with Ahab and its
aftermath in chs. 17–19,[6] which results in *Yhwh*'s instructions to Elijah to anoint
Elisha as his successor, Jehu as king of Israel, and Hazael as king of Aram. A
series of three episodes then follows.

A new episode begins in 1 Kgs 20.1, introduced by the phrase, 'and Ben-
Hadad (וּבֶן־הֲדַד), king of Aram, gathered all his army…', which then relates the
onset of hostilities between Aram and Israel in 1 Kgs 20.1-12. This episode initiates the consequences for Israel brought on by Ahab's apostasy, his support for
Jezebel, and their actions against *Yhwh*'s prophets. At this point, the immediate
narrative does not indicate that Ahab stands under judgment, but the literary
context of 1 Kings 17–19 has already informed the reader of *Yhwh*'s plans to
replace Ahab as king of Israel with Jehu. This would indicate that the episode in
1 Kgs 20.1-12 is meant to be read following chs. 17–19 in the synchronic literary
form of the text. The author of 20.1-12 may not have intended such a reading, but
the redactor or compiler of these materials seems to have had precisely such an
agenda in mind.

The appearance of a new character, an anonymous prophet, in 1 Kgs 20.13,
again introduced by a *waw*-conjunctive formulation, begins the next episode,
'and behold, one prophet (וְהִנֵּה נָבִיא אֶחָד) drew near to Ahab, king of Israel…',
which indicates *Yhwh*'s support for Ahab in the battle with the Arameans. Again,
the immediate narrative provides no clue that Ahab will die or suffer any punishment, but again the narrative context of 1 Kings 17–19 has already informed the
reader that Ahab is a marked man. Such a reading is hardly the intention of an
original author, but it is the product of a redaction that placed its sub-units in
sequence.

A third episode begins in 1 Kgs 20.35, which again employs a *waw*-conjunc-
tive presentation of another anonymous prophet to introduce a new episode that
finally takes up Ahab's condemnation for showing mercy to Ben-hadad, 'and one
man (וְאִישׁ אֶחָד) from the sons of the prophets said to his neighbour…' The initial
condemnation of Ahab by the anonymous prophet appears in 20.35-43 and, once
again, the reader already knows from 1 Kings 17–19 of *Yhwh*'s plans to replace
both Ahab and Ben-hadad. Although most interpreters would correctly consider
the Naboth's vineyard narrative in ch. 21 and the death of Ahab in 22.1-38 to be
separate texts on diachronic grounds, their respective formulation with initial
waw-consecutive sequences, 'and it came to pass (וַיְהִי) after these things that
Naboth had a vineyard…' (21.1), and 'and three years passed (וַיֵּשְׁבוּ שָׁלֹשׁ שָׁנִים)
without war between Aram and Israel…' (22.1), indicates that they are meant
to be read in sequence with 20.35-43 in the synchronic literary form of the text.
The three narratives in 20.35-43; ch. 21; and 22.1-38 would together constitute a

---

6. Most interpreters maintain that 1 Kgs 17–19 constitutes a coherent block of material that has
been worked redactionally into the larger tradition and literary framework. In addition to the works
cited above, see especially Steck 1968 and Hauser 1990.

three-part presentation of Ahab's condemnation, beginning with the initial condemnation in 20.35-43 by the anonymous prophet for sparing Ben-hadad, the reprieve for Ahab by Elijah in ch. 21 because of his repentance concerning Naboth, and the death of Ahab in 22.1-38 during the second Aramean invasion. The sequence explains both Ahab's condemnation and his early death prior to the demise of his dynasty as indicated by *Yhwh*'s words to Elijah at Horeb and Elijah's initial judgment of Ahab following his role in the murder of Naboth and the appropriation of Naboth's property. The narrative block in 1 Kings 17–19 introduces the entire sequence by informing the reader of *Yhwh*'s plans to replace Ahab as a result of his apostasy.

A synchronic reading of these narratives thus provides a certain narrative rationale for the literary arrangement of the presentation of Ahab's regnal account, namely, there is a concern to demonstrate *Yhwh*'s condemnation of Ahab, but there is also a concern to explain why, despite the apparent condemnation of Ahab's dynasty by *Yhwh* at Horeb in 1 Kings 19 and by Elijah in 1 Kings 21 following the Naboth incident, the narrative presents only Ahab's death and not the end of his entire house. At the diachronic level, many interpreters have argued that a redaction has secondarily portrayed the violent death of Ahab in battle against Aram.[7] At the synchronic level, however, the narrative builds considerable narrative tension into the presentation of Ahab's death and the demise of his house. It takes some three chapters for Ahab finally to die following *Yhwh*'s oracle to Elijah at Horeb, and it takes ten more chapters and a new prophet for the house of Ahab/Omri finally to fall in 2 Kings 9–10.

In order to understand the narrative purpose for that tension, we must now return to the question of 1 Kgs 16.34 and its place within the overall structure of the Ahab regnal account of 16.29–22.40. As noted above, the third person masculine pronoun in the phrase, 'in his days', indicates that the verse has a syntactical relationship with the introductory regnal account of 16.29-33, but the initial *waw*-consecutive formulation of 17.1 also indicates that the verse has a syntactical relationship with the following narrative block in chs. 17–19.

Most scholars agree that 1 Kings 17–19 constitutes a coherent, if redactional, narrative block.[8] It is noteworthy, therefore, that these chapters have a coherent literary structure that is built around the motif of the prophet's or *Yhwh*'s word. Indeed, 1 Kgs 17.1 begins with Elijah's statement to Ahab that there would be no rain in the land except 'by my word'. Of course, neither Ahab nor the reader has any reason to presume the credibility of Elijah's word other than the prophet's own claim that he serves *Yhwh*. Although most readers are likely well acquainted with Elijah from reading and rereading these narratives together with other presentations of Elijah in either Jewish or Christian tradition, the first-time reader has never heard of Elijah before and has no reason to assume that his claims are true. The following material in 17.2–19.21, however, is presented in a manner that substantiates Elijah's claims fully. Each episode in the narrative presents an

---

7.   See especially Miller 1966, 1967; McKenzie 1991: 88-93.
8.   See n. 6 and the literature cited above.

instance of *Yhwh*'s word to Elijah that then comes true. Each begins with an example of the prophetic word formula, 'and the word of *Yhwh* was unto Elijah, saying…', or a variant of this basic formula. The first example appears in 17.2-6 in which *Yhwh* tells Elijah to move to the Wadi Cherith where he will be supported by the wadi and the ravens, and it happens as *Yhwh* says. The second example appears in 17.7-24, which presents *Yhwh*'s instruction to move to Zarephath in Phoenicia where Elijah will be supported by a widow. It happens that Elijah must first provide food for the widow and save her son's life, but in the end, the woman, herself a Phoenician like Jezebel, affirms Elijah as *Yhwh*'s prophet and the truth of *Yhwh*'s word. The third episode appears in 1 Kgs 18.1–19.8, in which *Yhwh* instructs Elijah to confront Ahab, Jezebel, and the prophets of Baal/Asherah at Mt Carmel. The confrontation is successful as implicitly promised, but Elijah's success forces his flight to Horeb, where he receives the final word of *Yhwh* in the sequence. This fourth word appears in the narrative in 19.9-21 in which *Yhwh* instructs Elijah to anoint Elisha as his disciple, Jehu as king of Israel, and Hazael as king of Aram. The fulfillment of these words is only partially complete in the present literary context with the designation of Elisha, but the narrative ultimately finds its realization in 2 Kings 2, when Elijah goes to heaven in the fiery chariot leaving Elisha as his successor, 2 Kgs 8.7-15 in which Elisha plays a role in Hazael's assassination of Ben-hadad, and 2 Kings 9–10 in which Elisha instigates Jehu's overthrow of the house of Omri.

Given the interest in *Yhwh*'s and Elijah's word throughout 1 Kgs 17.1–19.21, it is striking that 1 Kgs 16.34 is also concerned with *Yhwh*'s word. Indeed, the notice presents Hiel's killing of his sons in the re-establishment of Jericho as fulfillment of the word of *Yhwh* through Joshua ben Nun. Insofar as both 16.34 and 17.1–19.21 share an interest in the fulfillment of *Yhwh*'s word, it would seem to provide a further basis for a relationship between the two texts. When read immediately prior to chs. 17–19, 1 Kgs 16.34 provides the reader with an initial basis for the claim that *Yhwh*'s word through Elijah will also be true. Its affirmation of the credibility of *Yhwh*'s word through Joshua thereby serves as a premise for the following concern with the credibility of *Yhwh*'s word through Elijah. But in fact it does much more than that. It also points to the need for *Yhwh* and Elijah to act against the apostasy introduced into the land during the reign of Ahab and his wife, Jezebel. His marriage to the Phoenician princess illustrates the violation of a fundamental norm of Deuteronomy—which informs the theological underpinnings of the entire DH, the prohibition of Israel's intermarriage with the seven Canaanite nations, since such intermarriage will result in Israel's apostasy against *Yhwh* (see Deut. 7.1-6). That is precisely what happens during Ahab's reign as a result of his marriage to Jezebel.

In this respect, Hiel's rebuilding of Jericho at this time takes on particular significance. Jericho was the first major Canaanite city given by *Yhwh* to Israel. Indeed, Mt Nebo or Pisgah in Moab, from which Moses viewed the land of Israel immediately prior to his death and Israel's entry into the promised land, is described as 'opposite Jericho' (Deut. 34.1, 3). The fall of Jericho to Israel represented the first instance of *Yhwh*'s fulfillment of the terms of the covenant laid out between *Yhwh* and the ancestors of Israel, that is, *Yhwh* would grant Israel the land of Canaan provided that Israel accepted *Yhwh* as its only Deity and observed *Yhwh*'s statutes. The rebuilding of Jericho, particularly with the sacrifice of the two sons of Hiel, represents the reversal of that relationship. Going back to the site of Israel's initial presence in the land of Canaan/Israel, it represents the re-Canaanization of the land and potentially the imposition of the covenant curses of exile, famine, and so on, articulated in Deuteronomy. The subsequent chapters make it clear that the curse of famine is already underway. Elijah, as *Yhwh*'s representative, has the potential to bring the people back to *Yhwh* and therefore to end the famine that threatens their existence in the land. The contest on Mt Carmel illustrates that role. When read in relation to Ahab's regnal account, 1 Kgs 16.34 signals the apostasy and reversal of covenant in Israel that Elijah and *Yhwh* must take action to combat.

And yet the reference to Joshua's curse indicates that 1 Kgs 16.34 is not read only in relation to its context in the Ahab regnal account, but also in relationship to the larger DH as well. Although some have argued that the Wadi Cherith, where *Yhwh* directs Elijah to live in 17.2-6, must be identified with the Wadi Qelt or another major wadi in the vicinity of Jericho, the lack of any specific reference for the location of the Wadi Cherith leaves the question open.[9] The fact of the matter is that the Wadi Cherith might be identified with any major wadi along the Jordan Valley, from the Wadi Yarmouk just south of the Kinneret in the Trans-Jordan to the Wadi Kidron that flows from Jerusalem into the northern portion of the Dead Sea, or the Wadi Udheimi that flows from the Transjordan into the northeastern portion of the Dead Sea. It is only 16.34 and Elijah's journey to heaven from Jericho in 2 Kings 2 that prompts scholars to conclude that the Wadi Cherith must be located in the vicinity of Jericho. Instead, the specification of Jericho in 1 Kgs 16.34 seems to point forward in the larger DH, insofar as Jericho and Ahab's apostasy figure in relation to narratives beyond the Ahab regnal account.

The next reference to Jericho in the DH appears in 2 Kgs 2.1-18, the narrative in which Elijah ascends to heaven in a fiery chariot leaving Elisha as his successor. The city seems to be the location of a band of prophets, who are twice described as 'the sons of the prophets who were at Jericho', which might suggest that they were based in the city. Upon witnessing Elijah's departure, Elisha picks up Elijah's mantle, strikes the waters of the Jordan so that they part, and the sons of the prophets declare that the spirit of Elijah now rests on Elisha. Within the present narrative framework, Elijah's ascent into heaven and his replacement by Elisha represents an important step forward in the fulfillment of *Yhwh*'s words to Elijah at Horeb, that is, to anoint Elisha as his successor. With Elisha now firmly ensconced as Elijah's successor, the following two words are now able to be realized, namely, the anointing of Hazael to replace Ben-Hadad as king of Aram and the anointing of Jehu as king of Israel to replace the house of Omri. Elisha ultimately undertakes both of these acts in 2 Kgs 8.7-15 and 9.1-13. Jericho thus

---

9.   For an overview of issues and discussion pertaining to the Wadi Cherith, see Younker 1992.

plays an important role as the site at which the fulfillment of *Yhwh*'s words, and thus the resolution of the problems in Israel manifested in the reign of Ahab, begins. Perhaps the specification of Jericho as the site for the resolution is the work of the compilers of the Elijah–Elisha tradition. Certainly, many interpreters note a redactional effort to join the narrative in 1 Kings 17–19 to the Elisha tradition by means of 2 Kings 2.[10] Indeed, Elisha's cry at the sight of Elijah in the fiery chariot—'Father, father! The chariots of Israel and its horsemen!'—appears also in 2 Kgs 13.14, when King Joash of Israel cries out at the sight of Elisha on his deathbed—'My father, my father! The chariots of Israel and its horsemen!' The phrase is apparently a reference to the heavenly army that must have been conceived to have accompanied Elisha and to have been the source of his power. Only on occasion was it visible to human eyes (see 2 Kgs 6.17).

But the narrative in 2 Kgs 2.1-18 seems to have implications beyond the Elijah–Elisha tradition as well. When Joshua and the people of Israel cross the river Jordan opposite Jericho in Joshua 3, the waters of the Jordan also split to enable the priests bearing the ark of the covenant and the people to cross the river on dry land. Indeed, immediately following the celebration of Passover at Gilgal, Joshua had a vision of the commander of the army of *Yhwh* at Jericho in Josh. 5.13-15. From a diachronic standpoint, such parallels suggest a common tradition history associated with the site of Jericho. From a synchronic standpoint, they suggest a relationship between the two narratives. Just as Joshua's conquest of the land suggests its sanctification as the holy land of Israel, so Elisha's emergence as prophet of *Yhwh* at Jericho suggests the beginnings of the process by which the land of Israel is to be resanctified. If one reads only to 2 Kings 13 or 14, such a process would be complete, especially when the regnal account of Jeroboam ben Joash in 2 Kgs 14.23-29 announces that the Israelite king controlled a land that extended from Lebo-hamath in the north to the Sea of the Arabah in the south, which would be a land roughly equivalent to Solomon's empire. Whatever problems may have emerged during the reign of the Omrides are resolved by this point.

Of course readers of the entire DH know that this is not the case. Northern Israel ultimately succumbs to the Assyrian empire, because of the sins of Jeroboam ben Nebat according to 2 Kings 17, and Jerusalem and Judah ultimately succumb to the Babylonians. The reason for the destruction of Jerusalem is particularly instructive; it is because of the sins of Manasseh (2 Kgs 21.10-15; 23.26-27; 24.3-4). Although the DH justifies the destruction of northern Israel by declaring repeatedly that all of the northern Israelite kings are as wicked as Jeroboam ben Nebat, the destruction of Jerusalem is attributed to one king, Manasseh, and his sins are explicitly compared to those of Ahab in 2 Kgs 21.3; 'he made an Asherah as King Ahab of Israel had done'. The analogy does not end there. Manasseh's grandson, King Josiah of Judah, is commonly recognized as one of the most righteous kings of the Davidic line, but his righteousness is not able to save Jerusalem because *Yhwh*'s decree is already decided during the

---

10. E.g. Miller, White, Otto, and others cited above.

reign of Manasseh.[11] Consequently, the prophetess Huldah informs Josiah that there is nothing to be done to save Jerusalem, but, as a righteous king, he will be spared from witnessing the destruction by an early death in a time of peace (2 Kgs 22.14-20). Ironically, this is the same reprieve granted by Elijah to Ahab following Ahab's repentance for his role in the crimes against Naboth (1 Kgs 21.21-29). It is perhaps no accident that the house of David should be treated like the house of Omri. Following the marriage of Jehoram ben Jehoshaphat of Judah to Athaliah, the daughter of either Ahab or of Omri (2 Kgs 8.18, which describes her as 'the daughter of Ahab'; cf. 8.26, which describes her as 'the daughter of Omri'), all members of the house of David are also descended from the house of Omri. Insofar as Elijah calls for the destruction of the entire house of Omri (1 Kgs 21.20-24), such a prophecy has grave implications for the house of David. It would seem that Manasseh represents the beginning of an attempt to fulfil just such a condemnation.

Although we do not see the full destruction of the house of David by the end of the DH, it is noteworthy that the dynasty ends its formal rule of Judah when King Zedekiah flees Jerusalem for the plains of Jericho where his army deserted him and where he was captured by the Babylonians (2 Kgs 25.1-7, especially v. 5). The true king of Judah, Jehoiachin ben Jehoiakim, was still alive as an exile in Babylon, but he was ultimately released from prison by the Babylonian king, Evil-merodach, and allowed to eat at the king's table. Many take this as a sign that there was hope for the future of the house of David.[12] Unfortunately, we must note that Mephibosheth ben Jonathan ben Saul, the grandson of King Saul of Israel and heir to the dynasty, was also granted the right to eat at King David's table (2 Sam. 9.1-13; cf. 19.24-30). Eating at the king's table represents control by the host monarch; as it happens, it also effectively marked the end of the dynasty of Saul. It is left to the reader to draw conclusions concerning the implications of such an act for the house of David.

III

In conclusion, we must note that Jericho plays an important role at the beginning and end of the DH. That role has implications for understanding the role of 1 Kgs 16.34 in relation to the DH as a whole, the purported Elijah–Elisha cycle, and the regnal account of King Ahab of Israel. It would seem that 16.34 was written to play a role in the Elijah–Elisha cycle and that it therefore functions at the head of Ahab's regnal account to express the re-Canaanization of the land of Israel during the reign of Ahab. When read in the larger context of the DH, however, it seems to signal a grave problem that emerges during Ahab's reign, but that is not resolved even by the conclusion of the DH, namely, Elijah's curse against the house of Omri is ultimately to be realized against the last line of Omri's descendants, the house of David, as well.

11. For fuller discussion, see Sweeney 2001: 40-63.
12. E.g. von Rad 1953: 74-91; Wolff 1975.

APPENDIX

Formal Analysis
Regnal Account of Ahab ben Omri: 1 Kings 16.29–22.40

A. Introductory regnal account	16.29-33
1. Regnal information	16.29
2. Regnal evaluation: evil	16.30-33
B. Body of regnal account	16.34–22.38
1. *Yhwh*'s/Elijah's response to Baalist apostasy in Israel	16.34–19.21
a. initial premise: Hiel of Bethel's re-establishment of Jericho by	
sacrificing his sons	16.34
b. Elijah/*Yhwh* take action	17.1–19.21
1) Elijah's statement to Ahab: no rain except by my word (premise:	
need to establish credibility of Elijah's/*Yhwh*'s word)	17.1
2) *Yhwh*'s first word to Elijah: go to Wadi Cherith for support from	
creation (premise: *Yhwh* controls creation, Baal does not)	17.2-6
a) account of *Yhwh*'s word to Elijah: instruction to live in Wadi	
Cherith	17.2-4
b) account of Elijah's compliance with *Yhwh*'s instructions	17.5-6
3) *Yhwh*'s second word to Elijah: go to Zarephath for support from	
Phoenician widow (premise: *Yhwh* provides food and restores life,	
Baal does not)	17.7-24
a) circumstance: wadi runs dry	17.7
b) account of *Yhwh*'s second word to Elijah and compliance: Elijah	
supplies widow with food/she can support him	17.8-16
(1) account of *Yhwh*'s second word	17.8-9
(2) Elijah's compliance: account of Elijah's support of woman so	
that she can support him	17.10-16
c) account of Elijah's actions to heal widow's son	17.17-24
(1) narrative introduction: account of son's illness	17.17
(a) son's illness	17.17a
(b) severity of illness	17.17b
(2) widow's statement to Elijah: rhetorical question/appeal for	
help	17.18
(3) Elijah's response: acts to save son	17.19-21
(4) *Yhwh*'s response to Elijah's actions: saves boy	17.22
(5) Elijah returns boy to widow/mother	17.23
(6) Widow's/Mother's affirmation of Elijah/word of *Yhwh*	17.24
4) *Yhwh*'s third word to Elijah: confront Ahab, Jezebel, and prophets	
of Baal/Asherah (premise: *Yhwh* brings rain, Baal does not)	18.1–19.8
a) *Yhwh*'s instruction to Elijah to appear before Ahab	18.1-2
b) Ahab's instruction to Obadiah to search the land	18.3-6
c) Obadiah's encounter with Elijah	18.7-16
d) Elijah's encounter with Ahab: confrontation with prophets of	
Baal/Asherah at Carmel	18.17-46
e) Elijah's flight from Jezebel	19.1-8
5) *Yhwh*'s fourth word to Elijah: appoint Elisha; anoint Hazael and	
Jehu (premise: *Yhwh* will defeat supporters of Baal)	19.9-21
a) *Yhwh*'s word to Elijah: Elijah's vision of *Yhwh*	19.9-18
b) Elijah's compliance with *Yhwh*'s instructions: designation of	
Elisha ben Shaphat as his successor	19.19-21

BIBLIOGRAPHY

Beck, M.
    1999   *Elia und die Monalatrie* (BZAW, 281; Berlin: W. de Gruyter).
Cogan, M.
    2000   *1 Kings* (AB, 10; New York: Doubleday).
Cross, F.M., Jr
    1973   'The Themes of the Books of Kings and the Structure of the Deuteronomistic
           History', in *idem*, *Canaanite Myth and Hebrew Epic* (Cambridge, MA: Har-
           vard University Press): 274-89.
De Vries, S.
    1985   *1 Kings* (WBC, 12; Waco, TX: Word Books).
Fohrer, G.
    1968   *Elia* (ATANT, 53; Zürich: Zwingli Verlag).
Fritz, V.
    1996   *Das erste Buch der Könige* (ZBKAT, 10.1; Zürich: Theologischer Verlag).
Gray, J.
    1970   *I and II Kings: A Commentary* (OTL; Philadelphia: Westminster Press).
Hauser, A.J.
    1990   '*Yhwh* versus Death—The Real Struggle in 1 Kings 17–19', in A.J. Hauser and
           R. Gregory (eds.), *From Carmel to Horeb: Elijah in Crisis* (JSOTSup, 85; Bible
           and Literature Series, 19; Sheffield: JSOT Press): 9-89.
Hentschel, G.
    1977   *Die Elijaerzählungen* (Erfurter Theologische Studien, 33; Leipzig: St Benno
           Verlag).
Long, B.O.
    1984   *1 Kings, with an Introduction to Historical Literature* (FOTL, 9; Grand Rapids:
           Eerdmans).
McKenzie, S.L.
    1991   *The Trouble with Kings: The Composition of the Books of Kings in the Deuter-
           onomistic History* (VTSup, 42; Leiden: E.J. Brill).
Miller, J.M.
    1966   'The Elisha Cycle and the Accounts of the Omride Wars', *JBL* 85: 441-54.
    1967   'The Fall of the House of Ahab', *VT* 17: 307-24.
Montgomery, J.A., and H.S. Gehman
    1951   *The Books of Kings* (ICC; Edinburgh: T. & T. Clark).
Otto, S.
    2001   *Jehu, Elia und Elisa. Die Erzählung von der Jehu-Revolution und die Kompo-
           sition der Elia-Elisa-Erzählungen* (BWANT, 152; Stuttgart: Kohlhammer).
Rad, G. von
    1953   *Studies in Deuteronomy* (SBT, 9; London: SCM Press).

Sweeney, M.A.

2001 *King Josiah of Judah: The Lost Messiah of Israel* (New York and Oxford: Oxford University Press).

Steck, O.H.

1968 *Überlieferung und Zeitgeschichte in den Elia-Erzählungen* (WMANT, 26; Neukirchen–Vluyn: Neukirchener Verlag).

Walsh, J.T.

1996 *1 Kings* (Berit Olam; Collegeville: Liturgical Press).

White, M.C.

1997 *The Elijah Legends and Jehu's Coup* (BJS, 311; Atlanta: Scholars Press).

Wolff, H.W.

1975 'The Kerygma of the Deuteronomistic Historical Work', in W. Brueggemann and H.W. Wolff (eds.), *The Vitality of the Old Testament Traditions* (Atlanta: John Knox Press): 83-100.

Würthwein, E.

1977 *Die Bücher der Könige*. I. *Könige 1–16* (ATD 11, 1; 2 vols.; Göttingen: Vandenhoeck & Ruprecht).

Younker, R.W.

1992 'Cherith, Brook of', in *ABD*, I: 899.

Part III

IN THE LATTER PROPHETS

Harvesting the Vineyard: The Development of Vineyard Imagery in the Hebrew Bible

Howard N. Wallace

Vineyards, grapevines and wine have always been part of both the talk about faith and the imagery of faith within the Judeo-Christian traditions. In the Christian faith wine has been one of the central symbols in its ritual activity. This essay will explore the imagery of vineyards, grapevines and wine to see how it has been used and developed in the language of faith over time. I dedicate this essay to my esteemed colleague Tony Campbell for at least two reasons. First, the study arises out of work with ministers and lay people trying to maintain the witness of the faith in what seems at times 'a barren land'. One focus of Tony's own work has been on the way scholarly biblical studies intersect with faith as it is lived within the community. Secondly, and somewhat frivolously, maybe Tony, whose preference is for drinking whiskey, can be persuaded to follow a more biblically based lifestyle and become a wine buff.

1. *Brief References*

The mention of vineyards, grapevines and wine is prolific in the Bible, and used in all types of literature. On many occasions the imagery is used to speak about the relationship between *Yhwh* and Israel. This happens in many brief references to the images of vineyard, grapevine and wine by way of proverb, saying, metaphor, simile and so on. There is also a small number of texts which develop the imagery at length. My focus will be on the latter, the many different connections between these texts, and the way the imagery develops over time. Before that, however, it will be helpful to glance at the way the imagery is used in the briefer references.

First, the image of the (grape)vine is used to represent the people or nations of Judah and/or Israel, often with negative overtones.[1] This is particularly the case in the prophets. For example, in Jer. 2.21 the people of Jerusalem are described as a choice vine planted by *Yhwh* (cf. Hos. 9.10; 10.1), which degenerates into 'wayward (shoots) of a foreign vine'. While the language is different, the passage is reminiscent of Isa. 5.1-7, although there the image is of a vineyard not just a vine. I will consider this passage in greater detail below. It is the growth of the

---

1.   In shorter references, it is rare to find the vineyard used to represent Israel. Jer. 12.10 is one possible exception.

vine that is the focus in Jer. 2.21. In other instances of the use of the vine as an image for the people of Judah it is the fruitfulness of the vine that is central. This is so in Jer. 8.13 where the lack of grapes on the vine represents the wickedness of the people. Hosea 10.1 also focuses on the fruitfulness of the vine but there the fruit is not the works of the people but the blessings on the nation which become a snare for them. The multi-layered function of the vine in metaphor is already apparent, although it is only the processes of natural growth which are the focus in these examples. This aspect of the metaphor is apparently quite ancient being employed in Deut. 32.32-33: 'For their vine comes from the stock of Sodom, and from the vineyards of Gomorrah; their grapes are poisonous, their clusters are bitter; their wine is the poison of serpents, the strong venom of vipers'.[2] The full extent of the metaphor is employed in this example, from vine to grapes to wine; although, with a possible allusion to the production of sour or bitter fruit, it is mixed with another metaphor in which poisonous drink is used to describe a deadly end.[3] In this case, the metaphor is associated with sinfulness by reference to Sodom and Gomorrah. That which is the image of something life-giving and sweet can also be used to allude to something sinful and ultimately deadly.[4]

The image of the vine is not only used for the people or nation as a whole. It is also employed in relation to kings in Israel and Judah. Judges 9.13 speaks by way of a parable of trees and vine of the possibility of establishing kingship in Israel. While there is an anti-monarchical sentiment behind the parable, it is the image of the vine as a source of life and joy that is employed. The vine is also mentioned as an important part of the agricultural bounty of the promised land (e.g. Deut. 8.7). As such, vineyards, grapevines and wine come to be used as a major set of images for abundance, peace and blessing in the land, especially in the expression of sitting under one's own vine (e.g. see Deut. 7.13 and especially 1 Kgs 4.25; Isa. 25.6; 36.16 = 2 Kgs 18.31; Mic. 4.4; Zech. 3.10; 8.12; and 1 Macc. 14.12). This same set of images is also employed negatively to portray the destruction of the land (e.g. Isa. 7.23). Finally, in Jer. 5.17 there is reference to the element of human labour in viticulture, where the overtaking of the vineyard by briers and thorns, a familiar image from Isaiah 5, is due to the lack of human care.

With this picture in mind, I will now turn to the more detailed portrayals of the images of vineyard, grapevine and wine.

2. Isaiah 5.1-7

The 'song of the vineyard' in Isa. 5.1-7 is central to any treatment of the biblical imagery of vineyards, grapevines and wine. The tradition of which it is an exemplar is foundational for many other passages employing the imagery. In some cases the Isaiah text itself is arguably influential in the formulation of other texts.

2. On the antiquity of Deut. 32, see, for example, Robertson 1972 and Albright 1959.
3. See, e.g., Isa. 51.17-22; Jer. 25.15-16; Ezek. 23.31-34 etc.
4. For a treatment of the concept of Israel as the vineyard of the Lord in Rabbinic Judaism see Petuchowski 1981.

Isaiah 5.1-7 is a well crafted, complex passage. There has been a great deal of debate over the genre of the passage. Suggestions have included a song, a love song, a drinking song, a satirical polemic against fertility cults, a lawsuit, a fable, an allegory and a parable.[5] The imagery of vineyard and wine production is central to the passage. However, the passage begins (v. 1a) with words of love and song suggesting another context, within which love is celebrated. The joyous celebration at the harvest festival has been put forward as a possible context in which many of these elements are brought together (Matthews 1999: 24). Within two verses of the start of the passage the scene has changed to that of judicial proceedings (vv. 3-6). Consequently, some scholars have suggested quite rightly that more than one genre is involved. Yee (1981) sees the passage as a 'song' about covenantal infidelity combined with a juridical parable.[6] This shift in context, and the change of the singer of the song from singer/prophet (vv. 1-2) to vineyard owner (vv. 3-6) only revealed as *Yhwh* in v. 6, back to prophet (v. 7), all serve to keep the reader/hearer constantly reassessing their interpretation of the passage.[7] Even in v. 7, where the prophet explains the imagery for the reader/hearer, further meaning can be gleaned by comparing the interpretation with the image itself as we will see below.

Both the natural and the human processes involved in viticulture are employed in the 'song of the vineyard'. The human role of preparing the vineyard, planting it, maintaining and securing it and preparing for harvest (v. 3) is given in more detail than in any other reference to viticulture. This detail is extended in a negative way in vv. 5-6 when judgment is outlined. The detail serves both to emphasize the effort expended by the vineyard owner on his property, a thought reiterated in the question of what more could have been done (v. 4), and to slow the story down, implying a lengthy wait by the owner. In the normal course of events it would have been some years before the vineyard was mature and ready to produce.[8] This human role is what is related to *Yhwh*'s role with Israel. The portrayal of the vineyard owner as an unspecified 'beloved' in the first part of the passage maintains anonymity.[9] The owner could be any ordinary landowner. This is only broken in v. 6b where the ability of the owner to command the clouds to withhold their rain clearly elevates his identity beyond the human. The delay in the identification of the owner, coupled with the detail given of the efforts the owner puts into his vineyard, serves to generate a deeper understanding in the reader of *Yhwh*'s concern for Israel when the meaning of the story is finally revealed. In contrast to the human role played in the vineyard, which in this case represents divine activity with Israel, the natural processes of growth in the vine

5. As well as the standard commentaries, see particularly Willis 1977 and Korpel 1988.

6. Cf. also Clements (1980: 55) who sees the passage as a parable with some allegory.

7. See Williams (1985: 463), who argues that the passage is constructed so that the reader constantly has expectations that are proven false and is frustrated in the interpretative process.

8. Matthews (1999: 24) suggests four to five years referring to Lev. 19.24-25, although it should be noted that this text is related to when Israel first enters the land.

9. Although Blenkinsopp (2000: 207) argues that the words 'beloved' in v. 1 (ידי and דודי) both occur in theophoric elements in biblical names and could suggest to an ancient audience that *Yhwh* is to be understood as the 'beloved' in that verse.

and fruit production are given short measure. Whereas the vineyard owner's activities are described in detail, a mere two words in Hebrew (ויעש באשים, 'it produced stinking things') are used to describe the result in v. 2b. They are repeated for emphasis in v. 4b. In spite of having fulfilled his part, the owner had no control over the fruit produced by the vineyard. The latter was clearly the cause of the problem.

The interpretation of the passage in v. 7, with the shift to justice, righteousness and so on, might seem to have little direct connection to the imagery of the vineyard, but that is not the case. The repetition of the verb קוה ('to wait, hope') in vv. 2, 4 and 7 ties the interpretation into the earlier description of the vineyard owner's activity. *Yhwh*'s waiting for justice is comparable to the owner's waiting for the vineyard to produce grapes. But further, I noted above that in some instances the lack of fruitfulness of the vine represents Israel's wickedness (Deut. 32.32; Hos. 10.1; Jer. 8.13). Here the 'stinking things' produced are defined clearly as injustice and unrighteousness. Israel has acted contrary to the expectations and intentions of *Yhwh*. The woe oracles collected later in Isaiah 5 include further references to wine (e.g. vv. 11-13, 22) but in the context of drunken revelry. These woe oracles have the effect of interpreting and defining the nature of the sin in v. 7. Just as the covenant with *Yhwh* has been broken and undone, so the imagery of wine with its joyous associations at the start of Isaiah 5 is also 'undone' with descriptions of the destructive side of wine in the community and its association with injustice. *Yhwh* now responds with punishment in terms of undoing all the careful work undertaken earlier (vv. 5-6).[10] The final act, withholding of rain in v. 6b, echoes covenant curses (Lev. 26.19-20; Deut. 28.24; cf. 1 Kgs 8.35). Viticulture in Israel and Judah, like other agricultural activities, was dependent on rain rather than irrigation (cf. Deut. 11.10-12), and hence on the gift of the *Yhwh*. The people had proved unfaithful, negating the faithful and hopeful acts of *Yhwh*. The long process of preparation of the vineyard and expectation of its fruitfulness by the owner/beloved underlines and justifies both faith in and a faithful response to *Yhwh*.[11] The owner not only prepares the ground for the vineyard, but has throughout the long period of waiting guarded the vineyard from being overrun by thieves and wild animals (cf. Isa. 7.23-25), kept weeds from destroying it from within and given it every opportunity to become fruitful.

3. *Developments within Isaiah*

a. *Isaiah 27.2-6*
It has long been recognized that Isa. 27.2-6 constitutes a post-exilic development of the song in Isa. 5.1-7. In concert with other material in the so-called Isaiah Apocalypse (chs. 24–27), 27.2-6 reinterprets earlier prophecy, even that in the Isaiah tradition, and in the process reverses what the earlier text said (cf. Sweeney 1987: 51-52; Clements 1980: 219). Blenkinsopp (2000: 374-75) concludes that

---

10. Note the interpretation of Carroll 1999. Also cf. Matthews 1999: 25.
11. This is the wider theme of Isa. 5–12 in relation to the Assyrian crisis (cf. Isa. 7.9b).

'In any case, 27.2-5, read as a radical revision or eschatological abrogation of 5.1-7, presents a theologically interesting case within the Isaian tradition'.

There are a number of problems associated with Isa. 27.2-6. The first is textual. There are several differences between the MT and the LXX, especially in vv. 3b-4.[12] The second problem is contextual, relating to the coherence of the units in Isaiah 27.[13] The connection between v. 6 and vv. 2-5 has been questioned, especially by Wildberger (1997: 583),[14] although with many others I believe that v. 6 functions as a conclusion to the preceding verses. In spite of the textual and contextual difficulties associated with Isa. 27.2-6, a number of aspects of Isa. 5.1-7 are echoed in the later text: the reference to singing and love-song in 5.1 and the command to sing in 27.2; the fertile location of the vineyard in 5.1 and the pleasantness of it in 27.2; and the suggestion of protection in the watchtower in 5.2 and *Yhwh*'s guarding the vineyard in 27.3.[15] However, none of these involve exact verbal correspondence. The only terminology shared by the two passages is in reference to 'thorns and briers' (5.6 and 27.4), a phrase exclusive to Isaiah (cf. 7.23-25; 9.17; 10.17). In addition, it is important to note that other passages earlier in Isaiah have also been suggested as influential on 27.2-6, namely Isaiah 1.17 and 1.24.[16]

The reflection of Isa. 5.1-7 in 27.2-6 has one other aspect to it. I noted how the 'song of the vineyard' in Isaiah 5 changed speakers as it progressed, from a singer (vv. 1-2), to the owner/*Yhwh* (vv. 3-6), back to the prophet in the interpretation of the parable (v. 7). A similar shift occurs in 27.2-6. It begins with a statement by the prophet or other individual calling a group of males to sing about a vineyard, referred to somewhat unusually by feminine singular pronouns (לה). In vv. 3-5, *Yhwh* speaks in the first person about his relationship with the vineyard, still referred to in the feminine singular. In v. 6, it is not clear if *Yhwh* is still speaking or the prophet has returned. In any case, the text now speaks about Jacob/Israel in the third person as the writer applies the previous account to Israel. If Isa. 5.1-7 can be classified in genre as a parable, albeit with other elements, then the writer of 27.2-6 is treating the earlier passage allegorically, employing the old text to speak to the new post-exilic situation (also Childs 2001: 197). In the development of the imagery, the general intent of 5.1-7 is reversed. No longer is the image of the vineyard used to speak of judgment, but it is now used to suggest a possible state of peace with *Yhwh*, if the people are willing to embrace that.[17] Not only is the meaning reversed but many of the familiar

12. See the standard commentaries for suggested emendations and translations.

13. Sweeney (1987) argues fairly convincingly for reading the chapter as a whole, while Leene (2000) argues that vv. 7-9 act as a transition in the chapter between material on the vineyard and that with the city as the subject.

14. A break in the text is also suggested by a space left by the scribe after v. 5 in 1QIsa[a] (Blenkinsopp 2000: 375).

15. See also Wildberger (1997: 583) for other points of comparability.

16. Sweeney 1987: 55-56 and Leene 2000: 216-17.

17. This eschatological hope is not without an element of judgment. Apart from the reference to *Yhwh* burning any thorns and briers produced (v. 4), the rest of the chapter introduces a note of judgment if it is taken as a whole (Sweeney 1987).

elements are reversed. Now *Yhwh* constantly waters the vineyard (27.3) and has no anger against it (v. 4). If thorns and briers are produced, it is no longer *Yhwh* who allows them to come in from outside (cf. 5.6) but they are generated within the vineyard (27.4). While the watchtower was provided for the vineyard in 5.2, now *Yhwh* is its constant guardian. Nothing will harm the vineyard now from outside, potential danger can only lie within. The call for making peace with *Yhwh* fits in here. In 5.7, *Yhwh* expected justice and righteousness from Israel/ Judah. From the rest of Isaiah 5, these values were defined in social terms, justice for the disadvantaged, and so on. In Isa. 27.5 the call is for peace with *Yhwh*. While this could be understood in terms of social justice and righteousness, the fact that the 'thorns and briers' come from within suggests that the peace referred to is essentially an inner peace with *Yhwh*. Finally, whereas the vineyard produced only 'stinking things' in 5.2 and 4, now the whole world is full of the fruit of *Yhwh*'s vineyard.

The image of the vineyard from Isaiah 5 has been maintained in 27.2-6. A different vocabulary is used for the most part but there are enough similarities to know that the later passage is a development of the older word associated with Isaiah of Jerusalem. In the process of re-appropriation, the imagery has been reversed and the interpretation no longer deals with the issue of injustice in the nation. Faith is now a matter of internal piety and obedience in the faithful community of post-exilic Jerusalem (Sweeney 1987: 58).

b. *Isaiah 63.1-6*

An important issue in the interpretation of a number of passages in so-called Third Isaiah is attention to references or allusions to other texts, especially those in Isaiah (Childs 2001: 515). In the case of 63.1-6, there is a connection with Isa. 59.15b-20 and possibly 51.9-11 and 10.6. The image of the divine warrior in 63.3-6 has received most attention. By way of contrast, the imagery of the wine-press and the treading of grapes has all but been passed over.[18] In my opinion, a possible connection to Isa. 5.1-7 should not be overlooked. The reference to the winepress is not just a passing metaphor, lost as the activities of the divine warrior come into sharper focus.

The vocabulary of viticulture permeates the passage and there are several commonalities with Isaiah 5. First, there is the reference to the winepress itself (פורה) in 63.3. The term is used only here and in Hag. 2.16. יקב is found in Isa. 5.2 and is often translated as 'wine vat'. However, יקב can also mean winepress (Job 24.11; Isa. 16.10; Jer. 48.33) and the same verb (דרך) is used with both nouns for the act of 'treading' the grapes. The mention of Edom in Isa. 63.1 sets up an alliteration with the word 'red' (אדום) in v. 2, which is associated with the red juice stain from the press. Similarly, mention of Bozrah recalls the verb בצר meaning 'to cut off' but also used of grape gathering (e.g. Lev. 25.5; Deut. 24.21). In Isa. 63.1, the one coming speaks in 'righteousness' (צדקה, often translated 'vindication'), which is one of the qualities sought by the *Yhwh* in Isa. 5.7.

---

18. A few commentators have mentioned it in passing and referred briefly to Isa. 5, and so on. These include Miscall (1993: 141) and Conrad (1991: 106).

The use of רמס ('to trample') in 63.3 (used in parallel to דרך, mentioned above) recalls its use in 5.5 where wild animals and passers by are allowed to trample the unproductive vineyard, while the verb שׁכר ('to become drunk') used in 63.6 recalls שׁכר ('strong drink') in 5.11 and 22 (both times parallel to יין, 'wine').

The allusions are strong enough to think that a reading of Isa. 63.1-6 would raise thoughts of Isaiah 5. In the earlier chapter the vineyard owner never had the pleasure of the joyful harvest and treading of the grapes which he anticipated. Rather, in his response he let others trample his vineyard to ruins. In 63.1-6, *Yhwh* takes revenge on the enemies of his people. This later passage could be read as the resolution of the vineyard imagery in Isaiah. The vineyard owner does complete his work, although the grapes he now treads are not those he initially intended to tread. In a further twist of the interpretation of the earlier song, *Yhwh* now treads those who have been allowed at various times to trample his own people. In similar fashion to the resolution of the problem created when *Yhwh* used the Assyrians to punish his own people (Isa. 5.26-30; 10.5-27a), now *Yhwh* brings to account those who carried out his judgment on his own people. It is not without notice that the verb רמס ('to trample') was also used in relation to *Yhwh*'s punishment of the Assyrians (10.6).

4. *Further Biblical Developments*

Several other passages are worth brief consideration. The first is Psalm 80. This community lament is divided into three uneven sections by a repeated refrain in vv. 4, 8, 20 (Eng. vv. 3, 7, 19).[19] The last section, vv. 9-19 (Eng. vv 8-18) tells the story of Israel's past experience with *Yhwh* in terms of a parable of a vine. The provenance of this psalm and the historical event behind it have long been debated. Some have suggested it comes from the old northern kingdom, others that it belongs to Judah and Jerusalem at the time of Josiah and Jeremiah and others that it is a composite psalm with pre- and post-exilic elements.[20] A more convincing tradition-history approach has been argued by Nasuti (1988: 97-102). He recognizes a number of references within the psalm and linguistic elements which connect it to other Asaphite psalms and what he calls an Ephraimite tradition. These include the reference to Joseph (v. 2 [Eng. v. 1]), the tribal names Ephraim, Benjamin and Manasseh (v. 3 [Eng. v. 2]) and also aspects of the vine image with its connections to Hosea and Jeremiah. However, he also notes two aspects of the Psalm which link it with a southern tradition, namely the reference to Benjamin in v. 3 (Eng. v. 2) and the shift in the image of the vine in v. 13 (Eng. v. 12). There is a shift from the vine to the vineyard and its walls. The language used to describe the destruction of the vineyard is similar to that used in Isa. 5.5.[21] Tate strengthens some aspects of Nasuti's argument with further connections

19. Although it should be noted that the title for God changes each time the refrain is repeated.

20. For summaries of the various proposals see, among others, Tate (1990: 309-12) and Kraus (1989: 139-41).

21. W. Beyerlin argues that the vine metaphor was the latest stratum of the psalm. Cited in Tate 1990: 311.

between Psalm 80 and the Jeremiah traditions, but concludes that the connection of Psalm 80 to the Ephraimite tradition does not help a lot in the end as this tradition, even in Nasuti's argument, 'was at home geographically both in the North and South and historically both in pre-exilic and post-exilic Israel' (Tate 1990: 311).

While in the end this discussion may not help with questions of the provenance and dating of Psalm 80, it is suggestive with regard to the vine and vineyard imagery. It would seem that in Psalm 80 two different images, which are nonetheless related by virtue of their subject matter, are brought together. Moreover, two facts support the suggestion that Ps. 80.13 (Eng. v. 12) and Isa. 5.1-7 reflect a common tradition. First, the psalm and Isa. 5.5 use similar language to describe the breaking down of the walls of the vineyard.[22] Secondly, in the section on the vine in the psalm, *Yhwh* is addressed in the second person as the one who brought the vine out of Egypt (vv. 9-10 [Eng. vv. 8-9]) and as the one who can deliver (vv. 15-16, 18-19 [Eng. vv. 14-15, 17-18]), while the trouble faced by the people is caused by a third party (vv. 14, 17 [Eng. vv. 13, 16]). However, in v. 13 (Eng. v. 12) it is *Yhwh* who has acted against his people. This matches the earlier statements of the psalm (vv. 5-7 [Eng. vv. 4-6]) where *Yhwh* was angry with his people and put them at the mercy of their enemies. In both these matters, Ps. 80.13 (Eng. v. 12) and Isa. 5.1-7 are in agreement. The Isaiah connection would suggest that this common vineyard imagery, as opposed to the vine imagery, is a southern tradition.

The way that the two traditions have been brought together makes no provision for confession on the part of the vine/people. No mention is made of any faithlessness on their part in the past as is the case in Isaiah 5. On the other hand, there is no implication that *Yhwh*'s action is unjust, and the pledge of faithfulness in the future (v. 19 [Eng. v. 18]) together with the possible allusion to a fuller vineyard tradition (and even Isa. 5?) in v. 13 (Eng. v. 12) could suggest that the people have been faithless.[23] In any case, the emphasis in the psalm is on *Yhwh* as the only one whose 'turning' or 'repentance' will save the people (v. 15 [Eng. v. 14]). A similar point is made to that in Isa. 27.2-6. Finally, if Isa. 5.5 lies behind Ps. 80.13 (Eng. v. 12), then the parable told in Isaiah is interpreted allegorically in the psalm, assuming that some destruction of Jerusalem is referred to, such as occurred in 587 BCE.

Two other passages require brief comment. They are Ezek. 15.2-8 and 19.10-14. Both develop the image of the vine in a new way. In the former, a parable is told about a vine. It expounds the worthless nature of the wood of the vine, except as fuel for a fire (15.4). This is the vine's uniqueness among the trees. Consistent with the tradition of the vine imagery noted in the brief references above, the focus here is solely on the vine. What is unique about the parable is that it speaks not about the vine's lack of fruitfulness or grandeur, which brings condemnation,

---

22. Both verses use a form of the expression פָּרַץ גָּדֵר ('to break down a wall'). Here I propose a slightly stronger connection than Nasuti (1988: 99).

23. Cf. Mays 1994: 263-64.

but its inherent worthlessness.[24] The application of the parable in vv. 6-8 is alle-gorical in nature and focuses only on the destruction of the vine signifying the destruction of Jerusalem. Ezekiel 19.10-14 presents another hybrid use of the vine imagery. In the latter half of a lament over the 'princes of Israel' (the kings of Judah in the context of Ezekiel), the image of the vine is applied to the 'mother' of the princes (19.10), that is, Jerusalem or Judah. Notions of a favour-able planting are combined with a notion of pride or even hubris associated elsewhere with the parable of the great tree (cf. 17.3-10; 31.2-9).

5. Beyond the Hebrew Bible

The influence of the Isaiah 5 version of the vineyard tradition on New Testament passages has been a matter of comment and debate. Its influence has been espe-cially noted in the parable of the wicked tenants (Mt. 21.33-46//Mk 12.1-12//Lk. 20.9-19) and in Jn 15.1-11. In the case of the parable in the Synoptic Gospels, it is the account in the Gospels of Matthew and Mark that is of most interest. Each of the three accounts begins with the statement that a man (householder) planted a vineyard. Before reference to his letting it out to tenants, Matthew and Mark both give detail on his preparation of the vineyard, namely that he set a hedge around it, dug a wine press and built a tower (Mt. 21.33//Mk 12.1). The detail of the preparation clearly reminds the reader of Isa. 5.1-7. The question that has been debated is whether the Gospel account, especially Mark, has been influ-enced by the MT or the LXX of Isaiah 5.

At this point we should note that the translators of the LXX made several changes to MT Isaiah 5 in their work. Of the changes made, those relevant for our study are the following. First, while the speaker in the MT changes several times throughout the text, the LXX translators have framed the entire parable as a first-person speech. Secondly, in v. 2 the LXX omits the words ויעזקהו ויסקלהו ('he dug it and cleared it of stones') but adds καὶ φραγμὸν περιέθηκα καὶ ἐχαράκωσα ('and I surrounded it with a hedge and staked it'). This could imply that the vineyard owner does not have to start work from scratch, but that land already prepared to some degree is involved.[25] In addition, the Hebrew word יקב ('wine-press/wine vat') in v. 2 is translated by προλήνιον ('vat'). The usual translation is by ληνός ('winepress').

In Mt. 21.33//Mk 12.1, where the detail of preparation of the vineyard is given, it is clear that LXX Isa. 5.2 is influential. The Gospels omit reference to dig-ging the land and clearing it of stones, which we find in MT Isa. 5.2, but include the statements καὶ φραγμὸν αὐτῷ περιέθηκεν (Mt. 21.33) and καὶ περιέθηκεν φραγμὸν (Mk 12.1), which are similar to the additional clause in LXX. On the

24. Cf. Greenberg (1983: 269), who notes what the writer could have developed at this point in the context of the book of Ezekiel.

25. Kloppenborg Verbin (2002: 143-53) details most of the changes and argues that in these there is a shift from the individual vine to the vineyard as a whole, which I do not think is a strong point, and that the change in preparation of the vineyard together with some terminology changes suggests the influence of agricultural practices from Hellenistic Egypt.

other hand, the Gospels use the third person rather than the first person as in the LXX. Further, Matthew renders the LXX προλήνιον by ληνὸν, while Mark has ὑπολήνιον. It seems likely that while the LXX of Isaiah 5 has influenced the versions of the parable in Matthew and Mark, it is not necessarily an exclusive relationship.[26] This influence may not have been the only one on Mt. 21.33-46// Mk 12.1-12//Lk. 20.9-19. Evans argues that the Targumic traditions of Isa. 5.1-7 connect the passage with the temple's destruction. This could well be influential in the placement of the parable in Mark between chapters dealing with the temple, and the quotation from Ps. 118.22-23 in Mt. 21.42//Mk 12.10//Lk. 20.17 (Evans 1984).

While the translators of the LXX of Isa. 5.1-7 have made several changes to the MT in their work, I do not believe they have made major changes to the vineyard imagery in the process, nor, if the above argument is accepted, have their changes greatly influenced the development of the imagery in the Synoptic parable. The majority of developments in the parable do not come via the LXX. As I have already noted, the Synoptic parable is similar to LXX Isaiah 5 at the start with the details of the vineyard owner's activity. The vineyard and the owner are the same (i.e. Israel and *Yhwh* respectively) as in Isaiah 5. While the owner does not do quite the same in the preparation of the vineyard as in MT Isa. 5.2, he nevertheless does all that is required. The difference in the Synoptic parable is in the leasing of the vineyard to tenants. The parable turns into a history of Israel with its prophets and messengers from God, and in this sense echoes Isa. 5.1-7. In the preparation by the owner, and in the freedom of both the vineyard itself and the tenants in their management and care, the parts played by God and Israel in that history are summarized. The parable then takes a turn, for unlike Isaiah 5 the Synoptic parable is not about the vineyard itself, which we can presume is fruitful. In Mark and Luke it is about the tenants, that is, the leaders of Israel, although in Mt. 21.43 the writer redresses this somewhat by including an application of the parable to the Kingdom of God, which is understood there really as a matter of election. The writer of Matthew maintains to some degree the spirit of the Isaian parable, wherein the people have not produced suitable fruit.

Finally, a brief word about Jn 15.1-11. The development in this passage is more dramatic. The vine and vineyard imagery come together as the writer develops a theology of the relationship between Jesus, the Father and Jesus' disciples. Jesus is now the 'true vine' (v. 1). God, the Father, is still the vine-grower. In contrast to the Synoptic parable discussed above, the 'son' is now the vine, and not just one of the messengers, albeit the most important one. The Father is pictured as the carer of the vine, pruning, removing useless wood, and so on (v. 2).

---

26. Contra Kloppenborg Verbin 2002: 154. He argues (pp. 156-57) against Aus (1996: 4-6 n. 4), who questions that Mark depends on the LXX, but while not all of Aus's arguments are convincing, neither are Kloppenborg Verbin's rebuttals, especially that to do with the third person in Mk 12.1 and the use of ὑπολήνιον. In the former, Kloppenborg Verbin cannot use the changes in person in MT Isa. 5.1-7 compared to the uniformity of Mk 12.1-9 to argue for LXX influence. In the latter, he cannot simply argue that Aus does not show dependence on the MT as support for LXX dependency, which is what in effect he does.

There is a strong emphasis on Jesus as the source of life for the people who are represented by the branches of the vine. In this sense the John passage picks up on Ps. 80.8-19 (Eng. vv. 7-18). The branches depend on the vine, and when they abide in him they are fruitful. They can do nothing apart from him (v. 5). Verse 6 reminds the reader of Ezekiel 15 and the uselessness of the vine wood (cf. also Jer. 5.10). A strong tie is developed between the Father (the vineyard owner), Jesus (who as the vine gives life to the branches) and the people (the branches themselves). The source of life now moves in that direction. In contrast to Isaiah 5, the owner does not just expect the vineyard to yield fruit, but life and fruit-fulness flow from the Father through to the branches via Jesus. But, while Jesus replaces the vineyard as Israel (as in Isa. 5.7), in the Gospel of John Jesus is also a symbol of the new Israel (cf. 1.47).[27]

While there are some connections to the Old Testament imagery here, there are new developments in John 15. The vine-grower is no longer the main actor. The fruitfulness of the vineyard is directly dependent on Jesus, the vine. More-over, the imagery of bearing fruit is changed. No longer directly referred to as justice, and so forth, bearing fruit is understood as giving glory to God in the course of discipleship of Jesus (v. 8).

6. *Conclusion*

It is little wonder that vineyards, grapevines and wine figure strongly in the imagery of the Hebrew Bible. These things were both commonplace in ancient Israelite life, as well as items valued for both their sustenance of life and the wonderful delights they brought to community and family life.[28] They were part of the God-given cycle of agricultural life in the land at the same time as being the product of human toil and care. In these many aspects, and in the interplay between them, vineyards, grapevines and wine were employed in literary images for the health and wellbeing of the people, or the lack thereof. In briefer refer-ences the vine and its fruitfulness proved useful to represent the people or monarch. In more lengthy texts the intricate relationships and processes in the domain of the vineyard, both human and natural, were explored.

From this discussion of the parables and other texts concerned with vineyards and vines, some further points may be gleaned. First, there is a consistent image of God as the vine-grower/vineyard owner in most of these texts. As such, God is involved in the care of the vineyard/vine and has plans and hopes for it. At the same time God is also subject to the vicissitudes of the vineyard/vine, finding his hopes thwarted (e.g. Isa. 5). Secondly, there appear to be two streams of tradition in the imagery associated with viticulture in the Hebrew Bible, one focusing on the vine with possible connections to the briefer references noted at the begin-ning, the other concerned with the vineyard. The latter could be a southern tradi-tion. It is exemplified by Isaiah 5 or some tradition very close to it and developed within the Isaiah traditions. This development allows for either a radical reversal

27. See further Brown 1966: 669-72.
28. See Matthews 1999 for a general discussion of viticulture in the ancient Near East and Israel.

of the parable and its various elements (Isa. 27), or a possible 'completion' of the parable in a new direction (Isa. 63). The former tradition of the vine possibly belongs to a northern or Ephraimite tradition, finding expression in Psalm 80, combined already with an aspect of the vineyard tradition, or in other southern exilic or post-exilic texts (Ezek. 15 and 19) developed in new ways. Within the broader Jewish context, further developments took place as evidenced in the LXX and Targum of Isaiah. Finally, in early Christian circles both traditions were taken in new directions. The Isaian parable of the vineyard influenced the Synoptic parable of the wicked tenants via the LXX, while the 'I am' statement by Jesus on the vine (Jn 15) combined elements of both traditions, but with the vine developed in a still newer direction. In all this there is constant interplay between tradition and context, and a constant sense of new harvests to be gleaned.

BIBLIOGRAPHY

Albright, W.F.
    1959   'Some Remarks on the Song of Moses', *VT* 9: 339-46.
Aus, R.D.
    1996   *The Wicked Tenants and Gethsemane: Isaiah in the Wicked Tenants' Vineyard and Moses and the High Priest in Gethsemane* (University of South Florida International Studies in Formative Judaism and Christianity, 4; Atlanta: Scholars Press).
Blenkinsopp, J.
    2000   *Isaiah 1–39* (AB, 19; New York: Doubleday).
Brown, R.E.
    1966   *The Gospel According to John: XIII–XXI* (London: Geoffrey Chapman).
Carroll, R.P.
    1999   'YHWH's Sour Grapes: Images of Food and Drink in Prophetic Discourses in the Hebrew Bible', *Semeia* 86: 113-31.
Childs, B.S.
    2001   *Isaiah* (OTL; Louisville, KY: Westminster/John Knox Press).
Clements, R.E.
    1980   *Isaiah 1–39* (NCB; Grand Rapids: Eerdmans).
Conrad, E.W.
    1991   *Reading Isaiah* (Minneapolis: Fortress Press).
Evans, C.A.
    1984   'On the Vineyard Parables of Isaiah 5 and Mark 12', *BZ* 28: 82-86.
Greenberg, M.
    1983   *Ezekiel, 1–20* (AB, 22; Garden City, NY: Doubleday).
Kloppenborg Verbin, J.S.
    2002   'Egyptian Viticultural Practices and the Citation of Isa 5.1-7 in Mark 12.1-9', *Novum Testamentum* 44: 134-59.
Korpel, M.C.A.
    1988   'The Literary Genre of the Song of the Vineyard (Isa. 5.1-7)', in W. van der Meer and J.C. de Moor (eds.), *The Structural Analysis of Biblical and Canaanite Poetry* (JSOTSup, 74; Sheffield: JSOT Press): 119-55.
Kraus, H.-J.
    1989   *Psalms 60–150* (Minneapolis: Augsburg).

Leene, H.
    2000   'Isaiah 27.7-9 as a Bridge Between Vineyard and City', in H.J. Bosman, H. van
                Grol *et al.* (eds.), *Studies in Isaiah 24–27: The Isaiah Workshop* (Leiden: E.J.
                Brill): 199-225.
Matthews, V.H.
    1999   'Treading the Winepress: Actual and Metaphorical Viticulture in the Ancient
                Near East', *Semeia* 86: 19-32.
Mays, J.L.
    1994   *Psalms* (Interpretation; Louisville, KY: John Knox Press).
Miscall, P.D.
    1993   *Isaiah* (Readings: A New Biblical Commentary; Sheffield: JSOT Press).
Nasuti, H.P.
    1988   *Tradition History and the Psalms of Asaph* (Atlanta: Scholars Press).
Petuchowski, J.J.
    1981   'Judaism as "Mystery"—the Hidden Agenda?', *HUCA* 52: 141-52.
Robertson, D.A.
    1972   *Linguistic Evidence for Dating Early Hebrew Poetry* (SBLDS, 3; Missoula,
                MT: Society of Biblical Literature).
Sweeney, M.A.
    1987   'New Gleanings from an Old Vineyard: Isaiah 27 Reconsidered', in C.A. Evans
                and W.F. Stinespring (eds.), *Early Jewish and Christian Exegesis: Studies in
                Memory of William Hugh Brownlee* (Atlanta: Scholars Press): 51-66.
Tate, M.E.
    1990   *Psalms 51–100* (WBC, 20; Waco, TX: Word Books).
Wildberger, H.
    1997   *Isaiah 13–27* (Minneapolis: Fortress Press).
Williams, G.R.
    1985   'Frustrated Expectations in Isaiah V 1–7: A Literary Interpretation', *VT* 35:
                459-65.
Willis, J.T.
    1977   'The Genre of Isaiah 5.1-7', *JBL* 96: 337-62.
Yee, G.A.
    1981   'A Form-Critical Study of Isaiah 5.1-7 as a Song and a Juridical Parable', *CBQ*
                43: 30-40.

JEREMIAH 40.1-6: AN APPRECIATION

John Hill

Among Antony Campbell's many contributions to biblical scholarship in Melbourne, one of the most important is his role as supervisor of post-graduate students in their dissertation research and writing. I count myself very fortunate to have had him as my doctoral supervisor. He made what might have been an unrelentingly arduous task interesting and absorbing because of his learning, his encouragement, his ability to distinguish the wood from the trees, and his willingness to be involved in new areas of research. It is a pleasure for me to make a contribution to this volume in gratitude for his work and scholarship.

Turning to Jer. 40.1-6, I want to continue the theme of appreciation. My essay is intended as an appreciation of the literary dynamics of 40.1-6, a passage often assessed rather negatively by Jeremiah scholars. It describes the release of Jeremiah from a group of Judeans on their way to exile in Babylon (v. 1). The release happens through the intervention of Nebuzaradan, a high-ranking Babylonian official, who then gives a speech explaining the reasons for Jerusalem's destruction at the hands of *Yhwh* (vv. 2-3). He further proceeds to offer Jeremiah the option of going to Babylon and living there under good care, or to settle wherever he wishes in Judah (vv. 4-5). After considering the offer, Jeremiah decides to settle at Mizpah and live there in the community under the governorship of Gedaliah (v. 6).

1. *40.1-6 and Jeremiah Scholarship*

40.1-6 has been examined mostly from the point of view of its compositional history, and the coherence of the larger narrative of which it is a part—namely, 39.1–40.6. While much scholarly ink has been spilt on 40.1-6, little attention has been given to explaining the meaning of the passage within the final form of the book. So, for example, Wanke has identified 38.28b; 39.3, 14a; 40.6a as an earlier form of the narrative of Jeremiah's release, to which was later added 39.14b and then 39.11-13 and 40.1-5. Subsequently 39.1-2 and 4-10 were added. At the same time the text was put into its present order and the superscription composed for 40.1 (Wanke 1971: 108-10). Thiel has proposed that the earliest form of the narrative consisted of 38.28b; 39.3, 14, into which was interpolated 39.1-2, 4-10 (Thiel 1981: 54-55). A later stage in the redaction added, in the following order, 39.11-13; 40.2a, 1b; 2bα, 4*, 5-6 (Thiel 1981: 58-59; similarly Holladay 1989: 283). A further stage saw the arrangement of the narrative into its present order, and the insertion of 39.15-18 and the superscription in 40.1a. The final form of the text which resulted from such redactional development is said to contain 'an absurd picture of the preacher going into exile', and a 'pious outburst' by Nebuzaradan (Carroll 1986: 599). In regard to 40.1-6 itself, its superscription is said to be unintelligible, and some of its grammatical constructions clumsy.[1]

Critics have also focused on the relationship between 40.1-6 and the narratives which immediately precede it. They have pointed out that in 39.11-14 we already have an account of Jeremiah's release from captivity, and so question the relevance of a second account in 40.1.[2] They note the presence in 40.1 of a prophetic word formula which is not followed by the usual prophetic oracle, and the unusual speech of Nebuzaradan in vv. 2-3.[3] Their interest in redactional issues has also been further generated by other features of 40.1-6 such as the awkward grammatical construction in v. 1, the precise meaning of v. 5a, and the text-critical differences between the MT and the various LXX versions (e.g. Stipp 1992: 176-81). The coherence of the original narrative has been destroyed, and the processes which have produced the present text indicate the redactor's lack of understanding of the material before him (Pohlmann 1978: 106-107). Such a concentration on redactional issues in the major studies of Jeremiah has led to a neglect of the text in its final form, and its function within Jeremiah 37–44.[4]

2. *Jeremiah 40.1-6—Literary Considerations*

What I am proposing is a reading of 40.1-6 in its present form in the MT. After situating the passage in its immediate context, I want to focus particularly on the following points: the explanation by Nebzaradan of Jerusalem's destruction (vv. 2b-3), the offer to Jeremiah to go either to Babylon or settle in Judah (vv. 4-6), and the significance of the community at Mizpah. The figure of Jeremiah is a multi-layered construction, so that what we encounter is not history but a complex character representation whose purpose is to further the theological agenda of the book. I will conclude with some observations about the function of 40.1-6 within chs. 37–44.

a. *The Context of Jeremiah 40.1-6*
Jeremiah 40.1-6 is part of chs. 37–44, the account of the siege of Jerusalem and its aftermath. More specifically, 40.1-6 is the bridge between events connected

---

1. According to Mowinckel, 40.1a is 'eine jetzt ganz sinnlose Überschrift', attributable to source C and originally belonging with 39.15 (Mowinckel 1914: 24 n. 2). The clumsy character of the text's grammar is pointed out by Wanke 1971: 108-109. See also Stipp 1992: 178.

2. See the discussion in McKane 1996: 985-88.

3. See Holladay 1989: 269-70, 294. He rearranges the text so that the speech of Nebuzaradan becomes an oracle addressed to the exiles at Ramah. A more extensive reordering of the text is suggested in *BHS*.

4. An obvious exception to this is the analysis of 40.1-6 by Hardmeier. While his primary concern is to investigate the world behind the text, he takes seriously its final form, and argues that 40.1-6 is an attempt to portray the legitimacy of the community which gathered under Gedaliah's leadership (Hardmeier 1990: 214-17). The final form of the text is addressed in passing by Holt 1999: 166-67; Keown, Scalise and Smothers 1995: 234-37; and Wells 1999: 274-78.

with the siege of Jerusalem and the situation in Judah after these events. Its more immediate context is the larger unit, 39.15–40.6. The limits of the unit are determined by the repetition of the verb ישב ('to remain, dwell') in 39.14 and 40.6. Jeremiah 39.14 concludes 'so he stayed (וישב) with his own people'; 40.6 ends with 'and he stayed (וישב) with him [Gedaliah] among the people who were left in the land'.[5]

Within 39.15–40.6, there are two smaller units, 40.1-6 and 39.15-18, which are both about an interaction between Jeremiah and a foreigner: Ebed-melech in 39.15-18 and Nebuzaradan in 40.1-6. The first is situated in Jerusalem; the second at Ramah, possibly a staging post for the exiles on their way to Babylon (Holladay 1989: 293-94; Keown, Scalise and Smothers 1995: 235). Both begin with the prophetic word formula, which usually functions as an introduction to a prophetic revelation.[6] Jeremiah 40.1 has 'the word that came to Jeremiah from the Lord, whereas 39.15 has the unusual word order 'to Jeremiah the word of the Lord came' (translation mine).

40.1-6 is introduced by the prophetic word formula (v. 1aα), and by information about the encounter at Ramah between Jeremiah and Nebuzaradan, the Babylonian official. En route to Babylon as a captive together with other deportees, Jeremiah is freed by Nebuzaradan (v. 1aβ and b), who then makes a short speech (vv. 2b-5a). Nebuzaradan's speech consists of two parts. The first, couched in typical Dtr language, is his explanation for the demise of Jerusalem (vv. 2b-3); the second is the choice he offers to Jeremiah either to go to Babylon or stay in Judah (vv. 4-5). The passage concludes with Jeremiah's decision not to go to Babylon (v. 6).

b. *Nebuzaradan's Dtr Speech (40.2b-3)*
Nebuzaradan's Dtr speech is found in vv. 2b-3, and it has two functions. It provides an explanation for what has happened to Jerusalem, and interprets the events as the fulfilment of prophecy. The speech contains language and ideas that are common to both the book of Jeremiah and the broader range of Dtr literature.[7]

In the speech Nebuzaradan announces that 'the Lord your God threatened this place with this disaster' (v. 2), and 'now the Lord has brought it about' (v. 3). Within prophetic literature the expression 'to threaten disaster' (דבר piel with רעה is found in Jer. 11.17; 18.8; 19.15; 26.13, 19; 35.17; 36.7, 31; 1 Kgs 22.35, while 'to bring about evil' (בוא hiphil, with רעה) is found in Jer. 6.19; 11.11, 23; 17.18; 23.12; 1 Kgs 14.10; 21.21; 2 Kgs 21.12; 22.16. Similarly the expression '[the Lord] has done as he said' (כאשר דבר—Jer. 40.3) in the context of the fulfilment of prophecy occurs in 1 Kgs 5.26; 8.20, 53; 9.5; 2 Kgs 7.17; 17.23; 24.13.

5.   The English translation used here is that of the NRSV. On the role of ישב in determining the divisions of chs. 37–40, see Graupner 1991: 112.
6.   This is the terminology of Hals for 'prophetische Wortereignisformel' (Hals 1989: 362). Carroll calls the expression the 'reception of the word formula' (Carroll 1986: 267). Other occurrences of the formula are given in Carroll 1986: 206-207.
7.   For a listing of these expressions in the book of Jeremiah, see, among others, Thiel 1981: 58-59.

The speech functions as a fulfilment of prophecy and an explanation of why the disaster came about. In Jer. 36.31 *Yhwh* promises to bring on Judah and Jerusalem 'all the disasters (כל־הרעה) with which I have threatened (דברתי) them...' The expression 'to threaten disaster' (דבר with רעה) occurs in relation to the threat of future disaster in a number of places earlier in the book: 11.17; 19.15; 35.17; 36.3, 31.[8] In 40.2-3 the prediction comes true and prophecy is fulfilled. This is the first explicit statement in the book that *Yhwh*'s judgment against Judah and Jerusalem has been realized by the Babylonian conquest of 587.

The speech also functions as the explanation: 'And now the Lord has brought all this about...because all of you sinned...and did not obey his voice' (40.3). The diction of Nebuzaradan's explanation is similar to that found in passages in the book of Jeremiah and the Dtr literature which are constructed around what Thiel calls the Question-and-Answer pattern (*Frage-und-Antwort-Stil*).[9] These passages consist of (1) a question which seeks a reason for *Yhwh*'s destructive action against the people or the land; (2) an answer, usually spoken by the prophet; (3) a concluding word of judgment.[10] The question usually begins 'Why (על־מה) has the Lord dealt (דבר/עשה) in this way...', and the direct objects of the verbs דבר and עשה are usually expressions such as 'all these things' (כל־אלה) or 'all this great evil' (כל־הרעה הגדלה). Although in Jer. 40.2-3 there is no explicit question, Nebuzaradan's explanation implies the question 'Why has *Yhwh* done this?' In his speech we find similar diction to that in the question element of the pattern. His speech begins 'The Lord your God threatened (דבר) this place with this disaster (את־הרעה הזאת, v. 2). In regard to the destruction of Jerusalem and the exile, Nebuzaradan says 'now the Lord has brought it about (ויבא), and has done (ויעש) as he said'. In v. 2 we have the verb דבר with רעה, and in 40.3 the verbs עשה and בוא hiphil are used to describe *Yhwh*'s action. A similar combination found in the question component in 16.10 (דבר with רעה) and עשה with יהוה as its subject is found in the question component in 5.19; 22.8; Deut. 29.23; 1 Kgs 9.8.

There are also clear similarities between Nebuzaradan's speech and the answer component of the Question-and-Answer pattern. According to his speech, Judah 'did not listen to his voice' (40.3), the same expression as that found in the answer component of 9.12. In some instances of the Question-and-Answer pattern, the judgment component refers to deportation to a foreign land and submission to Judah's enemies and their deities—for example: 'you shall serve strangers in a land that is not yours' (5.19); 'I will scatter them among nations that neither they nor their ancestors have known' (9.15; Eng. 9.16). While Nebuzaradan's speech refers only to 'this thing' (40.3), its context is exilic. 40.1

8. The verb בוא hiphil with רעה is found in Jer. 4.6; 11.11, 23; 19.3; 23.12 (instances also noted by Holladay 1960: 357-58).

9. The passages in question are Jer. 5.19; 16.10-11; 22.8-9; Deut. 29.23-24; 1 Kgs 9.8. For his treatment of the Question-and-Answer structure and its variations, see Thiel 1973: 295-300.

10. Thiel points out a variation in how the concluding word of judgment is represented in the pattern (Thiel 1973: 299-300). In some passages, *Yhwh*'s judgment is portrayed as a future event (Jer. 5.19; 9.11-15; 16.10-13), while in others it has already happened (Deut. 29.23-27; 1 Kgs 9.8-9).

situates Nebuzaradan's speech against the background of Jeremiah's release from a captive group being deported to Babylon.

In the interpretation of Nebuzaradan's speech, a major difficulty for some scholars is the superscription in 40.1. It begins with the prophetic word formula, which usually functions as an introduction to a prophetic revelation. The formula is usually followed by the messenger formula and/or by a *Yhwh* speech in the first person, which may contain a command to the prophet.[11] In 40.1-6 there is neither a messenger formula, a command to the prophet nor a *Yhwh* speech in the first person. Mowinckel proposed that the formula has been displaced, and was originally immediately followed by a prophetic oracle (Mowinckel 1914: 24 n. 2).[12] Thiel has argued that the present text is the result of the 'D' redaction of an earlier narrative whose elements have been reordered and expanded, and which is now introduced by the prophetic word formula in 40.1aα (Thiel 1981: 57-61). The difficulty is to explain what is the referent of the expression 'the word that came to Jeremiah'. What exactly is the word which came from *Yhwh* to him? As the present text stands, it can only refer to Nebuzaradan's speech. The representation of Nebuzaradan, a Babylonian commander, speaking like a Dtr prophet has been described as 'absurd' (Carroll 1986: 699). From the point of view of history, this may well be so, but in passages which contain the Question-and-Answer pattern, there are instances in which foreigners speak in the same way. In Deut. 29.23-27 it is 'all the nations' (כל־הגוים) who ask 'Why has the Lord done thus to this land?', and who then answer 'It is because they abandoned the covenant of the Lord…' (v. 25). In Jer. 22.8 the same question is posed by 'many nations' (גוים רבים) who then provide the same answer (v. 9) as given in Deut. 29.25.[13] In this way, Jer. 40.2-3 is similar to Deut. 29.23-27 and Jer. 22.8-9, and its point is clear. The significance of the Babylonians' destruction of Judah is so obvious that even non-Israelites can grasp it, while those who should have understood—*Yhwh*'s own people—have failed to do so (see also Holt 1999: 166-67).

Within the book of Jeremiah itself the privileging of non-Jewish characters is an important literary device used to express the extent to which *Yhwh* has abandoned his people.[14] In 25.9 and 27.6 Nebuchadnezzar is portrayed as *Yhwh*'s servant. Apart from the designation of the Deuteronomistic prophets as the servants of *Yhwh*, the term 'my servant' is used in the Old Testament only of Abraham (Gen. 26.24), Moses (Num. 12.7) and David (2 Sam. 3.18; 7.5, 8).[15] In

11. For example, 'The word that came to Jeremiah from the LORD: Stand in the gate…and proclaim…and say…' (7.1-2). See also 18.1; 30.1 (with the messenger formula). Even in a text such as 32.1, the chapter's long introduction, which begins with the prophetic revelation formula, leads to the messenger formula and a *Yhwh* speech in the first person.

12. For a readily accessible summary of the discussion of this question, see McKane 1996: 996-97.

13. Thiel distinguishes passages in which the prophet (or *Yhwh*) speaks and those in which the speaker is the 'unbestimmte Mehrheit' or some such group (Thiel 1973: 298-99).

14. Holt refers to the device as 'the code of ethnicity' (Holt 1999: 166)

15. For a fuller treatment of this, see Hill 1999: 106-10. See also the brief comments of Keown, Scalise and Smothers 1995: 234-35.

Jer. 39.15-18 we also have the oracle which Jeremiah was commanded to speak to Ebed-melech the Cushite: 'I will save you (הצלתיך)...you shall have your life as a prize of war (נפשך לשלל) because you have trusted in me'. Here Ebed-melech is addressed in terms which in the book of Jeremiah are reserved only for the prophet himself and his scribe Baruch. *Yhwh*'s promise to save Ebed-melech (נצל hiphil) mirrors a similar promise to Jeremiah (1.8, 19; 15.20, 21; 42.11). The expression 'to have your life as a prize of war' is found in 45.5, the conclusion of the oracle which promises divine protection to Baruch. However Ebed-melech receives a further compliment. His protection is the result of his trust in *Yhwh*. While the themes of trusting in falsehood and a refusal to trust in *Yhwh* are common in the book, Ebed-melech is the only person in the book who is said to have trusted in *Yhwh* (39.18). The privileging of non-Israelites, then, is not foreign to the book of Jeremiah. The representation of Nebuzaradan is not something idiosyncratic, but is an example of a literary device used both in the book of Jeremiah and elsewhere to illustrate the obtuseness of *Yhwh*'s people in the face of his judgment against them. If Nebuchadnezzar can be *Yhwh*'s servant, Nebuzaradan surely can be *Yhwh*'s spokesman.

c. *Nebuzaradan's Offer and Jeremiah's Decision (40.4-5)*
After releasing Jeremiah, Nebuzaradan then offers him a choice about where he might settle (40.4-5).[16] The prophet has the option of either going to Babylon where he will be cared for by Nebuzaradan, or of staying in Judah. The language used in the latter part of the offer is significant for an understanding of 40.1-6. Nebuzaradan says to Jeremiah:

> See, the whole land is before you;
> go wherever you think it good and right to go. (v. 4bα)

What is interesting about v. 4bα is the expression 'the whole land is before you' (כל־הארץ לפניך), which is found elsewhere in Gen. 13.9; 20.15; 47.6.[17] Each of these verses sheds light on the significance of Nebuzaradan's words, and requires attention here.

The first verse for consideration is Gen. 20.15. The context of 20.15 is the story of Abraham and his encounter with Abimelech (20.1-18), a passage in which Abraham is described as a prophet (v. 7). In 20.15 Abimelech, king of Gerar, says to Abraham: 'My land is before you; settle where it pleases you' (הנה ארצי לפיך בטוב בעיניך שב). Abimelech's actions are the result of a dream in which *Yhwh* appeared to him to reveal that Sarah was in fact Abraham's wife. While staying over in Gerar, Abraham had passed off Sarah as his sister and

---

16. There are some textual difficulties in vv. 4-5. The beginning of v. 5 is generally regarded as corrupt. Here, and in v. 4bβ, I have followed the emendations of Rudolph which have been subsequently incorporated into *BHS* (Rudolph 1968: 246).

17. The phrase in Gen. 13 9 is identical to that in Jer. 40.6. Gen. 20.15 has ארצי־לפניך ('my land is before you'), and 47.6 has ארץ מצרים לפניך ('the land of Egypt is before you'). 20.15 has טוב with עין. In a footnote Pohlmann comments that 40.4bα recalls Gen. 13.9 and 21.5, but says nothing further about their connection (Pohlmann 1978: 101 n. 247). Similarly, see Wells 1999: 278 n. 26.

Abimelech had then taken her to his bed. After giving Abraham slaves, sheep and oxen, Abimelech offers him land where he might live. In 20.1 Abraham is said to reside as an alien (יגר), but in v. 15 he is now offered the opportunity to settle more permanently. As in Jer. 40.4, we find the words טוב בעיניך ('good in your eyes') used in relation to settling in the land, and in the context of a prophet as the recipient of an offer of land.

There is also another link between Gen. 20.1-18 and Jer. 40.1-6. In the former, the foreigner Abimelech is portrayed as someone who fears God. Abraham felt the need to pass off Sarah as his wife because he felt in the land of Abimelech 'there was no fear of God' (v. 11). What the story shows is that his perception was wrong, and that Abimelech was someone who took to heart the message that Abraham's God revealed to him in a dream. Because of his fear of God, he not only gives back Sarah but offers Abraham an array of gifts, among which is the offer of a place for him to settle. A function of Gen. 20.1-18 is to show 'that the fear of God indeed exists even outside Israel' (Westermann 1985: 329).[18] As shown above, a similarly positive assessment of the foreigner is shared by Jer. 40.1-6.

The second verse for consideration is Gen. 47.6 from the Joseph stories. Pharaoh says to Joseph: 'The land of Egypt is before you (ארץ מצרים לפניך); settle (הושב) your father and your brothers in the best part of the land'. The context is the coming to Egypt of Jacob and his sons because of the famine in Canaan. In 45.16-28 Pharaoh offers Joseph and his family the best land in Egypt, and in 46.3 *Yhwh* directs Jacob to come down and take up the offer in Egypt where he will become a great nation. On their arrival the promise is fulfilled (47.7-12).

The third verse for consideration is Gen. 13.9. Abram says to Lot: 'Is not the whole land before you?' (הלא כל־הארץ לפניך). Here Abraham makes the offer to his nephew Lot as a way of settling conflicts which emerged when both clans lived in the same area of land. Abraham acts as the superior figure who initiates the process and gives Lot the opportunity to take whatever land he wants. After Lot decides to take the Jordan plain and Abraham the land of Canaan, they both settle (ישב) in their respective localities.

In Jer. 40.1-6, then, we have an allusion to three accounts from Israel's patriarchal traditions which deal with a landowner or land controller who offers a place to live to someone who is landless or is there as an alien. The action of Nebuzaradan, then, has a deeper significance than just the release of a prisoner who may have been seen to have pro-Babylonian tendencies. In response to Nebuzaradan's offer, Jeremiah decides to stay in Judah, and goes to Mizpah to the community under Gedaliah's leadership, and 'stayed with him among the people who were left in the land' (וישב אתו בתוך העם הנשארים בארץ). We can note a similar sequence in the passages above from Genesis. After Lot makes his

---

18. For his full treatment of the narrative, see Westermann 1985: 318-29. In regard to Abimelech's dream, von Rad writes 'it is audacious of our narrator to consider the heathen worthy of an address, indeed, of a personal conversation with Yahweh' (1972: 228). On Abimelech's fear of God and Abraham's corresponding lack, see Fretheim 1994: 483.

choice (Gen. 13.14), he goes and settles (וישב) there. In Gen. 47.11 it is Joseph who settles (וישב) his family and gives them land to own (אחזה) in Egypt. Because of the allusions in Jer. 40.1-6 to the patriarchal narratives about land in the book of Genesis, Nebuzaradan's action is represented as something more than just the convenient release of a quisling-like figure. In 40.1-6 Jeremiah is represented as a figure like those from the patriarchal narratives, who were guided by *Yhwh* and given land in which they could settle.

3. *Jeremiah 40.1-6 and the Community at Mizpah*

One of the functions of 40.1-6 is the validation of the community which settled at Mizpah under the leadership of Gedaliah. The validation is achieved by the narrative's identification of Jeremiah with the Mizpah group, as Hardmeier has argued (1990: 214-17). His conclusion is founded on the clear emphasis given in 40.1-6 to the choice offered to Jeremiah, the subsequent rejection of the offer to go to Babylon, and the decision to stay in Judah. Represented in chs. 37–39 as a prophet who had been severely tested by suffering, whose prediction had come true, and who had the chance to go Babylon, his decision to stay in Judah carries enormous significance. While I agree with Hardmeier's conclusion, I would add a further consideration. The validation of the community under Gedaliah's leadership in 40.1-6 is not achieved only by the decision to join it made by such a significant figure as Jeremiah the authentic prophet who had suffered because of his fidelity to his mission. The Mizpah community's claims are further enhanced by another aspect of the figure of Jeremiah, namely the linking of him with figures from Israel's ancient patriarchal narratives. His settling at Mizpah invokes the memory of the patriarchs, and especially that of Abraham and his settling in the land under the guidance of *Yhwh*. It has been more usual to associate the traditions about Abraham and settlement in the land with the cause of the exiles than with those who had remained behind.[19] However, here in 40.1-6 we see an example of how the patriarchal traditions about settlement in the land are connected with the cause of those who were left behind in Judah after the events of 587.[20]

The validation of the Mizpah community is further supported by Nebuzaradan's release of Jeremiah in 40.1. The presence in the text of this second account of the prophet's release has puzzled scholars, who have regarded it as a secondary addition which disturbed the smooth flow of an earlier version of 40.1-6. What

19. On the significance of the covenant in Gen. 17 for the exiles, see Boorer 1977: 14-18; Campbell and O'Brien 1993: 29 n. 20; Westermann 1985: 256-65. For the view that the promise to Abraham in Gen. 12.1-10 has an exilic provenance and has in mind the situation of the exiles in Babylon, see Albertz 2003: 257-59. On the significance of Gen. 15 (rather than ch. 17) and the figure of Abraham for the exiles, see Van Seters 1975: 265-69.

20. In Ezek 32.23 there is an appeal to Abraham on the part of the survivors of 587, but their claims are rejected in favour of those of the exiles. See also Albertz 2003: 247; Greenberg 1997: 688-90; Zimmerli 1983: 198-99. That Abraham as 'the ancestor of a multitude of nations' (Gen. 17.4) might represent not just the exiles, but all the inhabitants of the land, see de Pury 2000.

has not been properly acknowledged is the important function in 40.1-6 of the second account of Jeremiah's release. A comparison between the two accounts of the release will help us appreciate the significance of the second. In the first account (39.11-14) Jeremiah is freed by Nebuzaradan on the direct order of Nebuchadnezzar. Jerusalem is the locus for this episode, as Jeremiah is still locked up in the court of the guard in the city (v. 14). In 40.1 the locus of the action has moved. Jeremiah is freed while at Ramah, where 'with all the captives of Jerusalem and Judah' he is en route to exile in Babylon. Besides releasing him, Nebuzaradan gives him the option of going to Babylon or staying in Judah. Jeremiah chooses the latter, and thereby separates himself from the exiles. In 39.11-14, after his release, Jeremiah is given into the care of Gedaliah, who is described here as 'son of Akiham, son of Shaphan'. However, in 40.1-6 Gedaliah is not just 'son of Akiham, son of Shaphan' but is now the Babylonian-appointed governor residing at Mizpah. The first narrative of the release concludes in 39.14 with the expression 'and he stayed in the midst of the people' (בתוך העם). The conclusion of the second narrative is similar, but with one major difference: 'and Jeremiah stayed with him among the people who were left in the land' (העם הנאשרים בארץ בתוך). Whereas in 39.14 Jeremiah was simply 'among the people', in 40.6 he is now clearly situated 'among the people *who were left in the land*' (emphasis mine). The identification of Jeremiah with the Mizpah community is achieved in two stages in 40.1-6. The first is in the account of Jeremiah's release by Nebuzaradan in 40.1 where the prophet is separated from those going into exile. The second is in 40.6 where he settles at Mizpah and so becomes clearly identified with those who were left behind.

The standing of the Mizpah community under Gedaliah is further underlined by what follows in 40.7-12 (following Albertz 2003: 6-7). Judeans who had fled to Moab and other surrounding countries together with surviving Judean soldiers and their leaders went to Mizpah (vv. 7-8, 11-12). References in v. 10 to the work of harvesting and storing wine, fruits and oil, together with the taking over of unnamed towns, indicate the existence of a significant infrastructure. That there was an abundance of wine and summer fruit (v. 12) could well be an indication of *Yhwh*'s blessing. In the book of Jeremiah, Mizpah is not just a rag-tag community which consisted simply of the poor and bedraggled survivors of the Babylonian invasion.[21] Rather, under the leadership of the Babylonian-appointed Gedaliah, and supported by the Abraham-like figure of Jeremiah, it offered the possibility of a new beginning in Judah. In the representation of such a view, 40.1-6 is a key text.

Finally, the above interpretation of 40.1-6 and its representation of the Mizpah community has implications for our understanding of the redaction of chs. 37–44. It has been argued by Pohlmann that 40.1-6 form part of the *Golah*-oriented material in chs. 37–44. He maintains that the verses are a late addition which reflects kindly on the Babylonians, and so reinforces the pro-*Golah* orientation of

---

21. Here the viewpoint of Jer. 40.1-6 differs from that in 2 Kgs 25.22-26, which omits mention of any positive aspects of the Mizpah community (Albertz 2003: 6).

the book (Pohlmann 1978: 106, 196, 213, 224 n. C).[22] However, as I have shown above, one function of 40.1-6 is to separate Jeremiah from the exiles, and to locate him clearly in Judah at Mizpah. Even if v. 1 and vv. 2-6 might come from different stages of the redaction, neither of them suggests a pro-*Golah* tendency. In v. 1 Jeremiah is separated from the exiles, and in vv. 2-6 he is clearly associated with the Mizpah community. Whatever pro-*Golah* texts there may be in chs. 37–44, 40.1-6 cannot be included with them.

4. *Conclusion*

40.1-6 has an important function in the book of Jeremiah. The first part of Nebuzaradan's speech (vv. 2b-3) provides the first occasion in the book where the Babylonian conquest is equated with *Yhwh*'s judgment against Judah and Jerusalem. What had been previously threatened has now come to pass. The second part of Nebuzaradan's speech provides a validation for the community at Mizpah. The language of his offer to Jeremiah contains allusions to the Abraham traditions. Just as Abraham's decision to settle in land offered him by Abimelech was part of *Yhwh*'s plan for his people, so Jeremiah's decision to remain in the land of Judah and settle at Mizpah is likewise part of a divinely orchestrated plan. 40.1-6 is also important in its positive representation of the community at Mizpah. Possessing the necessary infrastructure for normal life, and seemingly blessed by *Yhwh*, it was the place to which exiles returned from Edom and surrounding lands. Under the leadership of Gedaliah and supported by the presence of Jeremiah, the settlement there offered the possibility of a new beginning for Judah.

Several features of 40.1-6, about which some scholars have been rather dismissive, are also important to note. One example is the representation of Nebuzaradan as speaking like a Dtr prophet. Here 40.1-6 provides another example of how non-Jewish people are represented positively in the book of Jeremiah, so that an ironic contrast is thereby set up between the obtuse Judahites who reject the prophetic message, and the supposedly ignorant foreigner who fully understands it. A second example is the account of Jeremiah's release (40.1). Rather than being just a duplicate of an earlier account of the same event, its function is to separate Jeremiah from the exiles, so that in v. 6 he can be represented as unambiguously attached to the community at Mizpah.

40.1-6 then should not be seen as an ill-fitting intrusion which has destroyed the coherence of an earlier form of the present text. Instead, it should be judged as a passage which has an important function in chs. 37–44, and especially in the Jeremian narrative of the trauma associated with 587 and its aftermath.

---

22. A similar view has also been put forward by Seitz 1989: 280-81. The hypothesis of a *Golah*-oriented redactions is critiqued by McKane 1996: II, 1029, 1046-48.

BIBLIOGRAPHY

Albertz, R.
 2003 *Israel in Exile: The History and Literature of the Sixth Century B.C.E.* (trans.
 David Green; Studies in Biblical Literature [Society of Biblical Literature], 3;
 Atlanta: Society of Biblical Literature). Originally published as *Die Exilszeit*
 (Biblische Enzyklopädie, 7; Stuttgart : W. Kohlhammer, 2001).
Boorer, S.
 1977 'The Kerygmatic Intention of the Priestly Document', *AusBR* 25: 12-20.
Campbell, A.F., and M.A. O'Brien
 1993 *Sources of the Pentateuch: Texts, Introductions, Annotations* (Minneapolis:
 Fortress Press).
Carroll, R.P.
 1986 *Jeremiah* (OTL; Philadelphia: Westminster Press).
Diamond, A.R., K.M. O'Connor and L. Stulman (eds.)
 1999 *Troubling Jeremiah* (JSOTSup, 260; Sheffield: Sheffield Academic Press).
Fretheim, T.E.
 1994 'The Book of Genesis: Introduction, Commentary, and Reflections', in *NIB*, I:
 319-674.
Graupner, A.
 1991 *Auftrag und Geschick des Propheten Jeremia: literarische Eigenart, Herkunft
 und Intention vordeuteronomistischer Prosa im Jeremiabuch* (BTS, 15;
 Neukirchen–Vluyn: Neukirchener Verlag).
Greenberg, M.
 1997 *Ezekiel 21–37: A New Translation with Introduction and Commentary* (AB,
 22A; New York: Doubleday).
Hals, R.M.
 1989 *Ezekiel* (FOTL, 19; Grand Rapids: Eerdmans).
Hardmeier, C.
 1990 *Prophetie im Streit vor dem Untergang Judas: erzählkommunikative Studien
 zur Entstehungssituation der Jesaja- und Jeremiaerzählungen in II Reg 18–20
 und Jer 37–40* (BZAW, 187; Berlin: W. de Gruyter).
Hill, J.
 1999 *Friend or Foe? The Figure of Babylon in the Book of Jeremiah MT* (Biblical
 Interpretation Series, 40; Leiden: E.J. Brill).
Holladay, W.L.
 1960 'Prototypes and Copies: A New Approach to the Poetry–Prose Problem in the
 Book of Jeremiah', *JBL* 79: 351-67.
 1989 *Jeremiah 2: A Commentary on the Book of Jeremiah Chapters 26–52* (Hermeneia; Philadelphia: Fortress Press).
Holt, E.K.
 1999 'The Potent Word of God', in Diamond, O'Connor and Stulman (eds.) 1999:
 161-70.
Keown, G.L., P.J. Scalise and T.G. Smothers
 1995 *Jeremiah 26–52* (WBC, 27; Dallas: Word Books).
McKane, W.
 1996 *A Critical and Exegetical Commentary on Jeremiah* (2 vols.; ICC; Edinburgh:
 T. & T. Clark).
Mowinckel, S.
 1914 *Zur Komposition des Buches Jeremia* (Kristiana: Dybwad).

Pohlmann, K.-F.

1978 *Studien zum Jeremiabuch: ein Beitrag zur Frage nach der Entstehung des Jeremiabuches* (FRLANT, 118; Göttingen: Vandenhoeck & Ruprecht).

Pury, A., de

2000 'Abraham: The Priestly Writer's "Ecumenical" Ancestor', in S. McKenzie, T. Römer and H.H. Schmid (eds.), *Rethinking the Foundations: Historiography in the Ancient World and in the Bible; Essays in Honour of John Van Seters* (Berlin: W. de Gruyter): 163-81.

Rad, G. von

1972 *Genesis* (OTL; London: SCM Press).

Rudolph, W.

1968 *Jeremia* (HAT, 12; Tübingen: J.C.B. Mohr, 3rd edn).

Seitz, C.R.

1989 *Theology in Conflict: Reactions to Exile in the Book of Jeremiah* (BZAW, 176; Berlin: W. de Gruyter).

Stipp, H.-J.

1992 *Jeremia in Parteienstreit: Studien zur Textentwicklung von Jer 26, 36–43 und 45 als Beitrag zur Geschichte Jeremias, seines Buches, und jüdäischer Parteien im 6. Jahrhundert* (BBB, 82; Frankfurt: Anton Hahn).

Thiel, W.

1973 *Die deuteronomistische Redaktion von Jeremia 1–25* (WMANT, 41; Neukirchen–Vluyn: Neukirchener Verlag).

1981 *Die deuteronomistische Redaktion von Jeremia 26–45* (WMANT, 52; Neukirchen–Vluyn: Neukirchener Verlag).

Van Seters, J.

1975 *Abraham in History and Tradition* (New Haven: Yale University Press).

Wanke, G.

1971 *Untersuchungen zur sogennanten Baruchschrift* (BZAW, 122; Berlin: W. de Gruyter).

Wells, R.D.

1999 'The Amplification of the Expectation of the Exiles in the MT Revision of Jeremiah', in Diamond, O'Connor and Stulman (eds.) 1999: 272-92.

Westermann, C.

1985 *Genesis 12–36: A Commentary* (Minneapolis: Augsburg Press).

Zimmerli, W.

1983 *Ezekiel 2* (Hermeneia; Philadelphia: Fortress Press).

THE CONCEPT OF *RUACH* IN EZEKIEL 37

T. John Wright

1. *Development of Language*

When we are dealing with any language, there are issues of communication, and on many occasions, of cross-cultural and diachronic translation which give rise to many problems. These problems become greater when the literature concerned is ancient (even if in the same language as that of the reader), and even greater still if the language is *in articulo mortis*. As Donald Cruse sees it, we are not in the position to ask the native speaker about 'intuitive semantic judgements' or to elucidate informative responses in a controlled situation. He argues: 'Probably the most disadvantaged researchers…in the field of linguistic semantics are those who study "dead" languages. Often virtually the only direct evidence available to them is a corpus of written utterances, of somewhat fortuitous make-up, and now probably fixed for eternity' (Cruse 1986: 9).

It is easy to read contemporary and contextually owned understandings and concepts into those of the ancient world, as if the scientific revolution had not taken place. Even if due recognition is paid to context, under some supposed law of immutability such as 'as it is now, so it was then', many attempt to read the writings and iconographies of the eras which may be termed 'pre-scientific' as if they were their own. In popular conceptions humans are perceived as the same, who think like each other, and always have. A word means what it says; what is the problem? There is perceived to be a continuity and sameness about words and language. The thought patterns are immutable; the ways of perception are identical.

But the 'meaning' of a lexeme or utterance is not static, it is constantly evolving. The ways of perceiving the world and relating to reality have altered over the centuries, and so the nature of meaning itself has changed radically (Prickett 1986: 86). Prickett argues, 'there have been historically fundamental and irreversible shifts in the metaphors by which we perceive ourselves and the world since Old Testament times' (p. 225). This change is greater if one travels back into the primal consciousness of even earlier times, or travels across into contemporary so-called primal cultures. At any one point in time, there are cultural differences in all these areas making cross-cultural communication difficult.

The issue of 'translation' is further complicated by including acknowledgment of the diorism between 'collective' and 'individual' enlightenment of language, even within one community. This is well expressed by the nineteenth-century

German philologist, Wilhelm von Humbolt: 'No one when he uses a word has in mind exactly the same thing as another' (cited in Prickett 1986: 227). This is the 'creative energy' or the illocutionary force of language. Whatever the community may understand by a word or 'utterance', it is not necessarily the same as the understanding of each individual. Yet a poet may well play on this aspect of language, almost tantalizing the hearer and reader. Ezekiel, as we shall see, is a master of this.

2. *Meaning Extension: The Traditional Understanding of the 'Development of Meaning' in Lexemes*

A further unwritten principle, which is also opposed somewhat to that of immutability, is that of the evolution of language in which, as depicted by most scholars, there is a development from the material reference to the immaterial. For example, traditional historians of language such as Locke, Emerson, Bentham, Spencer, and Müller, argue that figurative language has evolved or developed in four stages, from the concrete to the abstract. The stages are:

(1)   the born literal or the exclusively literal meaning which refers to a material object; the 'signifier' and the 'signified' come together;
(2)   the concomitant meaning, in which the literal meaning is retained along with the transferred meaning *as well as*, which is reflected in allegory and symbolism, moving from prose into poetry;
(3)   the substituted meaning *instead of*, where the original meaning has not quite vanished, but the emphasis is on the new connotation;
(4)   the achieved literal, where a new and significantly different exclusive literal meaning occurs which refers to 'objects', even though they do not exist materially.[1]

The starting point is thus the 'literal', moving through the second and third stages, the 'metaphorical' period, reaching a new 'literal', into what Barfield calls the 'achieved literal', 'a tissue of faded or dead metaphors' (Barfield 1960: 53; 1965: 118).

The semantic evolution of some lexemes may well have developed this way, especially those relating to human consciousness. This may be illustrated with the word 'emotion'. The 'born literal' meaning is a 'moving out, migration'. The concomitant meaning is 'a moving, stirring, agitation'. The substituted meaning becomes any movement or disturbance of mind. Finally, from the mid-nineteenth century, there develops the 'achieved literal' stage of what *The Concise Oxford Dictionary of Current English* (1976) defines as 'mental sensation or state; instinctive feeling as opposed to reason'.

This approach has been traditionally applied to the Hebrew word *ruach*, and also to some extent to the Greek *pneuma* and Latin *spiritus*. For Biblical Hebrew the generic meaning of *ruach*, as seen through the eyes of 'enlightenment' linguists reflected in our dictionaries and commentators of Hebrew language and

---

1.   This analysis owes much to Barfield 1960: 48-53; 1965: 117-21.

ideas, is one where a semantic development can be traced from 'air in motion' to 'wind' to 'breath', 'spirit', 'disposition' (Wright 1985).[2] These senses were soon associated with the divine. So 'wind' became an instrument in the hand of the creator, the controller of the elements, either:

(1)   to perform acts of creation:

> 'By his *ruach* the heavens were spread out' (Gordis 1978: 280),
> 'his hand pierced the fleeing (בריח) serpent' (Job 26.13);

or

(2)   to perform salvific acts:

> 'Moses stretched out his hand over the sea, and *Yhwh* drove the sea back with a strong east *ruach* all night' (Exod. 14.21),
> '*Yhwh*…will wave his hand over the Euphrates with his scorching *ruach* that they might cross dryshod' (Isa. 11.15);

or, more commonly,

(3)   acts of punishment:

> 'A scorching *ruach* from the bare heights in the desert,
> on to the daughter of my people,
> not to winnow, not to sift,
> such a *ruach*, a full gale, shall come from me' (Jer. 4.11-12).

The 'wind' from God now becomes a dramatic symbol of God's power. But as people experience this divinely originated wind, this *ruach from* God soon becomes the *ruach of* God, anthropomorphically the 'breath' of God. The poetic parallel to Exod. 14.21, namely Exod. 15.8, picks up the anthropomorphic aspect: 'and with the *ruach* of thy nostrils, the waters piled up'. It is the *ruach* of God which is in Job's nostrils (Job 27.3). All living creatures have the *ruach* of life (Gen. 6.17; 7.15), but idols do not (Hab. 2.19; Jer. 10.14; Ps. 135.17). When one's *ruach* departs, the body returns to the ground (Ps. 146.4), but the *ruach* goes back to its giver, God (Eccl. 12.7):

> The dust returns to the earth as it was;
> but the *ruach* shall return to the God who gave it.

This *ruach* is of and from God, it is the life force in animate beings, it is the breath of life, which is given by the creator in order to make all creatures alive.

So far, one can trace the development of *ruach* over the four stages listed above: wind, to wind from God, to wind of God, to life-giving, to a new 'literal'

---

2.   It should be noted that in light of my work in the current paper I would wish to modify the diachronic emphasis in that paper. One can also compare Zimmerli (1969: 1262-65; 1983: 566-68), who starts from the 'objective' meaning 'air in motion', 'wind', then to 'breath of life', the organ of decision of the will, which is then applied to God as his own *Geist*, which gives life, and empowers the prophet. Shoemaker (1904) attempts to trace, according to the date of literary sources, a development by 'analogic metonymy' from an initial sense of 'wind'. Wiggins (1999: 5) follows Shoemaker. Others start from 'breath' (e.g. Hill 1967: 206; Hildebrandt 1995: 6). Vriezen (1966: 53) suggests seeing the lexeme as a verbal noun, equivalent to 'blowing', and it is this concept which is the original and unifying factor. See *HALAT* for a fuller discussion.

breath from God. But this is not the end; a further 'achieved literal' is attained in both the divine and anthropological levels. In the case of the latter, *ruach* relates to the psychical aspects of life, referring to emotions, dispositions, thought, intelligence, and moral energy. In despondent and difficult situations, the *ruach* can become sullen (1 Kgs 21.5), grow dim (Ezek. 21.7), faint away (Ps. 142.3), fail (Ps. 143.7), be in a state of anguish (Job 7.11), be anxious (Dan. 7.15), or be angry (Eccl. 10.4). A person can be 'trustworthy in *ruach*' (Prov. 11.13). The one whom God looks for is one who is 'humble and contrite of *ruach*' (Isa. 66.2). The volitional aspect is also dominant, for example, in Prov. 1.23:

> Behold I will pour out my *ruach* on to you;
> I will make known my words to you.

A translation of 'thought' or 'will' is usually suggested, although 'breath (of speech)' has been proposed (Woodhouse 1991: 4).

One of the key passages where the sense of *ruach* is used in such a manner, is where the promises are made to the ideal king, which amplifies what is implicated for the first Davidic king (Isa. 11.2; cf. 1 Sam. 16.13; 2 Sam. 23.2-3):

> The *ruach* of *Yhwh* shall rest upon him;
> a *ruach* of wisdom and understanding,
> a *ruach* of counsel and power,
> a *ruach* of knowledge and the fear of *Yhwh*.

The intellectual endowment, administrative skills and the fundamental precepts of the moral life, which are fundamental to the task of ruler, are all granted, with the recipient being given the *ruach* of *Yhwh*. For this writer the whole of the life of this Davidic leader is a gift from God, including the inner, moral and volitional life, the inner 'spirits'. These are dependent on the external spirit or 'Spirit', and are needed for the ruler to carry out his divinely appointed and supported role.

In the case of the divine, a new 'achieved literal' occurs with the concept of the 'spirit', which is part of the nature of God, is also conceived of as having its life apart from the former. The hominal terms such as nostrils, lips, tongue, hand, are used of God, in much the same way as *ruach*. These may be seen as anthropomorphic projections onto the divine, and understood metaphorically. But at the same time, such terms achieve their own literalness, especially if, as some of them have, they have mythical and theophanic overtones. So Hermann Gunkel, assuming a 'born literal' meaning of 'wind', can talk about the spirit giving life as 'a real breath of God' and 'that wherever the activities of the Spirit are vividly experienced, the Spirit is visualized as substance [*Stoff*]' (Gunkel 1888: 49; 1979: 61). Further he says 'the Hebrew conceived of the Spirit as a kind of wind, more mysterious, more supersensual, perhaps, but nonetheless as a delicate, airy substance' (1888: 48; 1979: 60). For Gunkel (1888: 51; 1979: 64) this 'substance' is clothing for a 'concept', namely the power of God at work. The new 'achieved literal' in turn is the beginning of a new development in meaning.

We have just worked through a traditional understanding of the development of the meanings of the lexeme *ruach*. This approach makes many assumptions based on the theory of language, the development of meanings, and the history of consciousness. Its starting point is the literal; it moves through the metaphorical, into the new literal. Even though it is difficult to tie down the period of the changes in the use of a word or concept, most approaches hitherto do fit into a neat package reflecting the evolutionary model and the linguistics of the 'enlightenment'. This is complicated by the lack of a clear definition or understanding as to what 'spirit' might 'mean'.

3. *Sentient Language*

Barfield (1960: 48-57; 1965: 116-25), followed by Prickett (1986: 85-89; 1989: 39-40) and Prickett and Barnes (1991: 76-78), argues that the origin of many words, especially those which refer to nature, is not the 'born literal' where the object is perceived of as outside itself and which has an objectiveness about it. It is, in a far more personal, inward, and sentient manner, a participatory experience, in which God and the creation are mutually inter-present in language. This is a period where there is no disjunction between the outward and the inner. Accordingly, for words like *ruach*, *pneuma*, and *spiritus* there is conveyed 'a sense of a ghostly yet palpable presence all around the speakers' (Prickett 1989: 39-40), what Barfield terms 'spectre' (Barfield 1960: 55). The mind of the early person, was not one looking at the external world as a *tabula rasa*, wondering and asking 'scientific-type' questions, or as a 'lazy onlooker', but one which was a structural component of the very world of which it was part. The subsequent history of such words has been the polarization of the outer and inner with 'literalness' becoming the end product, rather than the starting point.

Hence, in this understanding, words such as *ruach* did not refer in the first instance to a literal 'wind', which then gradually picked up meanings of 'breath' and 'spirit'. Rather, the Hebrew word expressed both 'inner' and 'outer' meanings from the start. It referred to what was essentially a numinous force. Prickett (1989: 40) puts it this way: 'If we now try to ask ourselves what exactly words like "ruach" or "pneuma" meant, even in biblical times, we have to try and think the literally unthinkable: a word that because it meant *both*, rather than being a metaphor of one for the other, meant *neither* in our modern senses'.[3]

Consequently, for the ancients, 'wind' and 'breath' were not distinguished, neither from each other, nor distinct from the ghostly spectre or numinous presence. Abstract concepts like 'life' and 'spirit' were not conceptualized as distinct from what we would conceive as the more real entities of 'blood' or even 'breath'. This is not to say that there was not any definable desynonymy[4] appearing in the light of experience and growth. What it does say, is that just because in the post-romantic age we are familiar with the movement of desynonymy, we need to be cautious in assuming that the movement actually took place with any vigour or haste in the early periods of the history of a language, or of a particular lexeme.

---

3. See further Barfield 1928: 62-65.
4. A 'process of linguistic differentiation' according to Prickett 1986: 87.

4. *The Sense of a Lexeme*

What we have been discussing is what Cruse (1986: 16) would designate as the 'latent' meaning of a lexeme, in which it is not fully defined until it is explored in contextual relations. Cotterell and Turner (1989: 164-66), building on the work of Cruse, Lyons and others, distinguish between, and then define, the lexical sense, the contextual or discourse sense, and the specialized sense of any lexeme or expression. They are defining here what they term the 'descriptive' sense, which is in contrast to any affective or connotative meaning (1989: 145). They exclude terms such as 'and' or 'so'.

For a 'full' lexeme the following conditions are necessary in order to depict the 'lexical sense' (Cotterell and Turner 1989: 164):
(a)   It is a publicly established meaning.
(b)   It can be embodied in a verbal definition that includes both the essential and prototypical elements of the quality, event, object, or concept potentially signified by the lexeme.
(c)   Its sense relations to closely related lexemes may be specified.

For the 'contextual/discourse sense' the conditions are (Cotterell and Turner 1989: 165):
(a)   It is the contextually determined descriptive meaning (and both presupposition pools and cotext[5] may be part of the context).
(b)   It can be embodied in a verbal definition that includes both the essential and semantically focused elements of the specific 'token' (or 'type') quality, event, object, or concept actually signified contextually by the lexeme.
(c)   Its sense relations both to the lexical sense (whether semantic narrowing or extension or both) and to closely related senses may be specified.

The last category could be either idiolectic or communitarian in origin and context, giving rise to a 'sense' specific to a person (such as St Paul) or a particular group which has its own distinctive interests. In both cases there develop senses which are confined to, and understood by, a well-defined group. Particular theological writings, including some from the Bible, can be categorized under this. Both the lexical and discourse sense are implicated. David Crystal (1987: 412), *inter alia*, recognizes the specialized character of religious discourse by entitling it 'theolinguistics', the 'study of the language used by biblical scholars, theologians, and others involved in the theory and practice of religious belief'. Perhaps I might propose analogously that what we are exploring in this paper is an example of 'theosemantics'.

In the case of Ezekiel 37, it is not a matter of seeing how the 'latent meaning' of a lexeme might feed into a discourse, but to take the 'latent meaning' and explore how the author utilizes the lexeme for his/her own purposes. Recognizing the possibility that any lexeme in theory may have an 'unlimited number' of

---

5.   That is, the 'accompanying text'; the 'verbal context' (Finch 2000: 212; Cotterell and Turner 1989: 16).

potential senses, and at the other end of the scale that every lexeme 'has at least one relatively well-utilised sense', Cruse (1986: 68-69) helpfully distinguishes 'two kinds of contextual selection' in any particular utterance, 'passive' and 'productive'. The former occurs when a selection is made from 'among pre-established senses', the context acting 'as a kind of filter'. The latter covers the case where the 'selected sense is not established', with the context acting 'as a stimulus'.

Much of the thinking on the use of *ruach* in Ezekiel 37 may be illuminated by this analysis. The wind/breath/spirit issue in many translations shows that there are issues about which of the three 'pre-established' senses is the significant one. The context acts as a filter. But the issue here is that for many it would appear that all three pass through the contextual filter. As shown above, for many scholars 'wind' is the pre-established sense, and the other two are developed senses, which in turn became pre-established themselves, or new 'born literals'. The task of the translator is to determine that which best fits the context. Or the second approach, where admitting there is ambiguity and vagueness, the context is permitted to 'generate' the sense. But even in the case under consideration this is not sufficient since, for most, it still does not clear up the ambiguity, there being no certain sense able to be selected.

5. Ezekiel 36.26-27; 37.1-14

In Ezek. 36.26-27 and 37.1-14 *ruach* is a *Leitwort*. The variations between the translations reflect the difficulties that contemporary scholars have in coming to grips with the term. The LXX and the Vulgate translate the term by *pneuma* and *spiritum* respectively, with one exception in 37.9bα where the Vulgate reads *ventis* ('winds').

The promise made in 36.26, 'I will put in you a new *ruach*', is invariably translated by 'spirit, *esprit*, *Geist*', except in the case of the GNB which translates as 'mind'. However, the GNB does not use that word elsewhere in 36.26-27 or 37.1-14. This concept is imputed by some commentators noting the parallel with לב, the two words together denoting 'the person's internal locus of emotion, will, and thought' and other usages (e.g. Block 1998: 355; 1989: 31, 43-46; Eichrodt 1966: 349; 1970: 499; Joyce 1989: 109-11).

This promise is explicated in v. 27, 'my *ruach* I will put in you'. The term *ruach* is again translated as 'spirit, *esprit*, *Geist*', with the NIV and the LB now capitalizing the 'S', as they do in Gen. 1.2 and elsewhere in the Hebrew Bible where *ruach* is seen as epitomizing the divine.[6] This donation is the 'dynamic power of *Yhwh*' which will enable the people to respond to the demands of God.

Ezekiel 36.26-27 is part of the context in which ch. 37 is presently situated. In particular, 37.1-14 develops the gift of the *ruach* promised in 36.27a, and 37.15-28 depicts the political and geographical situation in which the obedience

6. Some commentators also capitalize the 's', including Block (1998: 350, see the discussion on pp. 360-61).

of 36.27b is to happen, with 37.14a and 37.24b functioning as the 'final captions' to 36.1-13 and 37.15-23 respectively (Allen 1993: 140; Renz 1999: 200).

The opening verse of ch. 37, a traditional introductory opening to a vision-report in the book of Ezekiel, declares that when the hand of *Yhwh* was upon Ezekiel, *Yhwh* 'brought me by/in the *ruach* of *Yhwh* (and placed me in the middle of the plain)'. The movement of the prophet (in a vision), with the *ruach* being a force of locomotion, occurs not infrequently in the book (3.12, 14; 8.3; 11.1, 24; 43.5). Again the translators and commentators translate *ruach* by 'spirit, *esprit*, *Geist*', with the RSV, NIV, LB, and Block (1998: 367, 371-72) all with a capital 'S'.[7] Woodhouse has suggested 'breath of *Yhwh*' partly because he sees that as the meaning of *ruach* in 36.27; 37.1-14 (except for 'wind' in v. 9), he sees it implied specifically in 36.27 and 37.10 (cf. 2.2), and partly because he associates such divine sourced breath with the speech aspects (Woodhouse 1991).[8] Greenberg (1983: 70, 187; 1997: 742) makes an interesting distinction in that *ruach* when used on its own implies locomotion, but when it is used with the divine name implies revelation reception. This attempt at a distinction is somewhat artificial. The context needs to play a determining factor in the significance of any lexeme.[9] In this case the agency of conveyance is implied by יד יהוה and ברוח יהוה.

The prophet is shown the vale of dry bones, and Ezekiel is told to prophesy to the scattered and lifeless bones with these words (37.5): 'Behold I will cause *ruach* to enter into you, that you may come alive'. The translations vary, most of which go for one 'meaning' and place other possibilities in the margin. Some consistently use 'spirit, *esprit*, *Geist*'[10] but most utilize 'breath, *souffle*, *Odem*', and a few 'breath of life'.[11] The functionalism of breath is the main concern in these renditions. Some translations precede the noun with the definite article thus identifying the concept.[12] The 'ambiguity' of the sense of the lexeme is often recognized (e.g. Block 1998: 376).The promise is reiterated in the next verse v. 6: 'I will put *ruach* into you that you may come alive'. Most of the translations do not differ from v. 5 in their respective renditions, except the three translations which had the definite article, now delete it, with BJ adding the indefinite article.[13] The ZB replaces *Lebensodem* with *Odem*. The LXX has a significant variation, reading πνεῦμά μου ('my spirit') being influenced by 36.27 and prefiguring 37.14. The MT does not make this identification until the interpretation of v. 14.

The prophet prophesied unto the bones and observed that they had come together, with sinews, flesh and skin covering them. Then he comments (v. 8b):

7. Of the translations consulted, the ZB here alone refers to other possible meanings: *Wind, Lebensodem, Geist* ('wind, breath of life, spirit').

8. I assume Woodhouse includes Ezek. 36.26 which is not discussed.

9. See, for example, the discussion in Cotterell and Turner 1989: 164-67; Crystal 1987: 107; Cruse 1986: 15-16.

10. E.g. Douay, NAB, BJ, NEchtB.

11. So Moffatt; *Lebensodem ZB*; *Lebensgeist* (Zimmerli, Eichrodt); πνεῦμα ζωῆς ('spirit of life' LXX).

12. JB, BJ, Moffatt, and English translations of Eichrodt (1970) and Zimmerli (1983).

13. The English translations of Eichrodt (1970) and Zimmerli (1983) retain the definite article.

'But there was no *ruach* within them'. The translations all have the same as in v. 6.[14] With this section, vv. 4-8, the prophet is thus told to prophesy to the bones. He did so; but there is still one vital thing missing, *ruach*. Since most scholars see this missing element as 'breath', this is the popular translation for this section, although 'spirit (of life)' is utilized by others.

The next section, vv. 9-10, is concerned with the provision of this missing element. As in vv. 4-5, in v. 9 the prophet is addressed by *Yhwh*, and told to prophesy, and what to say to the recipient. In the former case it was the bones, in the latter הרוח ('the *ruach*'): 'prophesy to the *ruach*, son of man, and say to the *ruach*...'

Both the tension and confusion of the translators increases at this point. Who is being addressed here?

(1)   Those which have used 'spirit, *esprit*, *Geist*' to this point still do so.[15] The ZB introduces *Geist* (not used since v. 1). Eichrodt for the first occurrence, translates *Geist*, and for the second continues with *Lebens-geist*.

(2)   Most of the other translations consistently retain 'breath, *souffle*, *Odem*'.

(3)   However, there are some which anticipate a further meaning which comes from the second part of this verse, namely 'wind, *Wind*' as the one being addressed.[16]

Following the command to prophesy, the message is given to the entity addressed, in this case the *ruach*. It is comparable to the message addressed to the bones in vv. 5-6: 'from the four 'winds' (רוחת [plural of *ruach*]), 'come, O *ruach*, and breathe upon these slain, so that they may come alive'. The one addressed is variously translated:

(1)   those who see hitherto the meaning as 'spirit, *esprit*, *Geist*' continue to do so, with the LB now introducing 'Spirit' for 'wind';

(2)   others carrying on from the context, see the 'breath' being addressed, though some of these had in v. 9a the one being addressed, the 'wind';[17] but more with 'breath, *souffle*, *Odem*' being addressed in both parts of v. 9.[18] The advantage of this translation is that it puts it into the context of the last clause of v. 8b, 'there is no *ruach* in them', that is, the need of infusion in order for there to be life.

(3)   The third group sees the translation as 'wind' as in v. 9a.[19] The LXX omits any addressee, with pneuma being carried through from v. 9a.

The confusion in the minds of the translators is easy to understand.

---

14. The LXX correctly omits the modifier μου ('my').

15. Douay, NAB, BJ, *NEchtB*, Allen 1990: 181.

16. So Greenberg 1997: 744, AV, RV, NEB, REB, LB, GNB, Moffatt and *HSLuth*.

17. So AV, RV, Moffatt.

18. So RSV, NRSV, NIV, NASB, JB, NJB, NJPSV, TOB, *HSLuthR*, Zimmerli and Eichrodt retain *Lebensgeist*.

19. NEB, REB, *HSLuth*. The LB has 'wind' in v. 9a and bα, 'Spirit' in v.9bβ, but paraphrases the beginning of v. 10: 'So I spoke to the winds as he commanded me'.

To add to the confusion is the use of the term רוחה, the plural of *ruach*. There are four of these, and they are generally taken to be the 'four winds', that is, the four quarters of the world. The LXX reads the plural πνευμάτων[20] and the Vulgate *ventis* ('winds'). The 'winds' are under God's direction, and part of his creative force, and so for some may represent the divine life-giving breath (Block 1998: 377). Some translate with a dynamic equivalent phrase such as 'every quarter',[21] 'every direction',[22] 'four ends of the earth' (Moffatt), 'quatre points cardinaux' (TOB), 'points of the compass' (Caird 1980: 44).

Just as in v. 7a where the prophet prophesied as commanded with the results being described in vv. 7b-8, so in v. 10a the prophet prophesies with the results in v. 10b, the apex of the vision: 'and the *ruach* came into them and they came alive'.

Most of the translations pick up what was said in v. 8b. What is missing there is here provided by *Yhwh*, be it 'spirit' or 'breath'.[23] The bones of vv. 1-8b and the bodies of vv. 9-10 have now been animated.

Except for the LXX, the identity and the authority of this *ruach* has hitherto not been explicated. Consequently, picking up the words of 36.26-27, in an explanatory promise, God is made to say in v. 14: 'And I will put my *ruach* within you, and you will come alive'. Most translations reflect those in 36.27, though some have a significant difference which may reflect the movement of the 'events'. So the RSV interestingly moves from 'spirit' to 'Spirit', while some others from 'spirit, *esprit, Geist*' to 'breath, *souffle, Odem*'.[24] In other words, this last group sees the overriding aspect of ch. 37 as the concern. The significance of this verse is the identifying of the source of the *ruach*, namely *Yhwh* himself. Those translations which identify *ruach* with 'Spirit', as well as seeing 37.1-14 as the fulfilment of 36.26-27, would appear to be influenced by a Christian concept of the Spirit, which is identified with the Holy Spirit, well exemplified by Block (1998: 360-61).

What the data isolated above show is that what the Western world understands as separate words with their own associative fields, goes back to one Hebrew word, *ruach*. The variations and the number of footnotes in the various translations show that 'European' minds, for whom the literalism of 'wind', 'breath', 'spirit', is quite distinct, overcome the difficulties by utilizing words like metaphor, symbol, and paronomasia. Some seem comfortable in the distinctive meanings; so, for example, G.A. Cooke (1936: 400): 'Of course *my spirit* [v. 14] is not the same as *the breath* (or *spirit*) of v. 9'. But the complexities of the situation

20. But Codex Alexandrinus reads the 'born literal' ανέμων τοῦ ουρανοῦ ('the winds of the heaven').

21. NEB, REB.

22. GNB; cf. Block 1998: 377.

23. The exceptions being the English translation of Eichrodt (1970) which has 'breath of life' in v. 8 and 'spirit of life' in v. 10—both for *Lebensgeist*. Allen (1990) apparently has 'breath' in v. 8 (see p. 185; v. 8b appears to be accidentally missed out on p. 181), and 'spirit' in v. 10 (p. 181). Greenberg (1997: 741) has 'breath' in v. 8 but 'wind' in v. 10 for reasons stated above. Codex Alexandrinus has πνεῦμα ζωῆς ('spirit of life').

24. NJPS, GNB, TOB, ZB, *HSLuthR*.

are ignored in this comment. A further example of distinction is Carley (1975: 36-37; cf. p. 70), who, after a helpful discussion on *ruach* in Ezekiel, concludes that for the translocation passages ' "Wind" rather than "the spirit of Yahweh" is the instrument effecting the prophet's movement…'

Others acknowledge and even rejoice in the 'ambiguity' (e.g. Block 1989: 29): 'One of the marks of Ezekiel's literary genius is his mastery of ambiguity. He uses many words with different meanings, frequently making the switch within the same context. In some of those instances one cannot be sure whether he intends a singular sense or if both possibilities are in mind.'

Block then discusses *ruach*. As well as 'ambiguity' (1989: 34, 38),[25] the term 'word play' is used (1989: 38, 45; Carley 1975: 30), and the use in ch. 37 is said to be 'not uniform' (Block 1989: 37). Others have similar phrases such as 'interplay of senses' (Woodhouse 1991: 18). David Aaron (2002: 199) has some wise words to say about 'ambiguity': according to him, 'ambiguity should not be treated as a defect… Rather, ambiguity is an inescapable characteristic of the human creation of meaning, and any attempt to define it out of meaning is only evasion.'

There are some translations and commentators who attempt to do this, keeping as much as possible to a homogeneous translation, rather than coming to terms with the discourse sense of the utterance. They are uncomfortable with ambiguity or *double-entendre*. Cotterell and Turner (1989: 179) state, surprisingly, that, 'As a rule of thumb we should recognize that, in any context, a word will only carry *one* of its possible senses; the question of which single meaning is the most appropriate to the context is what needs to be settled'.

Ambiguity itself is an 'evasion' for Cotterell and Turner, a fudging of the exegesis of the passage. They do admit, however, that it is possible to have '*double-entendre*' but it 'is relatively rare, and preferably only to be invoked when there are clear markers of it', citing Jn 3.8 as an example (1989: 175). They do not discuss Ezekiel 37.

To understand what the ancient Hebrews were saying in the passage under consideration, there is little point in isolating and juggling three primary senses of *ruach*, as does Block (1998: 376), among others. None of the words, 'spirit, *esprit*, *Geist*', can pick up the nuances of *ruach* or πνευμα; and in reverse, these two ancient lexemes do not cover all aspects of the modern English lexeme 'spirit'—such as 'angel', 'spunky', 'bravery', 'feeling', 'humour', 'alcoholic drink'. Further, the semantic range of the German and French lexemes do not coincide with each other nor with the English word. In the thesis of Barfield and Prickett there is a way out of the dilemma of the modern translations and the mental gymnastics of commentators. It is not that the word *ruach* has different meanings, but the word expresses a concept and reflects an 'entity' that is almost impossible for us moderns to grasp without dividing that entity up into signifiers of the literal.

The first ten verses of ch. 37 are a report of the vision experienced by Ezekiel, and as such it is the third of four significant vision reports in that book (1.1–3.15;

25. The word 'is absolutely ambiguous' (Moscati 1947: 308).

8.1–11.25; 37.1-14; 40.1–48.35). In all these, *ruach* is the locomotive force for the prophet, a depiction of his participatory involvement. In particular, in ch. 37, the prophet participates actively in the vision. This 'represents' God's involvement not only in the life of the prophet, but also in the life of the nation, with the activity of *ruach* in the life of the prophet becoming a paradigm for the new life of Israel (Carley 1975: 31; Fishbane 1985: 452; Renz 1999: 202-205).

The force is from the divine, a force which is, as discussed above, translated by 'spirit, Spirit' and by 'breath of *Yhwh*'. But it may well also be translated by 'wind' (Greenberg 1983: 70),[26] or 'spirit-wind' which Brownlee (1986: 168) defines as that which 'concerns…Ezekiel's physical sensation of being lifted and propelled toward his destination… [H]e felt the sense of levitation.'[27]

Yet Brownlee (1986: 168) distinguishes all this from the situation in 37.1 when he says that this 'inspired trip into the valley did not involve the sense of levitation, only an exalted frame of mind, which is attributed to "the spirit of Yahweh"'. As far as I can make out, the reason why Brownlee makes this distinction is because of the reference to the divine name, *Yhwh* (see also 11.5). Certainly, the source of the *ruach* is now mentioned, but why does it make it different in nature and kind? There is behind *ruach* here that awesome, unknown power from God, which can throw one down to the ground, and yet raise one to one's feet, transport one, both within visions, and indeed without them. It is where the 'son of man' meets the 'Father of man'; the created is confronted with the creator. It is that time when the latter can communicate with the former in ways which are almost beyond the limitation of words.

In the first commission to prophesy in 37.4-6, the prophet as the authorized messenger of God is addressed and told to prophesy to the scattered bones that they might come alive. How? With God causing a *ruach* to enter into the same (vv. 5, 6). Other than those who consistently see 'spirit' throughout the chapter (except 'the wind' in v. 9), the word is translated by 'breath (of life)' or 'spirit of life'. This is what we moderns understand was missing from these newly assembled corpses, and so what is needed needs to be provided. At the end of the report on the resultant action in the vision (vv. 7-8), the prophet advises that even though bodies may now have been recreated, there was still no *ruach* in them (v. 8).

And so the prophet receives a second commission to prophesy to the *ruach*, who is to be asked to come from the four רוחת and breathe on those lifeless bodies so that they might come alive (v. 9). In the report of the resultant action in the vision (v. 10), the said *ruach* enters, and the bodies do spring into life. This *ruach* is identified in v. 14 as the *ruach* of *Yhwh*.

Reference is often made to Gen. 2.7, where God provides the newly created man with the one vital thing, נשמה ('breath').[28] But why is this word not used here? Such a question is almost impossible to answer.

26. Where he refers to 3.12, 14; 8.3; 11.1, 24; 43.5; but he does not refer to 37.1. Woodhouse (1991: 13, 19) follows Greenberg.

27. See further Brownlee 1986: 25, 37, 53, 156 (but on p. 154 he renders 'a divine-wind'), 168, on Ezek. 2.2; 3.12, 14; 11.1. For 11.24a he translates as 'wind'.

28. See, e.g., Block 1998: 360.

נשמה occurs some 25 times in the Hebrew Bible, and almost always signifies 'breath' in people, and by association once in animals (Gen. 7.22), and hence by synecdoche to 'life', 'living being' (Isa. 57.16). It is basically 'life in the body'. In several passages the word is applied to God, it being the breath of *Yhwh* who creates (Job 33.4) or brings forth judgment (Isa. 30.33). It is God 'who gives נשמה to the people upon earth and *ruach* to those who walk upon it' (Isa. 42.5). Lack of *ruach* and of נשמה means death (Job 34.14-15). Although most of these references to this word are in the exilic and post-exilic literature, the word does occur earlier (Gen. 2.7; 7.22 [J[29]]; and see also 1 Kgs 17.17; Ps. 18.16 [Eng. 18.15]). It is the 'older and more common word for breath' (Shoemaker 1904: 25). Aubrey Johnson (1964: 28) argues that especially in the literature from the exile onwards *ruach* became a substitute for נשמה. If this was the case it could be one reason why *ruach* was preferred to נשמה, particularly if the author wishes to play on the 'senses'. In other words, one of the 'meanings' of the latter was included in the former, which in turn was compatible with the connotations of 'spirit' and 'wind'.

But this kind of argument may fall into the trap that one can differentiate between the two or three 'born literals' in *ruach*, and hence the variation in, and the problem of translation in passages like Ezekiel 37. It is not a question of which of 'wind', 'spirit' or 'breath' is the best translation for each occasion. The issue is whether there is something inherent in the lexeme *ruach* which enables it to be used. Prickett (1986: 67) argues: 'for the ancient Hebrews the wind was an essentially numinous force. The very idea of "wind" was for them inseparable from "breath" and, therefore, from a ghostly, magical, and mysterious immaterial presence for which the word *also* stood.'

The same 'ghostly, magical, and mysterious immaterial presence', the same awesome, life-giving power which Ezekiel experienced in his 'lifeless' body, is the one which is to give life to those 'lifeless' bones.

In Ezekiel there is a poetic edge to the language. Poetic language does not necessarily move with or follow the broader semantic development of language. The poet may recognize the possibility of semantic change by broadening or narrowing, or by the influence of cross-cultural 'contamination', and indeed may well utilize such change in any utterance. There may be movement two ways: back into earlier or archaic senses, or forward, playing with phonological, grammatical, and semantic aspects of language. However, a poet depends on idiosyncratic consciousness.

Earlier I expressed caution with respect to assuming a process of desynonymy. Yet it is quite possible that by the sixth century BCE speakers of Hebrew, when using *ruach*, were well aware of the distinct, achieved literal meanings of 'wind', 'breath' or 'spirit' or 'spirit of God', or 'disposition', and that most often the other connotations were not consciously present. This is illustrated by the discussion of נשמה above, by the use of *ruach* in 1 Kgs 19.11 ('The Lord was not in the

---

29. This refers to a proposed source of the Pentateuch, the Yahwist, which is customarily dated in the pre-exilic period to the tenth or ninth centuries BCE. However, some revisionists would date it to the exilic or to the early post-exilic periods.

ruach'),[30] and by the parallelism with סופה ('storm wind') in Isa. 17.13, normally dated to about 701 BCE (Kaiser 1974: 85). Particular winds had their own lexemes and there are pre-exilic references to these—especially קדים, the east wind (e.g. Gen. 41.6, 23, 27; Hos. 12.2; 13.15).

So, for a writer who is a rhetorician, a poet, one who plays games with words, it need not be surprising to discover a further level. The prophet is the one who cries out in distress 'Ahah! they are saying of me…"does not this man go on *mashaling meshalim*"', 'multiplying similitude upon similitude' (Ezek. 21.5 [Eng. 20.49]). Even though the accusation of the prophet by the people implies disdain for the prophet and his message, and also questions the intelligibility of his riddles or parables, it is at the same time rhetorically a recognition of the word craft of the prophet.

This craft is acknowledged elsewhere, especially in Ezek. 17.2 and 24.3. In the former passage the prophet is enjoined, by using two cognate phrases, to 'propound a riddle' (חוד חידה) and to 'compose a fable' (מְשֹׁל מָשָׁל). In 24.3 the latter phrase is also used to 'compose a parable'. On both occasions the resulting composition and imagery form part of a judgment oracle. But this approach is not simply noetic. There is a paradigmatic role. The audience/reader is involved, invited in by the richness of the language, to participate in the world of משל with its 'fecundity as meaning-spawning devices' (Polk 1983: 572).

What the author is doing in ch. 37 is rediscovering synonymy, and making the whole a riddle: the source of *ruach*, namely *Yhwh*, tells the receiver of *ruach*, the prophet, to prophesy to the *ruach*, telling it to come forth but from where, the רוחת. We might call this kind of riddling 'metasynonymy', something which goes beyond 'mere' synonymy.[31] It is not a play on words, paronomasia, nor even a play on meanings, but a kind of semantic circle which turns language in on itself, almost magical in intent. Whatever the prophet wants to say turns out to be the same, but in a way that keeps the distinct associations up in the air.

The *ruach* comes from *Yhwh*. In *ruach*, and through *ruach*, the lifeless meets the life-giver, meets that 'ghostly, magical, and mysterious immaterial presence'.

BIBLIOGRAPHY

Aaron, D.H.
    2002   *Biblical Ambiguities: Metaphor, Semantics, and Divine Imagery* (Leiden: E.J. Brill).
Allen, L.C.
    1990   *Ezekiel 20–48* (WBC, 29; Dallas: Word Books).

---

30. However, 1 Kgs 19.4-18 is possibly post-Dtr, based on an earlier core (see Campbell and O'Brien 2000: 397); others argue that it forms part of a pre-Dtr Elijah tradition, possibly modified by the Elisha circles (Gray 1964: 337). There are many clear pre-exilic references to *ruach* as wind (see Briggs 1900: 133-34; Shoemaker: 1904: 14; and for the Psalms, Wiggins 1999: 5).

31. I owe this suggestion to Dr Mary Dove, Reader in English, University of Sussex.

1993   'Structure, Tradition and Redaction in Ezekiel's Death Valley Vision', in P.R. Davies and D.J.A. Clines (eds.), *Among the Prophets: Language, Image and Structure in the Prophetic Writings* (JSOTSup, 144; Sheffield: JSOT Press): 127-42.

1994   *Ezekiel 1–19* (WBC, 28; Dallas: Word Books).

Barfield, O.

1928   *Poetic Diction: A Study in Meaning* (London: Faber & Gwyer).

1960   'The Meaning of the Word "Literal"', in B. Cottle and L.C. Knight (eds.), *Metaphor and Symbol* (London: Butterworths Scientific Publications): 48-63.

1965   *Saving the Appearances: A Study in Idolatry* (New York: Harcourt, Brace & World).

Block, D.I.

1989   'The Prophet of the Spirit: The Use of *rwḥ* in the Book of Ezekiel', *JETS* 32: 27-49.

1998   *The Book of Ezekiel: Chapters 25–48* (NICOT; Grand Rapids: Eerdmans).

Briggs, C.A.

1900   'The Use of רוח in the Old Testament', *JBL* 19: 132-45.

Brownlee, W.H.

1986   *Ezekiel 1–19* (WBC, 28; Waco, TX: Word Books).

Caird, G.B.

1988   *The Language and Imagery of the Bible* (London: Gerald Duckworth).

Campbell, A.F., and M.A. O'Brien

2000   *Unfolding the Deuteronomistic History: Origins, Upgrades, Present Text* (Minneapolis: Fortress Press).

Carley, K.W.

1975   *Ezekiel among the Prophets* (SBT Second Series, 31; London: SCM Press).

Cooke, G.A.

1936   *A Critical and Exegetical Commentary on the Book of Ezekiel* (ICC; Edinburgh: T. & T. Clark).

Cotterell P., and M. Turner

1989   *Linguistics and Biblical Interpretation* (Downers Grove, IL: InterVarsity Press).

Cruse, D.A.

1986   *Lexical Semantics* (Cambridge: Cambridge University Press).

Crystal, D.

1987   *The Cambridge Encyclopedia of Language* (Cambridge: Cambridge University Press).

Eichrodt, W.

1965–66   *Der Prophet Hesekiel* (ATD, 22/1-2; 2 vols.; Göttingen: Vandenhoeck & Ruprecht).

1970   *Ezekiel: A Commentary* (trans. C. Quin; OTL; London: SCM Press).

Finch, G.

2000   *Linguistic Terms and Concepts* (Basingstoke: Macmillan).

Fishbane, M.

1985   *Biblical Interpretation in Ancient Israel* (Oxford: Clarendon Press).

Fox, M.V.

1980   'The Rhetoric of Ezekiel's Vision of the Valley of the Bones', *HUCA* 51: 1-15.

Gordis, R.

1978   *The Book of Job: Commentary, New Translation and Special Studies* (Moreshet, 2; New York: The Jewish Theological Seminary of America).

Gray, J.

1964   *I and II Kings* (OTL; London: SCM Press).

Greenberg, M.
    1983   *Ezekiel, 1–20* (AB, 22; Garden City, NY: Doubleday).
    1997   *Ezekiel, 21–37* (AB, 22A; Garden City, NY: Doubleday).
Gunkel, H.
    1888   *Die Wirkungen des heiligen Geistes, nach der populären Anschauung der apostolischen Zeit und nach der Lehre des Apostels Paulus. Eine biblisch-theologische Studie* (Göttingen: Vandenhoeck & Ruprecht).
    1979   *The Influence of the Holy Spirit: The Popular View of the Apostolic Age and the Teaching of the Apostle Paul* (trans. R.A. Harrisville and P.A. Quanbeck II; Philadelphia: Fortress Press).
Hildebrandt, W.
    1995   *An Old Testament Theology of the Spirit of God* (Peabody, MA: Hendrickson).
Hill, D.
    1967   *Greek Words and Hebrew Meanings: Studies in the Semantics of Soteriological Terms* (SNTSMS, 5; Cambridge: Cambridge University Press).
Johnson, A.R.
    1964   *The Vitality of the Individual in the Thought of Ancient Israel* (Cardiff: University of Wales Press, 2nd edn).
Joyce, P.
    1989   *Divine Initiative and Human Response in Ezekiel* (JSOTSup, 51; Sheffield: JSOT Press).
Kaiser, O.
    1974   *Isaiah 13–39* (trans. R.A. Wilson; OTL; London: SCM Press).
Moscati, S.
    1947   'The Wind in Biblical and Phoenician Cosmology', *JBL* 66: 305-10.
Polk, T.
    1983   'Paradigms, Parables, and *mĕšālîm*: On Reading the *māšāl* in Scripture', *CBQ* 45: 564-83.
Prickett, S.
    1986   *Words and the Word: Language, Poetics and Biblical Interpretation* (Cambridge: Cambridge University Press).
    1989   'The Status of Biblical Narrative', *Pacifica* 2: 26-46.
Prickett, S., and R. Barnes
    1991   *The Bible* (Landmarks of World Literature; Cambridge: Cambridge University Press).
Renz, T.
    1999   *The Rhetorical Function of the Book of Ezekiel* (VTSup, 76; Leiden: E.J. Brill).
Shoemaker, W.R.
    1904   'The Use of רוּחַ in the Old Testament and πνεῦμα in the New Testament', *JBL* 23: 13-67.
Vriezen, T.C.
    1966   'Ruach Yahweh (Elohim) in the Old Testament', in *Biblical Essays: Proceedings of the Ninth Meeting of 'Die Ou-Testamentiese Werkgemeenskap in Suid-Africa' Held at the University of Stellenbosch 26th–29th July 1966 and Proceedings of the Second Meeting of 'Die Nuew-Testamentiese Werkgemeenskap van Suid-Africa' Held at the University of Stellenbosch 22nd–25th July 1966* (South Africa: Pro Rege-Pers): 50-61.
Wiggins, S.A.
    1999   'Tempestuous Wind Doing Yhwh's Will: Perceptions of the Wind in the Psalms', *SJOT* 13: 3-23.

Woodhouse, J.
  1991   'The "Spirit" in the Book of Ezekiel', in B.G. Webb (ed.), *Spirit of the Living God, Part One* (Explorations, 5; Sydney: Lancer): 1-22.
Wright, T.J.
  1985   'Rûaḥ: A Survey', in D.W. Dockrill and R.G. Tanner (eds.), *The Concept of Spirit* (Prudentia Supplementary Number 1985; Prudentia: Auckland): 5-25.
Zimmerli, W.
  1969   *Ezechiel. II. Ezechiel 25–48* (BKAT, XIII/2; 2 vols.; Neukirchener–Vluyn: Neukirchener Verlag).
  1983   *Ezekiel. II. A Commentary on the Book of Ezekiel, Chapters 25–48* (trans. J.D. Martin; Hermeneia; Philadelphia: Fortress Press).

The Genre of Jonah

Steven L. McKenzie

In a recent article on the future of form criticism, Tony Campbell calls for a refocusing of the method 'on the lasting insight and value that once contributed to firing enthusiasm for it' (Campbell 2003: 16). That insight, he goes on to explain, is embodied in two concerns: concern for the shape or structure of a text (German *Form*) and concern for its genre (*Gattung*).[1] The purpose of this article is to illustrate these and others of Campbell's insights with a form-critical analysis of the book of Jonah in hopes of demonstrating their validity and perhaps supplementing them with some additional suggestions. I will begin with the concerns of *Form* and *Gattung* that Campbell highlights.

1. *The Structure (*Form*) of Jonah*

The typical first step of form-critical analysis is determination of the unit to be studied. Since the unit in question is the book of Jonah, its beginning and end points are not at issue. However, Campbell's observation that 'the focus on the whole' was central to the initial attraction of scholars to form criticism and 'remains at the core of form-critical insight' is pertinent (Campbell 2003: 23). The book of Jonah may be composite (Sasson 1990: 16-19). The originality of the psalm in Jon. 2.3-10 has especially been called into question, although most scholars have now come to see the psalm as integral to the book as it now exists. The present analysis will have to reflect on the matter of the poem's original *Sitz im Leben*, but the primary concern in Jonah is certainly the nature of the book as a whole.

   A unit's beginning and ending are often key for form-critical considerations, and those of Jonah highlight the book's uniqueness. Jonah is among the prophets, and it begins like other prophetic books by noting that 'the word of *Yhwh* came to Jonah son of Amittai' (1.1). However, this is not a heading like those found at the beginnings of most prophetic writings (Isaiah, Jeremiah, Hosea, Joel, Amos, Obadiah, Micah, Nahum, Habakkuk, Zephaniah, Malachi). It does not say 'the word of *Yhwh that* came to Jonah '. Rather, it launches into the story: 'The word of *Yhwh* came to Jonah son of Amittai, *saying*…' In this respect, Jonah's begin-

---

1. Campbell uses the term 'nature' instead of 'genre'. I prefer 'genre' as a designation for literary category and 'nature' as a broader term encompassing the *Gattung* of a text as well as its purpose or function and *Sitz im Leben*.

ning is close to those of Haggai and Zechariah, only without a dating formula as in the latter books. This distinctive beginning highlights the fact that Jonah, unlike the other prophetic books, is essentially a narrative rather than a collection of oracles.

The ending of Jonah also suggests its uniqueness, as it is one of only two books in the Hebrew Bible that conclude with a question. The other one, Nahum, also concerns a prophet who utters an oracle against Nineveh. But while Nahum asks Nineveh whom its evil has not impacted, in Jonah the question is patently theological; *Yhwh* asks whether he (*Yhwh*) is not justified in being concerned for all the people and animals of Nineveh. This question has implications for the nature of the book.

There are two sets of expressions in the book that seem to function as dividers, such that the narrative falls into four episodes or scenes. The statement that opens the book, ויהי דבר יהוה אל־יונה, is repeated in 3.1 with the additional word שנית, effectively dividing the book in two. Then, the notices of Jonah's prayers in 2.2 and 4.2 divide each half in two. Thus, the book falls into four principal scenes:

1. Jonah on the ship (1.1-2.1 [Eng. 1.1-17]).
2. Jonah in the fish's belly (2.2-11 [Eng. 2.1-10]).
3. The effectiveness of Jonah's preaching in Nineveh (3.1–4.1).
4. Jonah's reaction to the Ninevites' repentance (4.2-11).

The symmetry between the two halves of the book reveals that Jonah is a well organized work of narrative literature.[2] It also shows clearly that Jonah is the central character of the work and suggests that its contents revolve around his interactions with the other characters.

2. *The Genre (*Gattung*) of Jonah*

Campbell observes, 'Without adequate reflection, it is frequently taken for granted that the focus of Old Testament narrative traditions is history' (Campbell 2003: 27). Certainly that is the case with Jonah, which has engendered frequent and heated debates about its narrative's historicity, especially as regards the possibility of a person surviving three days inside a whale. Yet, as Campbell goes on to point out, narrative can be the format for many different *Gattungen*—story, account, report or notice, legend and märchen [*sic*] among others, and he notes that distinguishing imaginative story from historical report in the Bible, though important, can be challenging (Campbell 2003: 27-28).

In Jonah, there are good indications that one is dealing with story. We have already seen that the Jonah narrative evinces a well organized literary structure. It is also full of word plays, what Halpern and Friedman (1980: 83) call 'an ornate tapestry of paronomastic techniques'. Jonah is, moreover, a tapestry of allusions to other biblical texts, including ones in Genesis, Exodus, Deuteronomy, the

---

2. For a much more detailed study of Jonah's symmetry than is possible here, see Trible 1994 (especially pp. 110-17). See also the synthesis of observations about Jonah's structure in Marcus 1995: 138-39.

Elijah/Elisha stories in Kings, Psalms, and other prophets, especially Jeremiah (cf. Feuillet 1947; Lacoque and Lacoque 1990: 16-19; Magonet 1976: 65-84). These structural and literary techniques do not exclude historical report but are more typical of the creative activity of storytelling. It is also widely recognized that there are patently unhistorical elements to the narrative, especially as concerns Nineveh, which came to prominence as the capital of Assyria only in the seventh century, over 100 years after the prophet Jonah of 2 Kgs 14.25 (Grayson 1992: 1119). The description of the city as three days' journey across (Jon. 3.3) is a gross exaggeration.[3] At its height, Nineveh's circumference was about 7.75 miles (Grayson 1992: 1118). The title 'king of Nineveh' is at best a narratological device rather than a historical designation (Sasson 1990: 248). Also, the reference to Joppa as Jonah's port of embarkation is problematic, since Joppa was apparently in Philistine, not Israelite, hands in the eighth century (*ANET*: 287). What is more, the Phoenician port of Tyre would have been closer to Gathhepher in the Galilee, Jonah's home according to 2 Kgs 14.25 (Wolff 1986: 77).

More to the point, the narrative in Jonah evinces very few details befitting historical or biographical report. No date or time frame is supplied for the story. There are no details about Jonah's life or career. The book does not explain when Jonah lived or where he was from; it never even calls him a prophet. While that information may have been assumed (2 Kgs 14.25), the author apparently considered it irrelevant to the point of the book. The ethnic origin of the sailors is not identified. We are also not told at what place on dry land the fish vomits Jonah up. Nor is the name of the king of Nineveh provided; indeed, Jonah is the only human character who is named.

On the other hand, the definition of story over against report is eminently appropriate to Jonah: 'Story moves from tension to its resolution, via plot; account, report, and notice do not' (Campbell 2003: 27). The tension in the story is brought about by Jonah's disobedience of *Yhwh*'s initial command to go to Nineveh and is resolved when *Yhwh* belays the 'evil' intended for Nineveh after its inhabitants repent at the preaching of Jonah (3.10). The plot details how *Yhwh* thwarted Jonah's attempted flight, Jonah's encounter with the sailors in that attempt, his consumption by the large fish, his prayer/psalm in the fish's belly, his reluctant acceptance of *Yhwh*'s commission, and the Ninevites' response to his delivery of the divine word.

A more specific designation that has been proposed as Jonah's *Gattung* is short story or novella, which is defined as a series of episodes involving a main character in interaction with other characters leading to a conclusion (Wolff 1986: 82). Other examples of novellas in the Bible are the books of Ruth and Esther and the story of Joseph in Genesis 37–50, each of which follows the main character's interactions with different people leading up to the resolution of a tension that is presented early in its narrative. The *Gattung* of Jonah as a whole, then, is short story or novella rather than historical report or account.

---

3.   Although the meaning of this measurement has been debated (e.g. Stuart 1987: 487-88), its reference to diameter seems clear from the next verse according to which Jonah walks a day's journey into the city.

What sets Jonah apart from other novellas is its final episode, essentially ch. 4. This episode consists of the dialogue between *Yhwh* and Jonah, the object lesson of the plant that *Yhwh* causes to spring up overnight and then kills with a worm, and the question that concludes the book. This final scene suggests that the story has a didactic or teaching function, and this observation in turn raises the question of the author's intent in writing the book.

3. *The Purpose or Intent of Jonah*

Jonah's *Gattung* as didactic novella is useful as far as it goes and is widely recognized, at least by scholars. However, this recognition by itself does not get at the lesson that the book aims to teach. For this, it is necessary to examine Jonah's contents. A close assessment of the characters and interactions that are integral to its *Gattung* should bring its didactic objective into relief. Nevertheless, there is much more disagreement among scholars over the question of Jonah's intent or purpose than over its *Gattung*.[4] One does well, therefore, to keep in mind Campbell's point that 'interpretation is an art, not a science' (Campbell 2003: 27).

There are four characters or sets of characters in the story of Jonah: Jonah, God, other people, and the animals. In what follows I will examine each of these characters, their natures, and the role each plays in an effort to discern the intended purpose of the story. Before focusing on these characters, however, some preliminary observations are in order.

There are plenty of examples of exaggeration and hyperbole in the story of Jonah. The exaggerated size of Nineveh has already been noted. The repeated use of 'great' in the book signals this tendency toward exaggeration. Examples include a great city (1.2), a great wind (1.4), a great storm (1.4), and, of course, a great fish (2.1 [Eng. 1.17]), to name a few. There are also examples of ludicrous imagery. In 1.4 the text attributes human characteristics to an inanimate object as it states that the ship 'thought about' breaking up because of the severe storm. These few examples serve to place the reader on alert for other ridiculous and exaggerated images associated with the characters and their interactions.

a. *Jonah*
Jonah is a ridiculous character, full of contradictions. He is a prophet who does not want to prophesy, a man of God who tries to run away from God. He is the only character in the book who does not obey God. While prophets are typically admired for their boldness and integrity in speaking the word of God, there is nothing admirable about Jonah.

Jonah blatantly disobeys the divine command to go to Nineveh and flees in the opposite direction.[5] This is most unexpected; it is exactly the opposite of the

---

4.   For an overview of the different proposals, see Marcus 1995: 148-56.

5.   There are several candidates for ancient Tarshish. The one likely intended here was Tartessos on the southern coast of Spain, which would have represented the westernmost nautical destination for Israelites.

obedience to God that one expects a prophet to model. While Moses and Jeremiah are reluctant to accept the divine call, Jonah is alone in direct disobedience. More to the point, his action is nonsensical. Jonah makes clear in his later conversation with the sailors that he believes *Yhwh* to be the God of heaven and the maker of sea and dry land (1.9). But if he believes that *Yhwh* is not confined by geographical boundaries, how can he hope to run away from him? Jonah's action is ridiculous and inexplicable, and the narrative does not offer any explanation for it at this point. He appears deluded, a character whose deeds do not match his beliefs.

On the ship, Jonah is so out of touch with what *Yhwh* is doing that he falls asleep in the hull, oblivious to the storm raging outside. It takes a non-Israelite, the captain of the foreign crew, to advise Jonah that he needs to get in touch with his God (1.6). Despite the captain's plea, there is no prayer on Jonah's lips at this point. His ethnic pride is obvious in his self-identification to the sailors (1.9), in which he boasts that he is a Hebrew and that he fears the very God he is fleeing (1.10). The fact that he has imperiled the ship and its crew seems to be of little significance to him.

The only time in the book that Jonah expresses gratitude is at the low point of the story for him—while he is in the fish's belly—and then it is entirely inappropriate. The prayer attributed to him in ch. 2 is actually a hymn of thanksgiving, which seems out of character for Jonah, especially in his current predicament. The words of the hymn are also not entirely appropriate to Jonah's situation. There is no mention of his mission or any of the events that placed Jonah in his predicament. Ironically, the first word of the poem is the verb 'I called' (2.3 [Eng. 2.2]); Jonah called to *Yhwh* in his distress—distress brought about by his failure to obey *Yhwh*'s order to 'call out' against Nineveh (1.2). It is *Yhwh* in the poem (2.4 [Eng. 2.3]), rather than the sailors as in 1.15, who threw the psalmist into the sea. There is no mention of the fish in the psalm; rather, the psalmist has apparently survived a 'near death' experience. The image of drowning in the psalm is simply a metaphor for death based on the comparison of the sea with the 'Pit' and 'Sheol'. Jonah, in contrast, does not yet know that he will survive his ordeal; he could die inside the whale. The references to *Yhwh*'s 'house' or 'temple' (2.4, 7) are also inappropriate to Jonah's situation. The temple was in Jerusalem, the capital of Judah, while Jonah was from the kingdom of Israel. Moreover, v. 9 mentions sacrifice at the temple and thus presupposes a setting back on land. This verse also refers to a vow to be paid at the temple—presumably one conditioned on the psalmist's recovery—of which there is no mention in the story of Jonah.

The original *Sitz im Leben* of the psalm in ch. 2 seems clearly to lie outside of the book of Jonah. It is impossible to know whether the poem is a later addition to the book or was borrowed from another setting by the author of Jonah. This is so precisely because the psalm's inappropriateness to Jonah's situation fits perfectly with the many ridiculous features of the story (Ackerman 1981). As Marcus (1995: 123-24) has observed, the poem is a linguistic parody in that it borrows metaphors common in other psalms but takes them literally. Most inappropriate and ridiculous of all, though, is the very picture of a man composing and then intoning a rousing hymn inside of a large fish that has just swallowed him. The humor of the scene is carried through its conclusion, when after three days *Yhwh* talks to the fish so that it 'vomits' Jonah up on dry land, thereby graphically illustrating *Yhwh*'s own disgust for the errant prophet (Ackerman 1981: 225).

Jonah displays no regret in the fish or on dry ground for having failed his mission and disobeyed *Yhwh*'s command. He is the only character in the book who does not repent. He remains obstinate. His attitude is unchanged. He learns nothing from his experiences. He goes to Nineveh when *Yhwh* commands him a second time, but only because he has no choice; fleeing has proven futile. His attitude toward the people of Nineveh and his task is reflected in his message in 3.4. Again, his behavior is stubborn and irrational and out of character for a prophet. Other prophets deliver extended oracles full of colorful language and vivid metaphors. Jonah has no intention of doing anything beyond the bare minimum. He marches a day's journey into the middle of Nineveh and utters the book's one brief oracle—only five words in Hebrew: עוד ארבעים יום ונינוה נהפכת ('Forty days from now Nineveh will be overturned'). The oracle is nonsensical, for while forty days is typically a round number for a long time in the Bible, the context or Jonah indicates that a short time is intended (Marcus 1995: 126). Also, the verb נהפכת is ambiguous; does it mean 'destroyed' or 'changed'?[6] There is no indication in the text that he repeats his message; he simply turns and leaves. Jonah refuses to prolong his message or his visit because he does not want them to be effective. Unlike other prophets, Jonah does not want his audience to listen or repent. He wants to see the Ninevites destroyed.

Despite his half-hearted effort, however, Jonah's prophecy is enormously successful—ridiculously so. He is the most successful prophet in the Bible by far. The entire city of Nineveh repents with fasting and prayer and sackcloth. Any other prophet would be ecstatic. But not Jonah. This turn of events strikes him as a 'great evil' (וירע אל־יונה רעה גדולה), and makes him angry (4.1). In 4.2, he explains the reason for his anger as well as for his initial flight. The explanation is even more absurd than his trying to run away in the first place. It is because *Yhwh* is merciful and forgiving, and Jonah wants the Ninevites destroyed, not forgiven. The verse cites what in other biblical texts (e.g. Exod. 34.6-7; Neh. 9.17) is a kind of credo or confession, but in Jonah's mouth it is a source of irritation. Jonah goes so far as to ask *Yhwh* to take his life. The prophet Elijah also asks for God to take his life (1 Kgs 19.4)—but because of failure as a prophet, not success like Jonah (Marcus 1995: 132). If God is not going to kill his enemies, Jonah reasons, God may as well kill him. Divine mercy makes life unbearable for him. His prejudice and hatred turn him into a ridiculous and pathetic character. The fact that *Yhwh* showed mercy to him when he directly disobeyed the order to go to Nineveh does not seem to occur to Jonah. Apparently hoping that the Ninevites will backslide so that he may still witness their annihilation, Jonah sets up camp overlooking the city.

6.   The ambiguity of this verb helps to counter the view that Jonah's anger is motivated not by bigotry but because he is worried about his prophetic 'record' (Burrows 1970). Even if Nineveh is not destroyed, it is certainly changed following the city's repentance at Jonah's preaching.

Of all of the ridiculous images in Jonah, perhaps the most ridiculous one concerns the bush that *Yhwh* appoints as an object lesson. Jonah cares deeply for this plant. He 'rejoices with great joy' over it (וישמח יונה על־הקיקיון שמחה גדולה, 4.6). Jonah's sense of priorities is ridiculous. He is more concerned about a bush than he is about people. He hates the myriads of people in Nineveh and longs for their destruction, but he holds deep feelings for a plant that gave him a little shade. His selfishness and callousness are incredible. He is so distraught over its death that for a second time he asks *Yhwh* to kill him (4.8). Life is just not worth living, as far as Jonah is concerned, without his plant. Again, he is an unbelievably ridiculous and pitiful character. *Yhwh*'s final interview with Jonah and the concluding question of the book are meant to show Jonah that his values are mixed up. While the question may be rhetorical, the fact that Jonah does not respond leaves the reader wondering whether he ever learned his lesson.

b. *God*

God in the book of Jonah is *Yhwh*, the God of Israel, who is also God of the entire universe, according to Jonah's confession in 1.9. Ironically, however, the Lord of the universe turns out to be an astounding micromanager in Jonah. He not only commands Jonah (1.1-2), but he also personally hurls the wind on the sea (1.4). He appoints (וימן) the great fish (1.1 [Eng. 1.17]) and then speaks to it so that it vomits up Jonah (2.11 [Eng. 2.10]). He also appoints (וימן) a bush (4.6) to shade Jonah and then, perhaps most ludicrous of all, appoints (וימן) a worm (4.7) to attack the bush. Finally, he appoints (וימן) a sultry east wind to afflict Jonah (4.8).

The idea of the Almighty personally sending out individual fish, plants, and worms on special missions and even speaking to them is ridiculous on one level. Yet, it provides a point of contrast that is important for the story. *Yhwh*, the God of Israel and also the God of heaven, the maker of sea and dry land, cares for and is involved in all of creation. His concern for the lowliest of creatures contrasts with Jonah's callousness toward his fellow human beings in wanting to see Nineveh destroyed. God's purpose in sending Jonah to Nineveh to 'cry out against it' is redemptive. He wants the Ninevites to repent so that he will not destroy them. On the way, he causes the sailors to revere him. He shows them his power but does not destroy them. When the people of Nineveh repent, he responds with mercy and saves the city. He expresses compassion for all of the people and the animals of the great city. However, the greatest display of *Yhwh*'s mercy in the book may well be in his treatment of Jonah himself. Despite Jonah's direct disobedience to a divine command and his selfish and arrogant attitude, *Yhwh* does not punish him but remains patient and to the end tries to instruct Jonah. The very mercy of God that so angers Jonah is what keeps him from being the target of divine wrath.

c. *Other People*

The two groups of people whom Jonah encounters in the story, the sailors and the Ninevites, are the opposite of Jonah, and their respective depictions are unexpected. Surprisingly, both groups make use of Israelite language and theology, as Marcus (1995: 128-30) has shown. The sailors are not the weathered, calloused lot that one might expect. They are more attuned to divine activity than Jonah. They perceive that the sudden, tremendous storm is not coincidental but is a divine response to something someone on the ship has done. The ship is in serious danger, so the sailors and everyone on board—except Jonah—are praying fervently.

The non-Israelite mariners, who have just learned about *Yhwh*, are more perceptive about his nature than his own prophet. They cast lots in order to discover the responsible party (1.7), and the lot falls upon Jonah. His confession to be a worshipper of '*Yhwh*, the God of heaven, who made the sea and the dry land' seems calculated to enhance the sailors' estimation of his own importance as well as their fears. And indeed, they become more afraid (1.10). These 'heathens' are immediately aware of the foolishness and futility of Jonah's attempt to run away from the Maker of heaven and earth. They are religious men who have been calling on their gods since the storm began and their ship became imperiled. Despite their devotion to the various religions, they convert immediately upon hearing Jonah's confession (1.9), and their prayers henceforth are directed to *Yhwh*.

The sailors also display a greater respect for human life than Jonah exhibits. They throw the cargo overboard when the storm becomes nasty (1.5). Their sense of priority—placing human life above profit—contrasts with Jonah's. Jonah tells them that they can calm the storm by throwing him overboard. One might expect hardened men such as sailors to comply immediately, especially considering Jonah's attitude of superiority. Yet these sailors are moral men. They do everything they can to save Jonah, rowing hard to try to return the ship to shore (1.13). It is only as a last resort and with great regret and fervent prayer to *Yhwh* that they toss Jonah into the sea. The sailors' fear of *Yhwh* and respect for human life contrast with Jonah's hatred and bloodthirstiness toward the people of Nineveh.

The Ninevites are also more righteous than Jonah. They are as pious and ready to convert as the sailors. Despite their great wickedness (1.2) they give heed to Jonah's message for them. They perceive, without his saying so, that he is speaking God's truth. His terse oracle evokes an incredible response. Everyone in the city repents, fasts, and puts on sackcloth as a sign of contrition (3.5), even before the king's order to do so. The king of Nineveh issues a decree mandating repentance (3.6-9). He does so without any certainty of the abatement of divine punishment but only in the hope that God will relent. The Ninevites thus rely on the very mercy of God that infuriates Jonah.

d. *The Animals*
It is not just the human characters other than Jonah who are obedient to God in the story. The animals and forces of nature also do God's bidding. The role played by animals in Jonah is especially remarkable both in its extent and in its character. The great fish appointed by *Yhwh* obeys him first by swallowing Jonah and then by vomiting up the distasteful prophet three days later when *Yhwh* speaks to it.

Most ludicrous of all is the image of the animals in Nineveh. The people of Nineveh are not alone in their response to Jonah's preaching. When news of Jonah's threatening message reaches the king of Nineveh, he issues a decree commanding all the people *and the animals* in the city to repent, fast, dress in sackcloth and pray to God for forgiveness (3.7-8). The idea that the animals in Nineveh dress themselves is, of course, quite ridiculous—much less that they would repent (or have sins to repent of for that matter), or fast, or pray. The animals of Nineveh highlight two points that are essential to the story in Jonah. First, they show the extent of the effectiveness of Jonah's message: everybody *and everything* repented. Second, they demonstrate the peculiarity of Jonah's character: everybody *and everything* else in the book obeys God.

Animals appear again at the end of Jonah, first when the Almighty appoints a worm and then in the rhetorical question that concludes the book: 'Should I not show compassion on Nineveh, the great city in which there are more than 120,000 people who do not know their right hand from their left *and many animals*?' This scene is part of an object lesson designed to teach Jonah that God cares for the people whom he (Jonah) detests—and not just the people but the animals as well. The animals are the last characters mentioned in Jonah, and they illustrate *Yhwh*'s concern for all of his creation.

This analysis of the characters in Jonah indicates that they are really carica-tures in service of the book's intent, which is to satirize Jonah or the people or attitude he represents. The book thus attacks the character of Jonah and is domi-nated by such unbelievable elements as absurdities, fantastic situations, and dis-tortions, as well as ironies, ridicule, parody, and rhetorical features, all of which are characteristic features of satire (Marcus 1995: 9-10).[7] Jonah's ridiculous, sometimes contradictory actions and words seem to be caused by his bigotry and hatred of the non-Israelite people in the book.[8] The other characters, as well as the exaggerations and ludicrous features of the story bring the foolishness of Jonah's prejudice and hatred into relief. Thus, *Yhwh*, the creator of all people, animals, and things, micromanages his creation in an effort to teach the obstinate prophet a lesson. The non-Israelites whom Jonah encounters turn out to be more pious and moral than he. The animals highlight the story's comical nature and ludicrous imagery and show *Yhwh*'s concern for all creation. While Jonah is the direct target of ridicule in the book, its real objective is the book's intended readership. The humor and hyperbole help the book's audience to perceive in Jonah the silliness of their own attitudes and the ridiculous lengths to which

7.   Marcus (1995: 97-141) systematically traces each of these features in Jonah.
8.   The view that the Jonah is primarily concerned to advocate divine mercy over justice as opposed to universalism over nationalism and bigotry (Crawford 1998; Simon 1999: vii-xiii) fails to appreciate the ethnic and national designations in the book: Jonah boasts that he is Hebrew (1.9); Nineveh can hardly be regarded as 'any big city' (Crawford 1998: 656) in view of Assyria's destruction of Israel. While the ethnic origin of the sailors is not given, the parallels between them and the Ninevites in the narrative indicate that they are 'not merely an accidental background' but are also 'representatives of the "pagan" world' (Magonet 1992: 938). Jonah, moreover, is hardly a compelling advocate of justice.

arrogance and prejudice can lead them. Jonah's character is thus something of a mirror for the book's audience. The author wishes to engage the audience with a ridiculous story, which will lead them to perceive a serious point.

4. *The* Sitz im Leben *of Jonah*

Jonah's name (יוֹנָה), meaning 'dove', contributes to the book's intent. The dove is sometimes used as a symbol for Israel (e.g. Hos. 7.11; 11.11), so that Jonah's character may represent Israel or at least some constituency of it. However, there is little to go on as regards the precise historical or social situation that the book was written to address. Jonah was drafted from 2 Kgs 14.25 as the story's main character perhaps because of the meaning of his name but also because he lived at a time when Assyria was reaching its apex.[9] Since Assyria decimated Israel in 721 BCE, it could be considered the quintessential 'evil empire' of foreigners. The fact that Jonah in 2 Kgs 14.25 was a nationalistic prophet who predicted the expansion of Jeroboam II's kingdom further enhanced his suitability as the target for a satirical portrait of a bigot. Still, by the time the book of Jonah was written, three centuries or more later, the real Jonah was a faint memory.[10] To judge from other writings of approximately this time (Ezra–Nehemiah, Chronicles, and perhaps Ruth), the question of *Yhwh*'s universal dominion and concern for all people seems to have become especially pointed. Jonah was likely written to contribute to this theological debate and may even have been intended as a response to the narrow perspective of Ezra–Nehemiah. Unfortunately, it is impossible to be more precise.

5. *Conclusions*

Jonah is a parade example of the way in which form criticism can enrich understanding of the Bible. A form-critical analysis of Jonah indicates that the real goal of form criticism is the discernment of an author's intent in a biblical text.[11] *Form* and *Gattung* are important dimensions of form criticism, but they may fall short of this goal, since a text's intent is not always implicit in its *Gattung*. Discernment of a text's intent is certainly not an objective science. This is because, as in Jonah, the composers of biblical texts could be quite creative—'knowledgeable, skillful, and presumably aesthetically aware' (Campbell 2003: 23).

---

9.   Jonah's patronymic, Amittai, may have furnished an additional, ironic motive for drafting him. It appears to be a shortened form of a sentence name meaning '*Yhwh*/My God is truth/faithfulness' (Fowler 1988: 165; Noth 1928: 162). In any case, it makes use of the root אמת, so that Jonah appears as 'son of truth', yet he is hardly true to his assigned task.

10.   The unhistorical nature of its details concerning Nineveh suggests considerable removal from the eighth century. The book is usually assigned a date in the post-exilic period (around 400 BCE) based on linguistic indicators, but even these do not yield certainty. For a review of the evidence, see Sasson 1990: 20-28.

11.   A text's meaning cannot be limited to its author's intent. Intent remains, however, an important part of the communication process from author to reader and the underlying reason for form criticism's attempt to discern a text's *Form* and *Gattung*.

Rarely do such texts explicitly articulate the intent behind their composition. Nevertheless, even a highly creative text like Jonah gives signals that allow careful readers to infer the author's intent from the work's content. In Jonah, exaggeration and caricature furnish these signs. The ridiculousness of the story is intentional and inherent to its satirical intent.

Campbell's stress on form-critical analysis of the whole of a work is important in this vein. The *Gattung* and intent of the book of Jonah are entirely different from those of any of its presumed composite parts. This stress on the whole may be applied fruitfully to other biblical books and perhaps entire corpora or *Gattungen*. I have in mind recent treatments of biblical history writing in the context of the ancient Mediterranean and Near Eastern world (Van Seters 1983). As with Jonah, the *Gattung* of historiography is widely recognized, but the assumption that its intent was to recount the past *wie es eigentlich gewesen ist* is a patently modern one.

Perhaps the most important aspect of form criticism in Jonah, and the closest to Tony Campbell's heart, is the implications it can have for faith. The debates over Jonah's historicity have often been heated because the very trustworthiness of the Bible is deemed to be at stake. These debates arise from misconstruals of the story's genre and misunderstandings of its intent. The problem, in other words, is not with the Bible but with its interpretation. The perspective on Jonah offered above is hardly new or unique.[12] Hence, it is surprising to find scholars these days, who still defend the historicity of the story.[13] This sort of monolithic approach to biblical literature not only misses the richness, if not the entire point of the book, but ironically also runs the risk of imposing upon the lay reader a 'faith crisis' that forces one to choose between the Bible and scientific accuracy or sensibility. Sensitivity to an author's creative use of *Gattung* for different intents can allow readers to recognize truth and value apart from historical or scientific accuracy (cf. Buss 1999: 411).

BIBLIOGRAPHY

Ackerman, J.S.
    1981   'Satire and Symbolism in the Song of Jonah', in B. Halpern and J.D. Levenson (eds.), *Traditions in Transformation: Turning Points in Biblical Faith* (FS F.M. Cross; Winona Lake, IN: Eisenbrauns).
Allen, L.C.
    1976   *The Books of Joel, Obadiah, Jonah, and Micah* (NICOT; Grand Rapids: Eerdmans).
Bolin, T.M.
    1997   *Freedom Beyond Forgiveness: The Book of Jonah Re-Examined* (JSOTSup, 236; Sheffield: Sheffield Academic Press).

12. See the list of scholars who have adopted the view that Jonah is satire in Marcus 1995: 145-47.

13. The list of commentaries arguing for historicity includes: Hasel 1976; Shank 2001: 325-63; Stuart 1987: 440-44.

Burrows, M.
1970   'The Literary Category of the Book of Jonah', in H.T. Frank and W.L. Reed (eds.), *Translating and Understanding the Old Testament: Essays in Honor of Herbert Gordon May* (Nashville, TN: Abingdon Press).

Buss, M.
1999   'Form Criticism, Hebrew Bible', in John H. Hayes (ed.), *Dictionary of Biblical Interpretation* (2 vols.; Nashville: Abingdon Press): I, 406-13.

Campbell, A.F.
2003   'Form Criticism's Future', in M.A. Sweeney and E. Ben Zvi (eds.), *The Changing Face of Form Criticism for the Twenty-First Century* (Grand Rapids: Eerdmans): 15-31.

Craig, K.M.
1993   *A Poetics of Jonah: Art in the Service of Ideology* (Columbia: University of South Carolina Press).

Crawford, S.W.
1998   'Jonah', in J.L. May *et al.* (eds.), *The Harper Collins Bible Commentary* (San Francisco: Harper Collins): 656-69.

Crenshaw, J.L.
1993   'Jonah, The Book of', in B.M. Metzger and M.D. Coogan (eds.), *The Oxford Companion to the Bible* (New York: Oxford University Press): 380-81.

Feuillet, A.
1947   'Les sources du livre de Jonas', *RB* 54: 161-86.

Fowler, J.D.
1988   *Theophoric Personal Names in Ancient Hebrew: A Comparative Study* (JSOTSup, 49; Sheffield: JSOT Press).

Good, E.M.
1965   *Irony in the Old Testament* (Philadelphia: Westminster Press).

Grayson, A.K.
1992   'Nineveh', in *ABD*, IV: 1118-19.

Halpern, B., and R.E. Friedman
1980   'Composition and Paronomasia in the Book of Jonah', *HAR* 4: 79-92.

Hasel, G.F.
1976   *Jonah: Messenger of the Eleventh Hour* (Mountain View, CA: Pacific Press).

Lacoque, A., and P-E. Lacoque
1990   *Jonah: A Psycho-Religious Approach to the Prophet* (Columbia: University of South Carolina Press).

Landes, G.M.
1976   'Jonah', in *IDBSup*: 488-91.
1978   'Jonah: A *Mashal*?', in J.G. Gammie *et al.* (eds.), *Israelite Wisdom: Theological and Literary Essays in Honor of Samuel Terrien* (Missoula, MT: Scholars Press): 137-58.

Limburg, J.
1993   *Jonah: A Commentary* (OTL; Louisville, KY: Westminster/John Knox Press).

Magonet, J.
1976   *Form and Meaning: Studies in Literary Techniques in the Book of Jonah* (Bible and Literature, 2; Frankfurt: Peter Lang).
1992   'Jonah', in *ABD*, III: 936-42.

Marcus, D.
1995   *From Balaam to Jonah: Anti-Prophetic Satire in the Hebrew Bible* (BJS, 301; Atlanta: Scholars Press).

Noth, M.
    1928   *Die israelitische Personennamen im Rahmen der gemeinsemitischen Namengebung* (BWANT, III.10; Stuttgart: W. Kohlhammer).

Person, R.F., Jr
    1996   *Conversation with Jonah: Conversation Analysis, Literary Criticism, and the Book of Jonah* (JSOTSup, 220; Sheffield: Sheffield Academic Press).

Sasson, J.M.
    1990   *Jonah* (AB, 24B; New York: Doubleday).

Shank, H.
    2001   *Minor Prophets* (The College Press NIV Commentary; Joplin, MO: Collegeville).

Simon, U.
    1999   *Jonah* (The JPS Bible Commentary; Philadelphia: Jewish Publication Society of America).

Stuart, D.
    1987   *Hosea–Jonah* (WBC, 31; Waco, TX: Word Books).

Sweeney, M.A.
    2000–   *The Twelve Prophets*, I (Berit Olam; Collegeville, MN: Liturgical Press).

Trible, P.
    1994   *Rhetorical Criticism: Context, Method, and the Book of Jonah* (Guides to Biblical Scholarship; Minneapolis: Fortress Press).

Van Seters, J.
    1983   *In Search of History: Historiography in the Ancient World and the Origins of Biblical History* (New Haven: Yale University Press).

Wolff, H.W.
    1986   *Obadiah and Jonah: A Commentary* (trans. M. Kohl; Minneapolis: Augsburg).

Part IV

IN BIBLICAL THEOLOGY

The Truth Trap in Interpretation[*]

Sean McEvenue

1. *Introduction*

Truth from the Bible, and true interpretation of the Bible, is very influential for good and evil in the affairs of this world and the next, and we must be grateful for all the advances over the past more than three hundred years in historical knowledge and hermeneutic method which have made possible an ever more textured understanding of ancient text. Many deadly anti-Catholic and anti-Semitic teachings have been based on studies of the Bible which have been honest, but following less informed methodology. In fact, according to a recent study, the development of hermeneutical speculation by Baruch Spinoza, which served to provide the philosophical basis for what became the 'historical-critical method', was motivated by his personal experience of persecution at the hands of the Catholic Church in Portugal, and the Rabbis in Amsterdam. In developing the theme that one could not claim to understand a biblical text until one had identified who had written it and in what historical context, Spinoza was primarily trying to free himself and others from an oppressive and life-threatening tyranny of dogma.[1] We must be grateful for this freedom.

On the other hand, this drive for truth is an arrogant effort. Unless we allow for its limitations, and provide further dimensions, it refuses any biblical message. Historical-critical method is an evolving application of the Enlightenment's discovery of objectivity in knowledge. Hard science was becoming the respected measure of truth, and all other truths were valued in a descending scale from hard science according to their degree of objectivity, with all personal reference meticulously removed. Thus, formal truth no longer induced knowledge learned by a revealing of what was hidden ('he finally admitted to his guilt'), or defined in terms of fidelity to what one had said ('he was true to his word'), or contaminated in any way by sentimental or emotive attachments (e.g. bitter truth or heartfelt truth), but it was triumphantly torn from its personal and subjective roots and viewed as the perfect correspondence between verifiable objective data and the formulations of words intended to depict them. Ingenious methods developed over the years for removing all bias, not only the bias of personal advantage but even the unavoidable bias of individual perspective. Thus the data henceforth

*   This essay has been written as an expression of respect and gratitude to Antony Campbell for his immense contribution to this effort through many years of precise scholarship, creative presentation, and unstinting labour in extremely useful publications.

1.   See Dungan 1999.

has to be observed as identical by several different people who live in different places, and so forth. In this perspective, truth has become a category reserved for things proven in these disciplined ways. This methodology has been extended and perfected for a multitude of diverse disciplines from physics to psychology. Wonderful things are achieved daily with it, but it harbours an in-built arrogance. It implicitly banishes from the realm of respected truth any knowledge except that which has been obtained as an impersonal and methodically derived answer to an objective question, every word of which is precisely defined. Thus we arrogantly decide in advance what we will know, what we will ask, how we will set standards of evidence and rules of inference. Knowledge based on affirmations by authority figures, or on intuition, or extended experience (let alone 'answer in prayer', extra-sensory perception and mental telepathy, etc.), may be interesting, but it is not respected at the level of truth. In fact most of what we know is excused from the category of 'truth'.

Without attempting a philosophical debate on this general observation, I would simply point out the most grossly obvious difficulty for finding truth in or about biblical text. In the first place, the historical data is so thin concerning ancient Israel during the biblical period that any historical affirmations which one can make about authors, or their specific contexts or the factual bases of their views, have only the most tenuous historical provability. The whole Bible suddenly seems to enter the realm of the partially possible and generally probable! And, instead of learning faith by reading an account of events in the Bible, must we first have faith in order to believe that those things happened?

Moreover, any affirmation in which the word 'God' appears is certainly not 'true' in this current sense of the word. God is a personal name, invoking a person defined as eternal, all-powerful, infinitely loving. This name cannot be properly used in an objective sentence, as its understanding within human thought is radically beyond our conceptualizations. God is not an object but a person known in an irresistible relationship or else not known. 'God' is a meaningful word only in the stance of I–Thou, that is, only as an invocation of another in which we cannot think and coldly define, but rather we must be swept out of ourselves towards the unlimited with awe and joy and hope. When we say anything through or about the biblical text speaking of God, we are either in a state of prayer (I–Thou, personal and subjective), or else discussing a mere virtual reality which we set up for purposes of discussion (no real object). Neither of these alternatives satisfies the scientific agenda.

Much has been written establishing the validity and nature of theological truth.[2] But most readers are not philosophers, and we often receive statements about the truth of scripture with an uncritical post-scientific and post-modern mind-set, ending then in confusion and scepticism. In what follows, I shall attempt to show that scriptural texts require of us a different approach from that

---

2.   Cf. Lonergan 1971. This important work provides the philosophical framework for the terms and definitions and epistemological reasoning in this paper.

which is easily defined in terms of scientific truth. I shall focus on a form of true knowledge specifically as this occurs in writing and reading/interpreting.

2. *Theory of Writing and Reading*

So-called academic writing presents, and describes with ever increasing accuracy, a material object (a text, a dated historical object, a chemical, a recorded experiment, an organism, statistical data, objectified psychological data, etc.), one which the reader can also find and observe or eventually learn that other researchers have verified. It also reasons about it, using a strict logic such as mathematics, in some productive way. There results a conclusion with an assigned degree of probability, or at least a hypothesis heading toward conclusions in the future. This is the general path of post-Enlightenment progress in human knowing. Journalists claim to follow the same path and to have the same ideals of truth, but with widely varying fidelity and rigour, ranging from recording the 'facts' with a solid measure of critical precision in a 'newspaper of record' to selecting and grouping them to make them seem intelligible within contemporary myths, and now, amid growing media competition, more and more blatantly extending to market for public appetites for sex, violence, paranoia, and so on. And when we think about 'truth' today, it tends to be thought of within that general model. In this culture, truth is measured by the degree of correspondence between the words and the material objects, and since both of these are usually fixed and, therefore, observable as often as needed, truth can indeed be measured. Truth advances as, on the one hand, the object is better categorized and selected and more precisely perceived and as, on the other hand, the words are better defined and become more and more technical and as the logical reasoning is refined. Most academic disciplines seek to formulate laws of nature, and they advance by a self-correcting process of ever more accurate formulation.

History too follows this same model. However, on the basis of verified objective data, history seeks to deduce, not laws which will hold in all identical cases, but rather the underlying relationships and causes which explain unique events which will never recur in identical form, and it advances by achieving ever more complete understanding and more precise accounting of these events.

Literary writing is totally different. It may not refer to facts at all, or when it does use facts or hard data, its primary focus is to evoke a personal (subjective) experience of them, a personal 'take' on them. And it does not record that experience objectively or phenomenologically so that the experience might be analyzed into its objective (true) and subjective (false) components, but rather it evokes the whole experience, using the resources of image and language so that the reader may share it. For this reason, literature is not usefully characterized as true or false, though those categories are sometimes used. Rather it is either good or bad! Literature is considered bad for one of two reasons. The first one is that it fails to evoke anything very much. There is a failure of language, of conceptualization, of image. What the author thinks to have expressed does not come across because even experts in reading cannot find in these words anything which leads them to a fresh experience, a new 'vision'. The second one is that the author's 'take' or 'experience' was trivial, or superficial, or perhaps perverse.[3]

Now contemporary theology is written in academic form, and categories of true and false are properly invoked in evaluating every sentence. But the Bible, its most normative source, was written in literary forms. Biblical texts either preceded the Socratic discovery of rigid logic, or else, even when written within the sphere of Hellenistic culture, retained their Jewish tradition of evocative and analogous thinking, and remained totally innocent of the canons of clear definition of terms and of syllogistic reasoning. And the Enlightenment, far from changing anything in the Bible, sharply enjoined upon us that we read the Bible as it was written, within its own thought patterns.[4]

Every page of the Bible is, at least in part, about God. God is not a material object. God cannot be described precisely and recorded. But God has been experienced and this experience of God can be evoked in literary forms. The Bible cannot be read as history, in our sense of that word, but rather as inspiration or revelation.

There is the experience of God which Jesus had through the hypostatic union of his two natures. His whole life evoked that experience through his attitudes and actions. His words in particular used the literature and thought patterns of ancient Jewish Old Testament culture to help those around him to share in the inspiration and revelation which he experienced and was. And the New Testament evokes in part the life and the words of Jesus, and in part that experience of Jesus' experience which drove his first disciples to become witnesses. The objective data of Jesus' experience can never be recovered and studied, and certainly the data of God can never be visually observed, but the shared evocation of that data has motivated the Christian Church through millennia.[5]

---

3. Literary scholars often will not consider this last category because it demands value judgments for which they do not feel competent, and it leads to censorship which is a contemporary taboo; but over centuries an exclusive canon of authentic literature is established just the same. For example, Victor Hugo's *Les Miserables* is certainly a mixture of story-telling with both accurate and misleading history, and yet it is undeniably a classic, classified as good literature no matter what critics may have noted about its various facets. Dan Brown's *The Da Vinci Code* uses the same ingredients, and is undoubtedly successful in evoking a vision, but we will not know whether his mixture is good or bad literature for many decades.

4. Even Bernard Lonergan (1971: 171), following Albert Descamps, recommends that we formulate biblical theology in this way. But to paraphrase literary texts is inevitably to miss their essence, and usually to falsify them, as has been brilliantly exposed by Cleanth Brooks (1975). Brooks argues that paraphrase presents the literary piece as though it were a statement which is either true or false, whereas these categories totally miss the point.

5. Meier (2001) has compiled a monumental presentation of the data of Jesus' life as accessible using objective historical methodology, but he names his three-volume work *A Marginal Jew: Rethinking the Historical Jesus* because such data is not the story of Jesus that has inspired the Christian faith. Wright (2003) has studied the resurrection as historical fact with truly marvellous sophistication, perception, and cogency. But even this fact, so uniquely basic to Christian faith, is lightly dismissed as fiction by serious historians who choose to not believe, that is, who reject the initial meaning of the biblical texts. History does not express the meaning of these texts, though history is the occasion of their writing. Faith is the meaning.

Similarly, Israel had become a nation and had lived over a thousand years of shared experience prior to Jesus, in which the awareness of God was invoked as a driving and normative force in their community life, and remembered in their literature. Archaeology can recover bits of data, and examine it, but it was its literary evocation by Israel's leaders and prophets, eventually retained in the Bible, which gave Judaism its founding inspiration and revelation, and which continues to do so today.

3. *Definitions*

By experience I mean that global awareness which may be personal or shared with others. On the one hand, it consists of a mixture of an objectified component of sensing along with emotions, thoughts, and decisions we derive from our senses, and, on the other, the unobjectified component of our mind which Lonergan calls foundational reality—that mass of emotions, neuroses, understandings, positions, expectations, images, archetypes, and so on, which form and inform our spontaneous attitude and our take on reality (Lonergan 1971: 267-69). Experience is the material about which we further think and decide.

By revelation I understand that special experience of heightened awareness and divine presence which we all experience at least at some points in our lives. It may be either personal or shared and may remain private or be made public. We may suppose it was experienced in ancient Israel and was described as inspiring Moses and Miriam to sing and dance by the Reed Sea (Exod. 15.19-21). The Early Church seems to have experienced it dramatically in the communal event celebrated as Pentecost, and in many stories we read in Acts. Paul speaks of it in terms of the love of God poured out in our hearts as the Holy Spirit (Rom. 5.5). Ignatius Loyola calls it 'spiritual consolation' and describes it as 'any increase of faith, hope and charity, and all interior joy…the soul inflamed with love of its Creator and Lord, and in consequence loves no created thing…in itself, but in the Creator of them all' and Harvey Egan, following Karl Rahner, describes it as mysticism whether it be the less conscious mysticism experienced in our transcendent orientation in every day life or special illumination by extraordinary grace.[6] In theological jargon, the word 'revelation' is sometimes specially applied to the prophetic illumination associated with the Bible. But it is useful to see it at the same time, not as something pertaining to a unique history, but rather as part of human experience which we all share, and to which we advert at some times during our lives, and to which we could perhaps be much more attentive.

Inspiration I understand as decisions or thoughts which are caused and contained within human consciousness but are directly dependent upon revelation.[7]

---

6.   Cf. Fleming 1978: n. 316; Egan 1987: 21-24; Roy 2003.

7.   For a clear description of this 'direct dependence', see the writings of Lonergan. For example, he shows how ordinarily one loves only after one knows, but in the case of transcendental knowing and loving one first loves through God's gift and then proceeds to love created things differently, and also to inquire about different questions and to know in a new way (Lonergan 1971: 115-17, 242-43, 340-41).

178 _Seeing Signals, Reading Signs_

4. *Concrete Applications*

All of this is an attempt at explanatory theory which now needs to be applied to the concrete reality of writing and reading biblical texts. We shall take several examples. First, the story of Saul, the first king in Israel, the first messiah, the subject matter of 1 Samuel 9–31. In the wider biblical context of the history of Israel, it serves to introduce the institution of kingship and, in particular, the momentous story of David, a king after God's own heart (1 Sam. 13.14).

a. *1 Samuel 9–31*

The institution of the kingship is presented in chs. 9.26–10.1 and 10.17-24 as carried out by Samuel at God's command, although it is in response to the people's fear of military enemies, involving a failure to trust *Yhwh*, and thus based on a habitual sinfulness of the people in which they reject *Yhwh* as their king (8.6-9; 12.18-25). And in ch. 8.1-5, it is explained that Israel is to be given a king because the generation of charismatic judges following Samuel has become corrupt.

The kingship, therefore, will be seen as a divine institution though rooted in Israel's sin, and it will go well or badly depending upon the behaviour of the people on the one hand and the king himself on the other (12.13-15). It is surprising that the whole image of anointing, namely, of messiah, and of royalty, that is, the adopted son of God (cf. Ps. 2), has so negative a backdrop. Of course it cannot be verified, proven true, either historically, since sins and divine interventions are conceptualizations which do not correspond visibly to observable data, or philosophically, since the whole notion of Infinite Love dealing with Israel and its government lies outside any academically acceptable political theory. Still, part of the author's insight is easily agreed to since it does seem that the human need for political power is often based on fear and loss of spiritual leadership (as was said to be the case in Israel) and that this will often invite violence and occasion grave injustice. Power is always something to be watched, feared, and limited. That is why our political lore knows that power corrupts and we resort to a 'division of powers'. Even this is dangerous, as it might turn into a multiplication of powers if there were no 'checks and balances'. So it makes sense that Saul's power was acquired and was partially abused, as the story indicates.

Moreover, the other part of this account might easily be agreed to by believing Jews and Christians, at least, as it can seem familiar: it fits into the familiar pattern of original sin where humans have sinned and thus God has instituted difficulty and suffering into this world. We are born and raised within the ambit of political (at least family) power, and this becomes a concrete instance of original sin: by nature we are good and made for paradise, but by history we cannot for an instant escape an origin and ambient which is characterized by dangerous power, and which can include violence. This can lead toward evil or good, depending upon how we behave on the one hand, and how the power (king, parents, etc.) behaves on the other. The pattern of thought is also analogous to that of a necessary evil in death. Death is instituted by God (Gen. 3.19, 21-23) but it originates in human sin (Wis. 1.13-16). This institution too will lead either to eternal life or real death depending upon how we behave. So it lies within the credible categories of biblical belief that the Saul story is true.

The account of kingship in 1 Samuel brings together two streams of thought: first, a human reflection on the facts of Saul, David, and Samuel, and second, a revelation of God's powerful involvement in our lives, violent and sinful as they are. The revelation stream was an elemental awareness of love which was given by God to this author and written by him into his inspired text by thematizing it in a pattern of thought found in other areas of biblical faith.[8]

The author wrote his text, not as a doctrine, and not as an objective history, but rather as an evocation of his faith experience, his memories plus his revelation, which enlivened him in his own lifetime, where heightened faith and hope and love enlightened his psyche, and he perceived his perilous human situation within the ambit of God's infinite and benevolent power. As he watches Saul rise and fall and David rise, he is filled with the conviction that we are not alone in this universe, and we may be motivated to act in order to preserve the good which God has created in us and in others, and to strive with full energy for the good and the love which God now provides for the future. That surely was the meaning of the text for the inspired author and editor, and therefore that is the meaning they intended for the readers—in other words, that is the meaning of the text.

Not that the text or its reader causes an experience of God. Only God through grace causes that. But when we read the text and feel nothing, experiencing no illumination, then we know that our interpretation is incomplete—so far the essence of this meaning has escaped us, and we simply have not understood. The scholarly reading of Shakespeare or Dostoyevsky is not expected to leave the reader cold, and the heat should be reflected by literary criticism. Similarly, the biblical scholar in an open university should not fail to experience and express what is evoked in a biblical text. If we are to read the poetry of Seamus Heaney, we must begin by hearing his voice. Only then will we adequately listen to his words.[9]

8.   To understand this better, we might consider the self-awareness of a widely respected Irish poet and literary theorist, Seamus Heaney. He says that poetry is a revelation of the self to the self, and he describes how the art of mixing streams of thought must be learned by the writer over time, portraying his own apprenticeship as a poet in terms of 'discovering one's voice' first by learning the 'craft' of writing which has to do with skill in the relating of words and the managing of their sounds and relationships, but then by learning 'technique'. By 'technique' he means 'a definition of his stance towards life, a definition of his own reality…the discovery of ways to go out of his normal cognitive bounds and raid the inarticulate…the watermarking of your essential patterns of perception, voice and thought into the touch and texture of your lines… Technique is what turns, in Yeats' phrase, "the bundle of accident and incoherence that sits down to breakfast" into "an idea, something intended, complete"' (Heaney 2002: 15, 21). He is aware of three streams here: a stream of words and a stream of objects to which they relate and a stream of self. Successful writing puts all three inextricably together to evoke an experience.

9.   Ignatius Loyola, in his *Spiritual Exercises*, instructs us to prepare ourselves for meditating on the scripture first by consciously adopting a reverent attitude, and then by a preparatory prayer that all our actions and intentions might by directed purely to God's glory, and then by a second prayer that we be granted the specific form of faith which corresponds to the text we will read: 'if the contemplation is on the Resurrection, one is to ask for joy with Christ in joy; if it is on the

In later years the Jewish community, and later still the Christian community, judged, not that what he wrote was verifiable objective truth, but rather that what he wrote did evoke for them an experience of God which was good, which was authentic and filled with the Spirit. The criteria for making this judgment can be very basic realizations that this reading experience leads one toward being more fully human, more alive, and more in harmony with the best of humanity around us.

Most of the story of Saul is a tale of failure and desperation, leading to his downfall and death. In the wider context, it serves as a legitimation of David: that is, that the succession did not pass to Saul's son Jonathan, but rather to the son of Jesse, because God had rejected Saul and chosen David. The author uses a number of literary techniques in making these connections visible in the text, of which only the simplest and most obvious will be mentioned here. The author was experiencing the confusion and chaos of a regime change. This surprises him: how could God choose Saul and then shortly after reject him? An answer is given to this question in 1 Samuel 13, a chapter in which Samuel is presented as a judge, and specifically in 13.7b-15a. God rejects Saul because Saul fails to do what God commands him. Another story in ch. 15 is very different in content and style (with Samuel presented rather as a prophet) and yet is tailored to make exactly the same point. The reader may wonder if one or both of these stories were created from whole cloth, or did they relate actual occurrences, or was each subjected to 'spin' in order to meet an editorial agenda. There is absolutely no way of knowing for sure.[10] But clearly the author, reflecting on the career of king Saul in comparison with that of David, has had an experience of understanding God's direct involvement in sinful human affairs within a paradoxical context of monarchy. His inspired take on his contemporary world expressed his enhanced faith and hope in the face of a life-time of objective deception and downfall and uncertainty.

How this understanding of the process of writing can be applied to authors who wrote other types of biblical texts, ranging through many genres from Proverbs to law codes, to Epistles and on to Apocalypse, is more than can be included in this article. However, two further rapid and uncomplicated examples, from two types of prophetic texts, may help to illustrate the notion that a text must be

---

Passion, he is to ask for pain, tears and torment with Christ in torment' (#3, 46, 48). One is struck by his belief that one needed first to pray, not once but twice, that one might be enabled to think properly and then pray properly. He understood that the text would not carry its meaning to the reader unless grace and acceptance of grace preceded.

10. Classical interpreters have shown a division of sources in the books of Samuel and Kings, each with its own continuity and agenda. This approach tends to leave the biblical text, as it now stands, incoherent and heading off in diverse directions. Campbell and O'Brien have introduced an important new idea here to make sense of this phenomenon, which occurs again and again in narrative texts. They envisage a institution of 'storytellers' who are to tell 'the story' on the basis of the biblical text but selecting and combining among variant accounts, and deciding between apparent contradictions, and filling out accounts which lack narrative colour, in order really to make whichever point is most helpful to any given group of listeners (Campbell and O'Brien 2000: 230-56 for Samuel, and especially pp. 6-7 for an illuminating description of this method; cf. also Campbell 2002 for a wider context and full bibliography).

perceived as written on the basis of an experience composed of both ordinary human perception and mystic illumination, and it should be interpreted as evoking a faith experience: Zeph. 3.14-18a and Hosea 1–3. They will each serve to illustrate that two types of knowing are united in a single experience, with a sense/knowledge perspective lending reality and immediacy, and a mystic perspective lending boundless dimensions and feeling.

b. *Zephaniah 3.14-18a*

Zephaniah too was experiencing and prophesying about regime change, to come on 'the day of the Lord' (1.7 and *passim*). *Yhwh* was about to punish the princes and the sons of the king (1.8) and also the wealthy (1.11-13).[11] However, his overall take on this event had a different tone than that of the author of 1 Samuel. Zephaniah, prophesying in the last half of the seventh century BCE, tells his listeners or readers in 3.14-15 what they must feel: exhilaration and delight, with no fear. But ever since 734 when the Assyrians made Judah its vassal, and especially since 722 when the northern kingdom fell, fear and foreboding had been felt and preached in Jerusalem without intermission for a hundred years. What made Zephaniah suddenly reverse the message? It may well be because his mind and imagination were filled with the dramatic change in political realities after the emperor Ashurbanipal died in 627. The power of Assyria went into irreversible decline. The Assyrians and the Egyptians had cooperated in a hegemony over the Eastern Mediterranean seaboard, and by this time Egypt effectively ruled over Judah. However, Babylon began to rise in power and ambition, and for some years, during the reign of Josiah in Jerusalem, conflict between Assyria, Babylon and Egypt left Judah free from oppression. Josiah was a wonderful and good king, a breath of fresh air after the evil Manasseh and Amon. Josiah even began to reconstitute the army of Judah and to recover Jewish control over some territories of the northern kingdom which had been separated since the death of Solomon. This was a singular window for joy, and Zephaniah may well have felt that the clouds had dissipated on his horizon. This is the sense/knowledge perspective.

However, 3.16-18a elevates the perspective: Israel is told not to fear, not because of political prospects, but rather because the saviour in their midst, *Yhwh*, is the one who is shouting for joy and ecstatically renewing them in his love! Now a reader who reads this may feel nothing at first. But the idea of God shouting for joy—shouting at a festival—makes the reader realize that some extension of perspective is required. S/he has not yet understood this text. It is not only about the history of Judah, though it is rooted in history. It is about exhilaration.

Zephaniah is drawing upon and expressing two sources of knowledge here: his observation of a current situation and his experience of a love poured in his heart,

---

11. Of course Isaiah had foretold a most famous regime change in the Immanuel oracle (Isa. 7), and Jeremiah spent many years reflecting on a total regime change in the overthrow of Jerusalem in favour of Babylon. In each case, the specific take on the event was the soul of the respective prophetic message.

a love which wants him joyous, a love which is itself joyous. One has not interpreted this text until one has allowed exhilaration to be the context in which it is heard. Zephaniah applies this to the current situation of Judah, and this is clearly the intent of the book as is made explicit in 1.1.

Still, what he has learned about God is always true about God. Readers in any situation can encounter Zephaniah's experience, ask for the grace of experiencing the same revelation, and eventually renew their 'take' on the situation of their own life-time. It is essential that the human and the divine dimension of the meaning are felt as one. Otherwise the human segment is irrelevant at least to later readers, and maybe historically uncertain; and the divine segment is pie in the sky. But his writing the two together is the literary achievement and core meaning. The key words about Israel in 3.14-15 ('shout', 'joy', 'no fear') are repeated in reverse order in vv. 16-18 (a literary technique which is common in Hebrew writing), but now with the difference that the joy and the shout are in God. At the level of experience, and caught up in the ordering of the words, God's joy and shout, and Israel's joy and shout, qualify and amplify each other. In literature the special energy of language, rooted deep in human consciousness, is used to evoke an experience which goes beyond direct description. The objective reality may not be ascertainable years later, but the experience can still be experienced. In biblical literature, the intended meaning and experience can be known only when sense and mystic grace are combined.

It may help to see another short example of this in a familiar verse. The song of the angels to the shepherds in Bethlehem is presented as follows:

Glory to God in the highest heaven,
and on earth peace among those whom he favours. (Lk. 2.14)

Both 'glory' and 'peace' taken separately can be utterly banal. God's 'glory' in heaven often sounds very abstract and paper-thin, and 'peace' on earth in most contexts means no more than an absence of overt violence. But the poetic line makes them strict parallels in the couplet; a creative effort of understanding is suggested so that they comment on each other and interpret each other. The divine glory solidifies with the presence of human voices, and the human peace swells with the Holy Spirit. And that is the literary meaning of the text. That is the intent of the writer, and it is demanded of the reader by the ordering of those words in parallel and within the conventions of Hebrew poetry.

c. *Hosea 1–3*
Very different is the revelation of Hosea 1–3. Without going into the debates about historical detail in these chapters, it seems that Hosea is married to an adulterous wife. He experiences betrayal with its attendant emotions. God invites him to perceive in this experience what God feels about Israel. The love of God which floods his heart has a colouring of hurt, of anger, but also of determination to win back the loyalty which is due to him. In this experience, Hosea understands something new about God's presence in Israel's life, and doubtless learns something new about the dimensions of his experience with the adulteress. The

text is full of diverse implications. But it is made clear in the words of the text itself that the reader has not understood this text unless he experiences it as a human disaster within its vast world of revelation. Both the human feelings and the divine horizons must be joined or else the experience of the text is simply not there.

Later Isaiah will write:

> I reared children and brought them up,
> but they have rebelled against me.
> The ox knows its owner,
> and the donkey its master's crib;
> but Israel does not know,
> my people do not understand. (Isa. 1.2b-3)

That seems to be a very similar experience of God, without necessarily demanding that Isaiah himself suffer betrayal. It may well be that this revelation was made easy for him by his reading and understanding of Hosea 1–3.

Sometimes the historical object which is being recalled is not as complex as broad political situations. For example, Jeremiah chanced to notice an almond tree, and a play on words occurred in his mind, namely that the Hebrew name for that tree is also the participle meaning 'watching' as a sentinel watches (Jer. 1.11-12). At the same instant he is filled with the realization that *Yhwh* has spoken to him about the future of Jerusalem, and he is electrified with certainty that the divine word was infinite in power. Similarly, the following verse tells of his thinking a metaphor upon noticing a cauldron boiling over. So he is overcome with foreboding and conceives a compelling conviction that *Yhwh* is intent on imminent doom. Both these certitudes, formulated in reference to otherwise trivial sense observations, offer concrete applications to the more general revelation of Jeremiah's responsibility in this political context described just before in 1.4-10.

Similarly Isaiah, who describes a complex realization of the meaning of God and of his own relationship to this infinite being and to Israel, in ch. 6 also relates the sense experience of a shuddering of the temple foundation and billowing smoke. It is not difficult to imagine how the physical phenomena could form a plastic representation in which the realization of his vocation is articulated. The reader who fails to put them together, and to feel both physical immediacy and limitless awe in the presence of this event, has not yet experienced what Isaiah experienced, or fully understood this text.

5. *Conclusion*

This study of Samuel, Zephaniah, and Hosea obviously does not preclude philological and historical questions whose answers, worked out over years of meticulous and often brilliant scholarship, may be true or false, and must be judged in those academic terms. (And such research is demanded of the community which believes in the value of this text as a sacred object.) However, this essay does intend to show that those discussions, whether they result in truth, falsehood, or total uncertainty, must not interfere with the central task of interpretation, that is, fully understanding by experiencing what the writer evokes through the text. Scripture is not primarily an intellectual puzzle. It is primarily a reminder of our deeper subjectivity, of who we are and where we come from, and a notification that God has intruded into our world which is first of all God's world. Whatever else it mentions is mostly by way of illustration.

BIBLIOGRAPHY

Brooks, C.
    1975   'The Heresy of Paraphrase', in *idem, The Well Wrought Urn: Studies in the Structure of Poetry* (New York: Harcourt Brace Jovanovich): 192-214.
Campbell, A.F.
    2002   'The Storyteller's Role: Reported Story and Biblical Text', *CBQ* 64: 427-41.
Campbell, A.F., and M.A. O'Brien
    2000   *Unfolding the Deuteronomistic History: Origins, Upgrades, Present Text* (Minneapolis: Fortress Press).
Dungan, D.L.
    1999   'Baruch Spinoza and the Political Agenda of Modern Historical-Critical Interpretation', in *idem, A History of the Synoptic Problem* (New York: Doubleday): 198-260.
Egan, H.D.
    1987   *Ignatius Loyola the Mystic* (Collegeville, MN: The Liturgical Press).
Fleming, D.
    1978   *The Spiritual Exercises of Saint Ignatius: A Literal Translation and Contemporary Reading* (St Louis, MO: The Institute of Jesuit Sources).
Heaney, S.
    2002   *Finders Keepers: Selected Prose 1971–2001* (New York: Farrer Straus Giroux).
Lonergan, B.
    1971   *Method in Theology* (London: Darton, Longman & Todd).
Meier, J.P.
    2001   *A Marginal Jew: Rethinking the Historical Jesus* (New York: Doubleday).
Roy, L.
    2003   'Can We Thematize Mysticism?', *Method: Journal of Lonergan Studies* 21: 47-66.
Wright, N.T.
    2003   *The Resurrection of the Son of God* (Minneapolis: Fortress Press).

ANTONY CAMPBELL'S *GOD FIRST LOVED US*
AND THE TASK OF BIBLICAL THEOLOGY

Rolf P. Knierim

The fact that Antony F. Campbell, a colleague and personal friend over almost half of my lifetime, has—surprisingly—arrived on the plateau of the septuagenarians, self-evidently causes me to want to be among the contributors for a volume in his honour, and to join all who congratulate him and wish him well for his future.

My contribution is concerned with the particular subject of the Task of Biblical Theology, not only because this subject has been the predominant concern of my own lifetime, but also because it has very much to do—as far as I see—with Campbell's whole life, a vocational life both personally and professionally. One may say that the number of our years is relative. It certainly includes the length of our lives in their entirety. And it excludes no part of their breadth.

Antony Campbell is known as a Jesuit priest and as a scholar of—what he calls in his book to be discussed below—the Older Testament (e.g. p. 8).[1] In his Church he has been active as a priest and as a biblical scholar. In scholarly circles he is known as a widely active and influential teacher and particularly as the author, in part co-author, of a broad-based collection of scholarly volumes and articles.

As interpreter of the Bible, Campbell is much more than merely an accomplished technician. I think one can safely say that his technical work is related to his understanding of the relevance of the Bible, in which the priest and scholar converge.[2] I find this convergence characteristically exemplified in his short book *God First Loved Us: The Challenge of Accepting Unconditional Love*.[3] This book could not have been written without what is said in it being controlled by its author's understanding of those aspects in the Bible—of the Christians[4]—that are

1. I use the word Tanak for the Bible of the Jewish people, and the words Old and New Testament for the two Testaments of the Bible of the Christians.

2. See *Afterword: The Bible's Basic Role* in his forthcoming commentary on 2 Samuel (FOTL, 8; Grand Rapids: Eerdmans).

3. Antony F. Campbell, *God First Loved Us: The Challenge of Accepting Unconditional Love* (New York: Paulist Press, 2000).

4. It is known that the *Vetus Testamentum* recognized by the Roman Catholic Church includes among its historical, didactic, and also prophetic Books more titles than those included in the Canon of the Protestant Churches. When mentioning 2 Esd. 8.1, 3, 34-36, 45, 47, Campbell (2000: 53-55) refers to texts in a canonical book of his Church.

conceptual in nature and represent the foundational condition for everything else said in the Bible, whatever its content, context, time, tradition, transmission, form, setting, genre, and style. This book's meditations show that the priest, positioned before and serving public audiences and readers, has not only applied the exegete of the biblical books rather than put him aside, but also that he has carried his exegetical expertise forward on to the level of biblical theology, and lastly on to the level of what theology has to say today in the movement of the Christians.

In the following I shall attempt to summarize the development of Campbell's book, thereby aiming at highlighting the essentials of its system, and conclude with a few remarks about the ongoing discussion. From among an endless number of issues addressed in this book, I must select those that are what I consider most important.

1. *Summary of the Development of Antony Campbell's* God First Loved Us

Under its title and sub-title, the book is unfolded in the sequential order of a *Preface* (pp. ix-xi); an *Overview* (pp. 1-6); eight numbered chapters (pp. 7-97); an *Afterword* (pp. 98-102); and a concluding chapter called 'Good Friday' (pp. 102-12).

Campbell's title emphasizes that it is God who 'loved' us—meaning: before we love God. This title's emphasis is specifically prompted by the questions of how—under the best of circumstances—the two loves are related, namely, of whose love for the other ranks 'first' and whose love would therefore rank second, or even, of whether both are the loves of co-equal partners. These questions are as urgent as the answers to them are not self-evident and often the opposite of what the 'Christian Faith' says.

Obviously presupposed in the title, and clearly supported by Campbell's entire book, is the notion that God's love for us is the one mode above all others in God's relationship with us, and not just one among its many modes, however important and whatever its rank may be. I do not think that Campbell's title focuses on the issue of love as just one among the kinds of God's relationship with us, regardless of how it is related to the other modes of God's overall relationship with us. It seems to say: 'Because of God's love, everything else matters. Without God's love, all else suffers.' This, too, belongs to what the 'Christian Faith' cannot do without, indeed, to what comes first in it.

The explicit emphasis on 'First' in Campbell's title is underscored and carried further by what is meant in his sub-title, namely, that 'Accepting' this 'First'— now called 'Unconditional'—love of God for us, is for us 'The Challenge'. According to Campbell, the need for us to accept that God 'First' loved us amounts not just to the challenge to accept the insight of a basic doctrine; it amounts to the challenge that we constitute this insight as the ethical, or moral, foundation of our existence. The challenge to accept being unconditionally loved surfaces in Campbell's perspective as the fundamental ethical requirement for us, as the basis for all other requirements, even before the requirement that we respond to God's love for us through our love for God and neighbour. This position could not be more radical.

For the further sake of seeing Campbell's focus in sharp relief, it may be noted that his focus on the challenge for us to accept that we are *loved* by God differs from the focus on our having to accept that we are *justified* by God through Jesus Christ. One can say that the acceptance of either of the two gifts of God, or of both together, represents an *ethical* stance—with none enabling us to boast. Still, the difference between the acceptance of love and the acceptance of justification remains, and therefore also the question of which of the two acceptances is the basis for which. Also, while the acceptance of our justification is said to happen through faith—whether faith is considered to be an ethical category or not—the question of whether the acceptance of God's love happens through faith too, or through something else, would have to be clarified. At any rate, however Campbell would define the relationship between love and faith—also the 'Christian Faith' often mentioned in his book—it is beyond any question that for him, there can be no (legitimate) faith that would not fundamentally rest on our acceptance of God's unconditional love for us to begin with.

Campbell's statement that God 'Loved' us says that God's love, also God's love 'First', preceded our love temporally, not only fundamentally. Which temporal fact is, and could be, meant, and why, must be sorted out. I assume that his formulation does not mean that because, or since, God 'loved', God has not, does not, and will not love us always.

He also says 'Us', by which he can only mean all—at least human—beings, and at all places and times from the beginning to the end of creation, and for that reason also each of Campbell's listeners and all of us, his readers, today—or God would not be God. That God's love is said to be 'Unconditional' is one thing; whether it presupposes all equally, therefore including us too—rather than 'us' before or at the expense of all others—is thereby not yet said, and deserves to be kept in mind.

In the *Preface* (pp. ix-xi), Campbell sets forth in condensed form his programme of 'The acceptance of God's unconditional love for us'. This sum is cast against the backdrop of the 'archaic', never and nowhere extinct religious conviction that says: 'Be good to the gods and they will be good to you'. It highlights the two aspects: first, of God's unconditional, also 'passionate' love for us (p. 13), God's love although, perhaps even because, we are damnable; and, second, of the 'major consequences for the religious spirit' which flow from our acceptance of God's love. (Note: these 'major consequences' themselves follow from the initial and fundamental consequence of the acceptance of God's love.) They challenge us to a level of commitment to the divine, almost unheard of in religious literature, to 'utter love' and 'absolute love' of God 'in return', to 'the vision' of a level of 'spirit-filled existence' and of 'our world', the vision of God's love for us and our love for God from which 'our behaviour flows'. This vision rises 'above the oldest archaism of the human spirit'.

One of the consequences for those who accept God's unconditional love is that they have to realize the mystery of God's unconditional love for the 'others' too, so that 'there is no escape from social justice and respect for human dignity and integrity', and that 'even this world of ours' itself must be seen as the place of 'God's beloved creation, crying out to be improved and made just'. Also, the vision of an unconditionally loving God is different from, if not in contrast to the idea of a divine judge, the idea that would leave this world open to our 'moral calculations'.

Thus far, I see in this programme the following:

First, Campbell does not speak about God's unconditional love alone. He speaks about both, God's love for us, first, and our love for God, in response. More precisely, he speaks about God's love as a mode of our human experience, itself the presupposition for our chance to accept God's love, rather than about God's love in abstraction from our experience. In other words, Campbell speaks about both God's love for us and our love for God anthropologically, not anthropocentrically, or, in an anthropologically understood theology of love, in which our human love of God appears not only as the natural 'outgrowth' from God's love for us, or as our 'response' to God's love first, but in which it may be understood as the very extension of God's own love for us in, or through, our love for God. Divine love through us, but no divinity of us.

Second, God's love is for all—humans—not only for 'us'. It is thereby not for us and also for all, but for all and therefore also for us, and me. At stake is whether God loves the world because God loves us, or whether God loves us because God loves the world. The difference between 'all' and 'us' in God's and our love is far-reaching.

Third, God's and our love reach into the arena of 'social justice' and 'respect for human dignity and integrity'. This aspect affects the assumption of the relationship between the theologies of universal social—also societal—justice and universal love. And it says that, while there might be degrees of justice without love, no love can ever happen without justice. Love appears as the foundation of the theology, and practice, of justice. (One may go on, for example, asking about the relationship between justice, love, and peace.)

Fourth, God's love presupposes 'God's beloved creation, crying out to be improved and made just'. Creation is more than all humanity, and both are more than us as human individuals. God's and our love have to do with what we call today ecology. Again, ecology may or may not have much to do with love, but love cannot do without ecology.

Fifthly, there is a difference, even a contrast, between the 'unconditionally loving God' and a 'divine judge', a not only loving but also punishing God or, as is said later, a God demanding 'redemption'. Whether love, also as a matter of justice, includes or excludes, or ultimately replaces the inevitability of punishing judgment, or redemption, is indeed a serious question. At least the basic structure of our human condition cannot exist with the justice also of punishment and redemption.

It is clear that Campbell speaks not only of love, God's and our love; he also speaks of all humans, of justice among all, of creation and the need for its ecology, of the God of love and the divine judge. He speaks in conceptualized categories, in concepts. These concepts are all seen as connected; none appears in isolation. Especially, they appear in his argumentation as aspects that—each related to all—belong to differing levels of priority, of super- and subordinate positions and, hence, of meaning and validity, and lastly of their extent and degree of truth. Campbell does not write to systematize the *Gestalt* of the levels of these concepts, but he operates on his view of the systemic nature of their relationship. His statements reflect a theoretical basis for a system of theological ethics.

Such a basis has nothing to do with abstraction from the ethos itself. It functions as the blueprint which is operative in everything said in the unfolding of the aspects of ethos. It is thereby known that thought, its expression and its action, are different. To think about, to speak about, and to act as one who accepts being loved are not the same. Last but not least, according to Campbell's programmatic *Preface*, when speaking about a 'level of spirit-filled existence', he refers to today's much talked about condition of spirituality. Two things are thereby distinctive: for Campbell, spirit-filled existence is defined by accepting being unconditionally loved by God, and by completely loving God in return, by nothing different and less. And, this spirit-filled existence is not experienced as something supra-rational, even irrational, or as something essentially supra-natural or mystical or emotional or meditative. It is a kind of experience that can be described and explained rationally.

In my ongoing discussion of the following units of Campbell's book, I want to stay on its programmatic level, thereby briefly referring to the aspects that confirm its major conceptual notions already identified, while pointing especially to those aspects that appear anew and must be added to the level of Campbell's system.

The *Overview* (pp. 1-6) elaborates on what has been said in the Preface. Continued in this section are Campbell's statements about—accepting—God's unconditional love and our love of God with its implications, such as the reworking of our self-image, our commitment to the poor and the rebellion against oppression and justice—anywhere—and the statements that the major changes of attitude, which are required by a commitment in faith to God's unconditional love for us, 'add up to a significant revision of the face of Christian faith' (pp. 2-3). This revision is said to touch our 'theological attitude' to human life in the stages of its beginning, its middle, and its end (p. 3). Regarding the 'middle' stage, it involves 'a rethinking...about our life...world...destiny' (p. 3).

What becomes explicit in these formulations of 'reworking', 'self-image', 'changes of attitude', of 'revision...of the face' of Christian faith, of 'theological attitude', of 'rethinking', and—exactly—also of 'the absurdity' (p. 2) of the faith of Christ crucified (1 Cor. 1.23-24; the first reference to a biblical passage in Campbell's book, and one involving a wisdom argument!), is that this concept of love is a rational concept. The same can be observed throughout the book, for example in the 'integrity' of the language of Christian faith (p. 12, see also pp. 19, 20, 23, 41 etc.).

Moreover, this concept is systemic. 'The face' (p. 3) of Christian faith means its structure, its *Gestalt*, its order, its system. Its vision is 'of bringing elements of faith together in brighter light and sharper focus' (p. 4). Elsewhere he argues the need for coherence versus the 'destructively incoherent' (p. 19), for the need of the 'choice' of 'what is primary in the language we use about God' (p. 19), whereby 'God's love' has for him 'to have priority over God's justice' (p. 19). Campbell operates on the background of a rational and systemic Christian theology of love.

This theology is generated by the inevitable recognition of distinguishable but related strata of values—more dominant and more subservient, primary and secondary and so on—which are not abstract from but intrinsic to the real experience of the notions or concepts themselves. In contrast to what he calls 'a level playing field', Campbell says that 'the theology of an unconditionally loving God...is faith that searches for its sense of God on a tilted playing field' and: 'By "a tilted playing field" I mean that priority has been given to a primary metaphor for God, to which others are subordinated' (p. 77).

New, from Campbell's *Overview* on, are the references to: faith, as Christian faith; Christ, in the *Overview*, Christ crucified; incarnation; and a biblical passage, from the New Testament, from St Paul specifically. These references, which from here on are found throughout the book, reflect conceptual notions which belong to Campbell's programme or blueprint, the systemic order for what he says throughout his book. One has to assume that these aspects are related to each other as well as to the five aspects already listed above, and one has to ask about their place in this 'playing field'.

In the eight numbered chapters, the concept of the book's topic is unfolded, progressing towards its ever more specific aspects: on the one hand, alongside types of the human experience of God's unconditional love and the challenge to accept it and, on the other hand, particularly in the later chapters, alongside the specific nature of the theology of God's love. Especially important is the fact that under each chapter title, and before Campbell's discussion, a chosen biblical word is quoted which obviously is to function as an exemplar for what is being discussed. This fact and the frequent biblical references in these chapters mean that the discussion of God's unconditional love takes place on the fields of biblical theology as well as of systematic theology or theological doctrine. And it points especially to the difference between the tasks of the exegesis of the theologies of the biblical texts and of biblical theology built from the exegeted texts and their own theologies.

In Chapter 1, *Introduction* (pp. 7-17), super-scripted by Exod. 34.6—'A God, abounding in steadfast love and faithfulness'—Campbell drives his point home that 'God's unconditional love for us', is 'the best' on which 'Judeo-Christian faith' has to be centred (p. 7). It is not one among other experiences, least of all of that of fear of a judging God (pp. 8, 11—the two terms of a loving and a judging God are polarized on p. 11). It is 'the best' and 'central' experience. And while its images are found in the Tanak, it is directly expressed 'from the Christian beginnings' in the New Testament of the Christians, especially in

1 John, which closely approximates Campbell's emphasis (pp. 8-9). Campbell is thereby clearly aware that Exod. 34.6, in its context and in similar passages considered inter-textually, speaks not of God's love exclusively but also of God 'visiting iniquity' (pp. 13-14).

In Chapter 2, *The Preliminaries* (pp. 18-28), super-scripted by Ps. 89.1—'I will sing of your steadfast love, O LORD, forever'—Campbell discusses 'the issue of our priorities' (p. 18) under four aspects. In coherent 'God-Talk', he says that 'for me, God's love has to have priority over God's justice' (p. 19). In 'Priorities are important', he focuses on the primary metaphor of 'God as loving' (p. 21), and the need for choosing what is primary (p. 19). In 'Experience is important', Campbell, confining himself to his own experience, especially regarding 'confusing' influences as to how our words relate to God, discusses the (incoherent) union of opposites, not in the mystery of God but in his own experience: 'Is there any point in begging for forgiveness', rather than giving thanks for forgiveness already granted by the loving God? The fourth aspect is discussed in ch. 3.

Chapter 3, *The Fear* (pp. 29-39), is super-scripted by 1 Jn 4.18—'There is no fear in love, but perfect love casts out fear; for fear has to do with punishment, and whoever fears has not reached perfection in love'. In light of 'God's love for us', central in Christian faith, fear (of God) 'puts restraints on love' (p. 30). That is, fear of a powerful God, a demanding God, even fear of God's self 'gets in the way of accepting God's love' (p. 33). And 'Scripture and liturgy don't necessarily help much to banish fear'. We are confronted with the issue of fear of God in the exegesis and theology of the Tanak and the New Testament—in light of God's love for us and for all unconditionally and equally!

Chapter 4, *The Vision* (pp. 40-49), is super-scripted by 1 Jn 4.19—'We love God because God first loved us'. Here is found the formulation for the title of Campbell's book. In this chapter, Campbell speaks about the 'visions' (p. 44) of 'our world' and 'ourselves' and 'our God' (pp. 46-47) 'as unconditionally loved by God' (p. 40-41) which exist in the 're-visioning Christian Faith' (p. 41). This re-visioning 'is in the Bible' (p. 40). 'The seed has always been there in Christian scripture' (p. 99). 'It cannot come out of modern fantasy; it has to have roots in the scriptures, in the traditional experience of God, and in the incarnation of Jesus Christ' (p. 41).

It is the vision of our 'thoroughly fouled-up world' and our sinfulness 'as we are' which, for a loving creator, 'are lovable, can be loved, could be created' (pp. 1, 45-46). 'A God who so loves and does not intervene is a God of mystery' (p. 47). Instead of punishing sins, the love—of the creator!—forgives; forgiveness opens the way to salvation, to being in a right relationship with God (p. 41), and 'creation leads to incarnation' through which 'God became one of us because of unitive passion' (p. 42), and that in the birth and life of the human being Jesus. And 'the final steps'—in this event of incarnation—'are Christ's passion, death, and resurrection and the continued presence of Christ in the eucharist' (p. 42).

According to Campbell, as I read him, forgiveness belongs to the love of the creator for his ('fouled-up') creation; it belongs to creation theology. It opens the way to salvation in the event of incarnation, which is the incarnation of Christ. Forgiveness in creation leads to salvation in incarnation. Christian soteriology evolves out of theological protology. Indeed, the theology of incarnation itself appears to belong to the theology of creation (cf. Chapter 6).

Chapter 5, *The Challenge* (pp. 50-63), is super-scripted by Isa. 43.3—'Because you are precious in my sight, and honored, and I love you'. In this chapter, the subtitle of the book, the challenge to us humans of accepting God's unconditional love is fleshed out in light of particular aspects. God's love is challenged by the philosophy of human beings' innate goodness, by the myths that life was better in its origin and will be better in its end-time than it is today, by ineradicable injustice, and by the—at least—insufficient idea of redemption with its 'overtones of buying back and repayment' (p. 52). The theology of redemption conflicts with the theology of salvation: 'Only justice insists on redemption' (p. 53). God's gift to us is God's forgiving us 'in our mess' (p. 53). Such is the vision of incarnation, which is 'not a means of divine redemption but an expression of divine Love. God so loved the world that God entered the world and took human flesh, becoming one of us… The incarnation is the unique and unsurpassable expression of God's love for us' (p. 53). We are challenged to accept incarnation, not justice, as the reality of God's love for us.

Chapter 6, *The Incarnation* (pp. 64-75), is super-scripted by Jn 1.1, 14—'The Word was God… And the Word became flesh and lived among us.' What he already had prepared in Chapters 4 and 5, Campbell now discusses directly. Redemption is understood to happen 'at a price' (p. 64). But 'A loving God does not need to redeem us; a loving God forgives us… Only justice insists on redemption, on repaying what is owed, paying for the fault. Love, like the father of the prodigal, moves to forgiveness' (p. 65). While the language of redemption should be 'relegated to subordinate status' (p. 66), 'the ultimate expression of God's love for humankind' (p. 66) should be found in 'the incarnation of Jesus Christ' (p. 67). Incarnation '(God's embracing human life) necessarily includes—beyond Christ's birth—his death and resurrection' (p. 67). If death as redemptive sacrifice is necessary, its necessity must be shown. 'Christ's death cannot be isolated from Christ's incarnation' (p. 67), from the totality of Christ's life from birth to resurrection presence in the Eucharist. 'Passion and death are part of incarnation' (p. 99). 'It is the task of exploring the shape of the Christian faith when primacy is given to incarnation over redemption' (p. 69).

Chapter 7, *The Difference* (pp. 76-85), is super-scripted by Song 1.2—'Your love is better than wine'. In this chapter, Campbell elaborates on the methodological side of the task of comparing the identified notions, concepts, aspects, or doctrines. Stating the need for a 'tilted playing field' (p. 77), he speaks about 'priority', the 'primary metaphor' for God that has been 'given', to which (not only one but) 'others are subordinated' (p. 77). In terms of method, we speak of as many levels of the 'field' as must be identified, of the recognition of their different 'values' in their interrelations. Through relating and comparing, we ourselves have to make the choices about what has priority and what appears to be subordinate and is therefore to be subordinated by us. Also, Campbell recognizes the category of the 'level playing field, a different kind of relationship' that might be 'sketched as analogy' (p. 78). It is the method of recognizing the systemic nature of the many aspects, and of having to systematize their order, for the sake of coherence, meaning, and truth. It is the method of the well known, already ancient, genre of the 'better sayings', as in Song 1.2.

Chapter 8, *The Mystery* (pp. 86-97), is super-scripted by Isa. 54.10—'For the mountains may depart and the hills be removed, but my steadfast love shall not depart from you'. Elements of the mystery are: 'our need to choose among our options for our God' (p. 86), that it 'stretches minds' (p. 87), that 'God is mystery' (p. 88), the inactivity of God, the theory of an all-powerful God versus the experience of a non-coercive God (p. 90); and also 'human life' (p. 89), the question of why we should be as we are' (p. 92), and more. I would add: the experience of God and God's salvation for the world and us as the experience that we are not, and do not possess and control the presence confronting us, of the ultimate truth of the world.

The *Afterword* (pp. 98-102) reiterates the essential thrust of Campbell's interpretation but adds (p. 101) that:

> Emphasis on God's unconditional love can contribute to bridging one of Western Christianity's deepest doctrinal divides. Divine grace, so important in the language of Roman Catholic theology, can be appropriately understood in terms of the activity of God's love. Love is not earned; it is a sheer gift of grace. Justification by grace, so central to Reformation theology, can be understood as appropriately expressed in the language of acceptance in faith of God's unconditional love. Love is not proved; it is taken on faith.

The book concludes with a meditation about the persons involved on Good Friday along with passages from the Gospel of John: Jesus; Pilate; Soldiers; Mary, His Mother; Mary Magdalene; the Beloved Disciple; and Jesus. And it is super-scripted by a word from 1 Cor. 1.23-24—'we proclaim Christ crucified, a stumbling block to Jews and foolishness to Gentiles, but to those who are called, both Jews and Greeks, Christ the power of God and the wisdom of God'.

2. *Remarks*

It is obvious that all chapters of the book, with the varying foci of their contents, are based on the concept of the two aspects already thematized in the book's title and sub-title, and of the unchangeable order in which these two aspects are related. This order is not compromised by the fact that the author in the course of his presentation switches back and forth from one of these two aspects to the other, nor that he describes the aspect of the challenge more than the aspect of the nature of God's gift of unconditional love—whereby the severity of the challenge may be the more bearable the more one puts forth the picture of the glory and triumph of God's gift, so broadly attested to in the New Testament as, for example, in Rom. 8.31-39. At any rate, the book must be read with the order in mind of the indissoluble kind of relationship of its two basic aspects.

The fact that the two main aspects are conceptually related is also true for all other aspects in these meditations. It underlies their discussion, and is often mentioned in the meditations themselves. Furthermore, the aspects are part of a structure, a *Gestalt*. Their relatedness is inherently systemic. They need for that reason to be critically compared, so that the degrees of their validity can be recognized, or prioritized. In as much as they have to do with his decisive focus on love, Campbell assesses issues such as justice, opposition to injustice, redemption, forgiveness, incarnation, and justification, in their position in relation to his theology of love. He systematizes his arguments. As far as the biblical roots are concerned, the comparison of these aspects includes all available texts; it proceeds inter-textually.

Thus, Campbell finds it inevitable to invoke the method of prioritizing and hence, also, of subordinating. His discourses are based on the method of systematization, by relating issues and aspects and discerning their priorities or subordinate positions. The book is, then, filled with references to the 'priority' of love over justice (pp. 11, 19, 20, 53, 91); to 'primary' (pp. 19, 65); 'primacy' (p. 11); 'central' (p. 34); 'subordinate' (p. 66); 'ultimate' (p. 66); 'over' (p. 69); 'better' (p. 74); 'tilted playing field' (pp. 77, 80) (all pages selective). This method of systematization involves a value-system, in which love is not one among others but the highest, the 'ultimate' (p. 66) value. The *better sayings* result from this method. As far as Campbell's use of the Bible is concerned, the method is not imposed upon the Bible from outside; it, and its criteria, evolve from what is found in the Bible itself. Of course, he is right in following this method.

Campbell operates within the horizon of the theological doctrine of his Church and also within the horizon of what needs to be called biblical exegesis and theology. I want to confine myself to a few remarks about how the Bible appears in his treatment of his subject. It appears in the passages introducing his chapters, in frequent references to biblical passages, and also in conceptual aspects contained in the Bible.

For the biblical ground of his topic, Campbell uses passages from across the Bible, essentially along each of his topic's two aspects. In a sense, he uses the entire Bible synoptically. Nevertheless, his programme could not be biblically substantiated unless he sees it grounded in those biblical passages and the concepts implicit in or resulting from them, which represent the decisive criterion for this programme. These are not just passages which say that God loved, or loves (whomever) before God is, or should be, loved; or, generally, that God loves the world because of or through Jesus Christ. They are those passages that, in text or concept, specifically say that God '*first loved*' us—all human beings— through the incarnation of Christ in his total life, as the life of an individual human being, two millennia ago. Without this specific root in the Bible, Campbell could not say what he says.

Operating as a biblical theologian from that decisive vantage-point, Campbell can, then, potentially, draw on all the varying aspects of God's love for humans and their love for God from within the total landscape of the biblical literature and its traditions. This specific biblical vantage-point functions as the first and fundamental word of the entire Bible. And it is the criterion for beginning to recognize the degree of validity of all other words within all biblical texts and traditions themselves, multilayered as they are. It represents the fundamental vantage-point from which to read the theologies in the Bible as a tilted playing field.

Campbell the exegete knows that no texts or concepts in the Tanak, neither the texts he refers to nor any others, nor the Tanak as a whole, can fulfil this criterion. This is evident from passage to passage mentioned by him. He does not say in what sense he uses the passages to which he refers. To this question, our hermeneutic has provided a range of options. It is obvious, however, that, by choosing his passages also from the Tanak—rather than forgetting and abandoning them and leaving them behind in their original places and times and communities and contexts and concepts—Campbell claims them as rightfully belonging to the way toward the vision of God's unconditional love for all in its ultimate and most universal and inclusive dimensions.

Campbell the exegete also knows that in the New Testament too not all aspects, which fall under the criterion of God's unconditional love and the challenge to accept it, are sufficiently addressed, if at all. The gift of God's love is unconditional, but love's saving effect is lost for the person who does not believe. This loss may be self-inflicted or it may be the result of God's punishment. The various aspects of this argument pervade the New Testament. Most importantly: is the reconciliation of all evil, the ultimate enemy, included when God first 'loved' us? As 'God is Love', and Love is 'the greatest' in the new creation (1 Cor. 13), can love exclude the ultimate enemy of God? And, does the truth of the ultimate love of God depend on the New Testament's expectation of the impending coming of the reign of God or of the second coming of Christ, or is this love present in our world at all times, regardless of the mythological, already outlived, view of the impending cataclysmic end of our universe?

We are familiar with the idea of the many kinds of the reality of evil, and also —to limited extents—with the experience of its power. And while we experience that love is unable to eliminate the reality of evil in the world, we know above all else that love replaces the right of evil to exist as the judge of truth. Such beliefs are everything but abstract speculations. For us, being challenged to accept being unconditionally loved means that we depend on that love at the outset, always and on love only, precisely because our own response in love of God and neighbour and enemy never matches the love of God for us. Even in our Christian faith, and even in the best of our response, we fail, like all other enemies of God, and still remain loved. We live by love as grace, by this kind of love alone, by pardon, or we do not exist rightfully. This involves much more than our being accepted as—however imperfect—human beings. We are accepted despite never deserving it. Only so, by pointing the finger against our own chest, will we quit pointing it against the others, the unbelievers, the evildoers and evil empires, and start loving. I think that's the direction of Campbell's argument, and he could not be more right.

I need to take exception to Campbell's understanding of redemption. He correctly objects to a kind of understanding of redemption in which we have to pay the price for our salvation and which conflicts with the understanding that God 'first loved' and 'unconditionally' loves us. It is also clear that redemption always involves payment of a price, be it for damage or hurt done by one to another person or by humans to God. Also, the notion that it is humans who have to pay the price, to make restitution, to atone for their breaking away from God, in order for them to restore their relationship with God so that they may be forgiven, reconciled, and even loved, certainly belongs to the elements of the structure of 'archaic' religiosity (cf. p. ix).

However, the biblical traditions know that, while the price must always be paid, it can either, and normally has to, be paid by the 'sinner', or it can be paid by way of substitution, and is made possible to be so paid, in order that the 'sinner' is free. One has to remember especially the structures of the sacrificial cult. The concept of substitution is considered as a basic legal and forensic category. Also, the act of pardon, by which the 'sinner' is freed from having to pay the price for her/his guilt, does not mean that no price is being paid. The damage has happened, and whoever has been damaged carries, that is, absorbs the loss without demanding restoration by retribution and/or punishment. Pardon is a forensic, not a sentimental act. The same is true for forgiveness. It too is a forensic act. Whoever forgives someone for damage suffered does not make the damage something that did not happen. By absorbing the damage oneself, one forfeits being compensated and demanding punishment, and also forfeits the right to such compensation and the justice of punishment. One pays the price oneself for the damage suffered, and the guilty person is free. After being struck on the cheek, a person offers the other cheek—for the rightful satisfaction of the law of compensation. Whoever sacrifices one's life for the enemy, rather than only for one's friends, pays the due price from the enemy, so that reconciliation happens by justice being fulfilled.

The issue of incarnation—of the pre-existent Son of God becoming human—must not be overlooked. It is thereby clear that an understanding of incarnation in the sense of a development of the incarnate person's total life, from birth to death throughout its phases, as if it were exemplary of the normal life of human beings, has no ground in any texts of the New Testament. The structure even of the gospels is not based on such a concept. Nor are they interested in presenting the end of Jesus' life like the normal ending of the lives of all human beings, which, to be sure, would not be too unusual even in the slaughter of innocents. The suffering servant is already significant as the one who suffered *instead of us*, not as the one who innocently suffered the fate of unfortunate mortal human beings, typically human as the picture of his extreme suffering may be.

As far as the texts themselves are concerned, the issue of incarnation is by far not as pervasive in them as is their overwhelmingly documented focus on Jesus' death *for our* sins, for our *enmity against God*. And where it is expressed, including the Gospel of John, it still stands in the service of Jesus who came to carry the sins of the world (cf. Jn 1.29, 35; 3.13-14). The entire New Testament speaks about the death of Jesus Christ *for our sins*. The death of Jesus through *his crucifixion for the sins of the world* is understood as the revelation once and for all of the righteousness and justice of God. It is the kind of justice through which we are free, because the deity paid the price itself for our enmity, thereby redeeming us to God. It is the kind of justice in which redemption does not make God's unconditional love for us impossible, but through which redemption on our behalf, rather than by us, is the fulfilment of the rightfulness of God's unconditional love for God's enemies. There are substantial reasons why these most fundamental texts do not see a conflict between redemption and unconditional love, but why they consider God's reconciliation of the world to God as the fulfilment of God's love for the world in its redemption through the sacrificial death of Jesus Christ.

On substantial as well as on exegetical grounds, it should be very questionable to conclude that the concept of redemption contradicts the concept of God's unconditional love. Redemption expresses the actualization of God's love just as much as the incarnation of the pre-existent Son of God. The question is how redemption and incarnation are (to be) related. According to the texts, perhaps except a text like Phil. 2.5-11, the incarnation, with its particular emphasis on the real human being Jesus, seems to serve, to be subordinate to the purpose of the redemption of the world. This may or may not be so. The question must be discussed, not just when we differ, but because it is important as such. Whichever better answer is found, it will be another case in the practice of biblical theology.

BIBLIOGRAPHY OF WORKS BY
ANTONY F. CAMPBELL, SJ

1964–65   'Homer and Ugaritic Literature', *Abr-Nahrain* 5: 29-56.

1969   'Jeremiah's Use of the Covenant Formula', in *Lectures on the Covenant Formula given by Norbert Lohfink S.J.* (Polycopied presentation; Rome: Pontifical Biblical Institute).

1969   'An Historical Prologue in a Seventh-Century Treaty', *Bib* 50: 534-45.

1975   *The Ark Narrative (1 Sam 4–6; 2 Sam 6): A Form-Critical and Traditio-Historical Study* (SBLDS, 16; Missoula, MT: Scholars Press).

1976   'Bultmann and the Old Testament', *Colloquium* 9: 34-36.

1979   'Psalm 78: A Contribution to the Theology of Tenth Century Israel', *CBQ* 41: 51-79.

1979   'Yahweh and the Ark: A Case Study in Narrative', *JBL* 98: 31-43.

1979   'The Yahwist Revisited', *AusBR* 27: 2-14.

1980   'Our Changing Understanding of an Unchanging God', *Word in Life* 28: 131-35.

1981–82   'The Old Testament and Women Today', *Compass Theology Review* 15.4: 1-9.

1982   'God's Anger and Our Suffering', *The Australasian Catholic Record* 59: 373-85.

1985   'A Paradigm for Language in Talking of the Spiritual and Psychological', in Edmond Chiu (ed.), *Psychiatry and Religion: Proceedings of a Conference, 27–28th June 1985, St Vincent's Hospital, Melbourne* (Melbourne: St Vincent's Hospital): 132-38.

1986   'From Philistine to Throne (1 Sam 16.14–18.16)', *AusBR* 34: 35-41.

1986   *Of Prophets and Kings: A Late Ninth-Century Document (1 Samuel 1–2 Kings 10)* (CBQMS, 17; Washington: Catholic Biblical Association of America).

1987   'The Literary Approach to the Old Testament', in Erich Osborn and Lawrence McIntosh (eds.), *The Bible and European Literature: History and Hermeneutics* (Melbourne: Melbourne Academic Press): 147-51.

1987   'Who Dares Wins: Reflections on the Story of David and Goliath and the Understanding of Human Freedom', in Edmond Chiu (ed.), *The Psychological and Theological Meaning of Freedom: Proceedings of Second Conference, Psychiatry and Religion, 10th October, 1986* (Melbourne: St Vincent's Hospital): 59-66.

1988   'Job: Case Study or Theology', in Edmond Chiu (ed.), *Psychiatry and Religion: Proceedings of Third Conference, 23rd October, 1987* (Melbourne: St Vincent's Hospital): 38-44.

1989   'God, Anger, and the Old Testament', in Edmond Chiu (ed.), *Psychiatry and Religion: Anger–A Psycho-Theological Analysis. Proceedings of Fourth Conference, 2nd September, 1988* (Melbourne: St Vincent's Hospital): 15-19.

1989   'Poverty and the Old Testament', *Compass Theology Review* 23: 21-28.

1989   *The Study Companion to Old Testament Literature: An Approach to the Writings of Pre-Exilic and Exilic Israel* (Old Testament Studies, 2; Wilmington, DE: Michael Glazier [republished in 1992 under the same title by Liturgical Press]).

1989   'The Reported Story: Midway Between Oral Performance and Literary Art',
        Semeia 46: 77-85.

1990   'God: Judge or Lover?', *The Way* 30: 92-102.

1990   '1 Samuel', in R.E. Brown, J.A. Fitzmyer and R.E. Murphy (eds.), *The New
        Jerome Biblical Commentary* (Englewood Cliffs, NJ: Prentice–Hall): 145-54.

1991   'Old Testament Narrative as Theology', *Pacifica* 4: 165-80.

1991   'Past History and Present Text: The Clash of Classical and Post-Critical
        Approaches to Biblical Text', *AusBR* 39: 1-18.

1993   (with M.A. O'Brien) *Sources of the Pentateuch: Texts, Introductions, Annota-
        tions* (Minneapolis: Fortress Press).

1993   'The Priestly Text: Redaction or Source?', in G. Braulik, W. Gross and
        S. McEvenue (eds.), *Biblische Theologie und gesellschaftlicher Wandel: Für
        Norbert Lohfink SJ* (Freiburg: Herder): 32-47.

1994   'Martin Noth and the Deuteronomistic History', in S.L. McKenzie and M.P.
        Graham (eds.), *The History of Israel's Traditions: The Heritage of Martin Noth*
        (JSOTSup, 182; Sheffield: Sheffield Academic Press): 31-62.

1997   'Structure Analysis and the Art of Exegesis (1 Samuel 16.14–18.30)', in Henry
        T.C. Sun *et al.* (eds.), *Problems in Biblical Theology: Essays in Honor of Rolf
        Knierim* (Grand Rapids: Eerdmans): 76-103.

1998   (with M.A. O'Brien) '1–2 Samuel', in W.R. Farmer *et al.* (eds.), *The
        International Bible Commentary* (Collegeville, MN: Liturgical Press): 572-
        607.

1998   (with M.A. O'Brien) '1–2 Kings', in W.R. Farmer *et al.* (eds.), *The Interna-
        tional Bible Commentary* (Collegeville, MN: Liturgical Press): 608-43.

2000   *God First Loved Us: The Challenge of Accepting Unconditional Love* (New
        York/Mahwah, NJ: Paulist Press).

2000   (with M.A. O'Brien) *Unfolding the Deuteronomistic History: Origins, Up-
        grades, Present Text* (Minneapolis: Fortress Press).

2000   'Women Storytellers in Ancient Israel', *AusBR* 48: 72-73.

2001   'Preparatory Issues in Approaching Biblical Texts', in Leo G. Perdue (ed.), *The
        Blackwell Companion to the Hebrew Bible* (Oxford: Basil Blackwell): 3-18.

2002   'Invitation or…?: The Bible's Role', *AusBR* 50: 1-9.

2002   'The Storyteller's Role: Reported Story and Biblical Text', *CBQ* 64: 427-41.

2003   *1 Samuel* (FOTL, 7; Grand Rapids: Eerdmans).

2003   'Form Criticism's Future', in Marvin A. Sweeney and Ehud Ben Zvi (eds.),
        The Changing Face of Form Criticism for the Twenty-First Century (Grand
        Rapids: Eerdmans): 15-31.

2003   'The Book of Job: Two Questions, One Answer', *AusBR* 51: 15-25.

2004   'Ignatius Loyola and the Unconditional Love of God', *The Way* 53.1: 31-42.

2004   *Joshua to Chronicles: An Introduction* (Louisville, KY: Westminster/John
        Knox Press).

2004   *2 Samuel* (FOTL, 8; Grand Rapids: Eerdmans).

forthcoming   (with M.A. O'Brien) *Rethinking the Pentateuch* (Louisville, KY: Westminster/
        John Knox Press).

Professor Campbell has also been a regular contributor to:

        Eureka Street, a magazine of public affairs, the arts and theology, published ten
        times a year by Jesuit Publications, PO Box 553, Richmond, Victoria 3121,
        Australia.

        Madonna, a magazine of theology and spirituality, published six times a year
        by Jesuit Publications.

INDEXES

INDEX OF REFERENCES

2 Kings (cont.)		21.5-6	14	*Nehemiah*	
18.22	23	21.10-15	111	9.15	65
18.23-24	23, 24	21.12	132	9.17	164
18.25	23, 24	22–23	84		
18.26-28a	23	22.14-20	112	*Job*	
18.28b-32	23, 24	22.16	132	7.11	145
18.28b	24	22.25-26	16	24.11	122
18.29-30	24	23.4-5	15	26.13	144
18.31-32a	24	23.5	84	27.3	144
18.31	24, 118	23.8-9	84	33.4	154
18.32b	24	23.10-12a	17	34.14-15	154
18.33-34	23, 25	23.12b-14	17		
18.36	23	23.15	16, 17	*Psalms*	
19.6-7	21	23.16-18	16	2	178
19.21b-28	21	23.19-23	16	10.1	62
19.21b-22	21	23.20	84	18.15 Eng	154
19.23	22	23.24-25	16	18.16	154
19.24	22	23.24	84	22.1	62
19.25a	22	23.26-28	16	80	5, 123,
19.25b-26	22	23.26-27	5, 111		124
19.27-28	22	23.36-37	16	80.1 Eng	123
20	19	24.1-2	16	80.1-18 Eng	127
20.1-11	19	24.3-4	5, 16, 111	80.2	123
20.1	20	24.8-9	17	80.2 Eng	123
20.2	20	24.13	132	80.3	123
20.3a	20	24.18-20	16	80.4-6 Eng	124
20.3b	20	25.1-7	105, 112	80.4	123
20.4	20	25.1-2	16	80.5-7	124
20.5-6	20	25.3-5	16	80.7	123
20.5	20	25.5	112	80.8-19	127
20.6	20	25.8-13	13	80.8-18 Eng	123
20.7-11	20	25.10-11	12	80.8-9 Eng	124
20.7	20	25.14-17	13	80.8	123
20.8-11	20	25.22-26	139	80.9-19	123
20.8	20	25.24	16	80.9-10	124
20.12-21	19	25.25-30	5	80.12 Eng	123, 124
20.12-13	20	25.27-28	16	80.13	123, 124
20.14-19	20, 21	25.29-30	17	80.13 Eng	124
20.14	21			80.14	124
20.15	21	*2 Chronicles*		80.14 Eng	124
20.16-18	21	20.13	32	80.14-15 Eng	124
20.19	21			80.15-16	124
20.20-21	20	*Ezra*		80.15	124
21	5	9.1-2	79	80.16 Eng	124
21.1-3	17	9.1	79	80.17-18 Eng	124
21.3	111	16.19-21	79	80.17	124

INDEX OF AUTHORS